THE POWER OF FORGETTING

THE POWER OF FORGETTING

Six Essential Skills to Clear Out Brain Clutter and Become the Sharpest, Smartest You

MIKE BYSTER

with KRISTIN LOBERG

HARMONY

BOOKS · NEW YORK

Copyright © 2014 by Brainetics, LLC

Published in the United States by Harmony Books,
an imprint of the Crown Publishing Group,
a division of Random House LLC, New York,
a Penguin Random House Company.
www.crownpublishing.com

Harmony Books is a registered trademark and the Circle
colophon is a trademark of Random House LLC.

Library of Congress Cataloging-in-Publication Data
Byster, Mike.
The power of forgetting : six essential skills to clear out brain
clutter and become the sharpest, smartest you / Mike Byster
with Kristin Loberg.
pages cm
1. Attention. 2. Memory.   3. Thought and thinking.
I. Loberg, Kristin. II. Title.
BF321.B88   2014
153.1'25—dc23
2013032193

ISBN 978-0-307-98587-3
eBook ISBN 978-0-307-98586-6

PRINTED IN THE UNITED STATES OF AMERICA

Book design by Jaclyn Reyes
Cover design by Kelly Sue Webb
Cover photograph: Getty Images

3   5   7   9   10   8   6   4   2

First Edition

To my wife, Robin, and my son, Josh,
who have always believed in me and encouraged
me to take a chance and go for it.

To my dad, Dave, and my sister, Beth,
for their constant love and support.

And especially to my mom, Gloria.
She taught me I could accomplish anything,
as long as I never gave up and I kept my
hair combed and my shoelaces tied.

I couldn't have done it without any of you.

CONTENTS

Memory is the mother of all wisdom.

—AESCHYLUS (525–456 BC)

A Forgettable Story

Kathy M. gets up at 5:00 a.m. so she can sneak in a forty-five-minute jaunt on her treadmill while responding to overnight e-mails, checking her Facebook page, and catching up on the morning news. By the time she lands at her desk at 9:00 a.m.—after she's made breakfast for the family, showered, dressed, lost and found her keys, sent several texts, shared a few photos online, opened some apps, downloaded key documents to her iPad, organized the kids' lunches, and dropped them off at school—she's already dealt with volumes of information and competing demands via her cell phone and home computer. Now at work, she struggles to prioritize her tasks amid the flurry of to-dos, incoming calls, and e-mails. She saves the review of an important file until later in the day because she fears her brain cannot concentrate on it yet.

Lunchtime hits and she wonders where her morning went, as she finds herself halfway through the day but feels far behind the eight ball in terms of how much she's accomplished. Scatterbrained, she tries to calm herself back into full focus by grabbing a coffee and scrolling through her favorite Web site. But then more distracting e-mails come in. And when her boss enters the office around four o'clock and asks her a quick question, she draws a total blank in a response. Her brain has shut down. Correction: Her brain never really got to work that day.

This, unfortunately, is typical not just of Kathy but of millions of us who are blessed and cursed in our hyperkinetic world, where there's just too much information to process and expectations to address 24-7. But the good news is there's an answer to this modern plight. There's a way to cut through the clutter in your brain and develop a laser focus and concentration. A way to power through tough problems so that you can move on to enjoying the rest of life and not let issues linger more than they need to. The solution lies in a little-known phenomenon: forgetfulness. That's right: When we learn to forget information, we have the ability to remember what we need to work faster and smarter through our day.

I don't know anyone who doesn't feel overwhelmed by responsibilities while at the same time drained by trying to keep up (and barely doing so). And although we think we're doing ourselves good by, say, taking a time-out at work to troll the Internet or respond to messages from friends, we could actually be doing a great disservice to our brains. Creativity and insight cannot be born from a brain living in a culture of distraction. Nor can fast, productive thinking happen when we're under the duress of stimulating activities. We are living with the same brains that our caveman forebears developed for us centuries ago, and those brains are not adapted to the realities of our modern era that have us navigating so many sources of information and stimulation.

Brain clutter is a costly condition. While it may not have an official diagnosis in the medical world, it most definitely has an undeniable list of symptoms: brain fog, inability to focus or concentrate, lack of productivity and innovation, stress, anxiety, nervousness, angst, worry, dread, and even depression. (A doctor will give you more grave-sounding technical conditions.)

The average working professional spends roughly 23 percent of the workday on e-mail and glances at the in-box about thirty-six times an hour. It takes most of us more than a minute to return to a task once we've stopped to read a new e-mail. Imagine gaining back all that time and energy! And imagine what it can do for the next generation. This is serious, folks. I like to think of myself as a fun and hip guy who tries to crack a few jokes when teaching, but I cannot express the severity of our current crisis. In fact, my desire to reverse this trend is the whole point of writing this book.

If we can learn to minimize the idle, ineffective clutter and maximize the stuff that future successes are made of, then we can go far. Mastering the art of forgetting, as you're about to find out, will be the ultimate key to that achievement. What's more, training your brain to operate faster, focus intently and immediately when you need it to, and unleash its fullest potential doesn't hinge on genetics, inherited IQ, access to the best schools, or even medical breakthroughs. The one skill that trumps all others in becoming smarter, more productive, and exceedingly more imaginative is, in fact, *forgetting*. I realize that this may sound absurd and quite counterintuitive. How can forgetfulness and efficiency coexist? Aren't these two concepts absolute opposites? Far from it.

In this book, I'm going to teach you everything you need to know to get your brain working more effectively for you. You'll be able to maximize the full power of your brain and get a lot more accomplished every minute of your day. And being able to forget will provide the foundation.

Let me be clear: This is not a "memory" book. I'm not here just to teach you a trick to memorize the Declaration of Independence so that you can recall it in a heartbeat. What you're going to learn—using a variety of exercises, shortcuts, and tools—is the art of forgetting. This single skill alone will help you become a better, more effective individual in all that you do. The "forgetting" lessons and their related exercises will enhance your ability to communicate, innovate, impress others, stand out in a crowd, get ahead of your peers, move up the corporate ladder, magnify your employability and moneymaking capacity, make excellent decisions, solve problems, plan for the future, speak publicly with ease, be a stronger player in games and sports, ask for what you want, adapt to new situations, handle crises, work under pressure, be independent, and more.

There are hundreds of abilities that can be elevated by mastering the power of forgetting. Throughout the chapters, I'll point out specifically why you're learning a given stratagem or being told to do something that seems impossible or impractical (such as multiply two-digit numbers in your head), but regardless of the specific lesson you're reading about on any given page, I want you to always keep your eye on the bigger—and much more monumental—picture and prize: Developing a mind that works super fast will allow you to live up to your greatest, most innovative potential.

Will you become the next Einstein, Edison, Oprah, Jobs, or *Fortune* 500 CEO? I can't make any promises, but I will pledge that if you read this book, wholeheartedly think about its material, and try my exercises (more than once!), you will begin to optimize the inherent power of your brain and allow your creative, inventive, and imaginative self to propagate in directions you never thought possible. You'll also be able to achieve multiple goals smoothly without feeling like your multitasking efforts are backfiring, sapping your energy, and destroying your peace of mind. The lessons in this book will help you to set the right tone every day for what you want to accomplish and give you the skills to stay focused despite distractions so you finish that list of important tasks.

Using your brain the way I am going to teach you will open you up to mastering anything in life, from speaking foreign languages to playing music, cooking, negotiating, communicating, and even establishing better relationships with others. You will also be giving your health a boost, because my exercises will give your brain a good workout. You'll finish this book with much more confidence in yourself, and that is perhaps the best gift I can give you. With confidence, you'll have the courage to strive for anything—to do and be whatever you want.

I've seen these lessons help people from just about every walk of life, from young students to retirees hoping to preserve their mental faculties, from entry-level employees to executives, CEOs, and those in serious leadership or political positions, and from parents to teachers, mentors, entrepreneurs, inventors, doctors, lawyers, restaurateurs, writers, and philosophers.

By the end of the book, you will have amassed your own unique collection of tools that make sense to you—and that work! And you'll never think about "forgetting" in quite the same way again. Indeed, the act of forgetting creates the defining line between the cool cats who accomplish a lot in life and the harried people who are constantly set back by their frenzied attempts and who always feel rushed.

HOW I TRAINED MY BRAIN

In the third grade, my teacher, Mrs. Carlson, told the class that we had to memorize the planets of the solar system. I vividly recall her instructing us to move to the back of the room, saying, "Don't return to your seats until you have all of them memorized." She then added that we should think about the following sentence: "My very educated mother just served us nine pizzas."

Obviously, she had given us the clue to getting all of the planets stitched into our brains quickly. It took me about five minutes to memorize the list from Mercury to Pluto (which technically is no longer a planet, but it was back then). In the fourth grade, my class was sent home with the task of committing all fifty states and their capitals to memory. Contrary to what you might think, I still didn't know how to make this easy for myself.

I studied all night long, staring at the list of states and capitals: Bismarck, North Dakota; Columbia, South Carolina; Salem, Oregon . . . Some states seemed to have unlikely capital cities, while others were just plain hard to remember, let alone spell (Montpelier, Vermont?). I thought perhaps the words would magically melt into my brain if I just glared at them long enough.

My parents kept coming into my room yelling, "Michael, get to bed already!" But I wouldn't give up.

The next day I felt defeated, tired, and overwhelmed. I didn't have the capitals memorized, and trying to push all that information into my brain at once made me barely able to recall anything at all (except for my own state's capital of Springfield)! Thankfully, my mother came to the rescue and helped me to come up with a song that would allow me to recall all of the capitals accurately and on the spot. And it worked.

From that moment on, I knew that I'd have to find not only my own ways of remembering information but also my own ways of organizing and filing away important data. It was also then that I began to really hone my skills in pattern recognition and make it an addictive habit. I became adept at finding hidden codes, formulas, and shortcuts to performing quick mathematics, playing with words in a different order to exercise my mind, and making up weird and bizarre stories or poems to store information I'd need to recall later.

If I were to ask you to picture a green apple in your mind, you would have already done so by the end of this sentence. That's about how fast I can solve lots of complex math equations. I know—it's a bit freaky and unbelievable. When I perform these feats for live audiences, the crowd always roars: "No way. You've got to be kidding me. That's not possible. I bet you were just born this way!" But then I have to tell them the truth: I was not born this way.

When I look back and try to pinpoint the moment I realized that forgetting was the linchpin to my brain's capacity, I
keep coming back to a moment from college. I was sitting on
a bar stool with a group of friends around me. I asked one of
them to give me a four-digit number, which I then squared in
a matter of seconds (e.g., 3,567 times 3,567), and I arrived at
the correct answer. Making this calculation in my head isn't
about being a "human calculator," which is what my buddies
liked to say. Much to everyone's surprise, it's about knowing
shortcuts that entail lots of *forgetting*. How so? Well, when I
perform this math in my head using an alternative route (no,
I'm not lining up the numbers and performing traditional
math whereby I carry the one and drop the zero), I actually
have to do a lot of forgetting—using certain numbers in my
step-by-step process while I leave behind others mentally and
stop pondering them.

Another way to think of this process in very practical
terms is to consider a scenario where you're challenged to
go buy a basket of strawberries as fast as possible. You bypass the meat and packaged-food section, and as you enter
the produce section of your supermarket, you don't look at
anything but the destination. You don't let the apples, or-
anges, bananas, or pears distract you. You dash right past
all the other colorful fruits and vegetables until you reach
the prize in the shortest distance possible. That's a crude
way of explaining what I do in my head when I make quick
calculations. I take the most direct route to the answer and
I don't let other inbound thoughts interrupt my process or
sidetrack my journey to the end result. In the case of Kathy,
the woman I mentioned at the beginning, she let too many
distractions in her morning send her brain into overdrive. By

the time she tried to focus on real work, she'd seen too many fruits and vegetables, so to speak, and she'd let too many of these colorful interruptions steal precious energy from her creative mind. But if she'd known to avoid these mind-numbing intrusions by dodging the allure of the Internet and mundane e-mails before 9:00 a.m., she could have arrived at work ready for action (and ready to tackle everything with aplomb). She probably would have enjoyed her morning with her family more, too.

Rest assured, I'm not here to tell you when you should and should not check e-mail or surf the Internet. I'm not going to tell you what you can and cannot do in this book; this isn't a "diet." But I will give you plenty of ideas for setting healthy boundaries in your digital life so you preserve as much mental energy as you can throughout your day. That way, you always have reserves ready to fire on all cylinders when important to-dos need to get done. (And unlike most diets, these ideas won't leave you feeling deprived or restricted!)

The exercises outlined in this book are much more than play. When researchers at Princeton determined back in the 1980s that I could do things with my mind that most people can't, such as multiplying big numbers in my head and reciting the letters of long words in alphabetical order within seconds (e.g., taking the word "rainbow" and spelling it as follows: abionrw), they were stunned to learn that I was the only self-taught person in their study. It's generally accepted that either you're born with a brain like mine or an "accident," such as a seizure or concussion, cracks opens previously inaccessible areas of your brain to unleash its full power. I'm living proof of a third option: self-training the brain to utilize more of its potential. And now many of my students are also living proof. I hope that—very soon—you will be, too.

HOW TO USE THIS BOOK

The book is organized into two parts. The first part, "The Power of Forgetting," will set the foundation for your journey. It will take you on a quick tour of how ignoring certain information at the right time while continuing to think and concentrate plays into memory and a high-functioning brain.

Part 1 will also help you recognize patterns in words and numbers that will help you distinguish between what's important and what's irrelevant. This will ultimately help you to streamline your brain's ability to organize, focus, and problem-solve quickly (as well as ace the next part of the book).

In part 2, "Mastering the Six Skills of a Productive Thinker," I'll share the six vitally important learning skills that are rarely taught in formal education and are essential for unleashing your full potential: focus, concentration, data retention, thinking outside the box, organization, and forgetting. My hope is that you'll feel like you are on a guided expedition: You'll learn as much from the narrative as you will from the activities and exercises. Every chapter includes indispensable information for anyone—whether you're about to enter the schoolroom or the boardroom. You'll discover:

- How to stimulate and optimize the brain's natural capacity for multitasking (despite the conventional view that it's impossible) so that multitasking takes on a life of its own

- How to enlist your imagination in the task of memory building, which will unlock an infinite capacity to retain vital information
- How to organize your racing thoughts and ideas to spur creativity and become a productive thinker
- How to spot patterns with your eyes even if you don't think you're a visual person, which is key to continually removing brain clutter and preserving the mental energy your brain needs to run efficiently
- How to catalog and manage an overwhelming stream of information so you can distinguish between what's important and what's not
- How to automatically avert distractions and be able to focus and concentrate at a moment's notice
- Effortless ways to quickly remember names, faces, telephone numbers, schedules, facts, and other pieces of information that will make you stand out—from the boardroom to a networking event
- And much more . . .

I've created a mix of exercises in this book, from easy to very difficult, and I doubt that they will all appeal to everyone.

So if you find yourself trying to complete a brain workout that frustrates you or drives you crazy (and makes you want to hurl the book across the room), don't beat yourself up. Skipping a few of the exercises won't be the end of the world. You'll still gain a tremendous amount of knowledge and smarts simply by reading and trying your best.

That said, let me remind you that in some cases a hard exercise might be a terrific way for you to identify a problem area in your life, so sticking with these harmless, low-stakes exercises even if they're frustrating at first might help you overcome an obstacle that you didn't know was keeping you from great success. Even though I'll be showing you how to conduct some wild math in your head, such as squaring a four-digit number instantly, these exercises are designed to work your brain in the very ways that help you to expand your overall brainpower. And I'm talking not just about mathematically inclined brainpower but about all kinds of mental acuities that allow you to retain massive amounts of information, be sharper and quicker at work and more engaged at home, maximize your creativity, and maintain a sense of clearheadedness. Obviously, I don't want you to throw this book across the room when you encounter a wall in solving any of my problems, but take note when you in fact *do* come across a particularly difficult exercise. This is likely a sign of where you can work harder and "spot-treat" an area in your brain that needs attention and strengthening. Everything about your brain will benefit when you do so.

My program can help anyone—anyone who tries, that is. As I'll reiterate throughout the book, the lessons and strategies presented here work best if you find ways to apply them to your own life.

If a certain technique doesn't work for you after you've tried it a few times, then dump it from your personal toolbox. Move on to another, more effective method that will help you to "forget."

Keep in mind that if you cannot seem to get the right answer to a certain exercise, that doesn't mean it's not working. These lessons (and their relevant exercises) do have to be practiced and learned. Back during your years of formal education, my bet is you were much more willing to accept setbacks as part of the learning process and to just keep trying. As adults, however, we tend to be more impatient. We want quick results. We're inclined to avoid what is difficult or what we don't think we're good at and instead spend our time on what comes easily and effortlessly. Most of us in the adult world haven't been in a traditional learning setting for a long time.

Give yourself permission to fail a few times. Pretend you're trying to get on a bicycle for the first time. Eventually, these skills will become part of your daily habits—and you won't even know it, but you'll experience the tremendous positive outcomes of allowing yourself to learn something new that did not come easily.

As students of life, we are never really done with learning. We are confronted with new information daily, increasingly so in our modern digital age. I hope you will return to this book to remind yourself of certain strategies and to refresh your forgetting skills. Having the tools to navigate through the influx of data we encounter—and forget what's not important—increases our chances for success. Whether you're a parent, a teacher, a student, an executive, or simply an "average" person hoping to enhance the speed, effectiveness, and overall health of your mind, this book will equip you with a set of skills that will return multiple benefits to you in the future.

And that future can be as early as today.

So turn the page and let's start with a quick quiz to gauge just how good your ability to remember things is now. Fair warning: I predict you'll score about a C on this test, which I share with lots of audiences, but by the end of the book you'll be able to pass it with flying colors.

POP QUIZ: HOW WELL CAN YOU RETAIN INFORMATION, REMEMBER, AND *FORGET*?

Let's try a little experiment. I want you to read the following list of ten items to yourself once—just once. It should take you no more than fifteen seconds. (Ideally, this exercise shouldn't be done in a book, because there's too much room for cheating; so please follow directions here. Ahem!) After you've looked through the list, I want you to turn away from the book, take a two-minute break, and then come back and see how many of those items you can write down on a piece of paper. Okay, ready? Here's the list:

silver tray
six crystal glasses
bar of soap
banana
chocolate pudding
laundry detergent
dental floss
loaf of bread
red rose
tomato

When you come back to the book, don't let your eyes see any of the words again. Do what you can to write them all down, giving yourself just half a minute to do so. How many words did you remember? This exercise is much harder than it appears at first, and I'll make you feel better by saying that it's nearly impossible to remember all ten items if you don't employ some strategy (as I quickly realized when I first heard this list at a cocktail party long ago). So don't feel stupid if you didn't come close to writing down all ten. And if you did, then did you get them all in the original order? Now, that's an added challenge!

Most people get about half of the words. If you recalled at least seven, you're way above average. But if you knew the secret here, you could have scored a perfect ten.

Later in the book, I'll teach you how to remember lists of items easily without rote memorization. In doing so, you'll be "forgetting" the actual words on the list and remembering something else about them that instantly commits them to memory.

PART I

The Power of Forgetting

CHAPTER 1

The Essence of a Productive Thinker

How It's Possible to Develop a Clear, Quick Mind Regardless of IQ

We now accept the fact that learning is a lifelong process of keeping abreast of change. And the most pressing task is to teach people how to learn.

—PETER DRUCKER

Take a moment to imagine what it would be like to finish projects on time, keep track of to-dos without waking at 3:00 a.m. stressing over everything that's on your plate, quickly find stuff that you misplace, manage time like a pro, stay on task no matter how many distractions rush into your head, and enjoy many moments of total relaxation. Now, I don't know about you, but I'd call someone who can do this a productive thinker. It's the person who seems to have everything under control despite the frenzy of modern life and who doesn't let anything get in the way of keeping priorities in check and accomplishing what matters. It's someone who rarely seems to be overwhelmed yet manages to complete an enormous number of projects. And it's the individual who uses his or her brain to its highest, most efficient capacity.

The average worker today wastes about three hours per eight-hour workday, not including lunch and scheduled break time. Not surprisingly, the Internet interferes the most with our ability to stay focused, followed by coworkers, socializing, and just plain old spacing out. Although humans have always weathered hardships and taken on enormous numbers of responsibilities through the ages, I think it's fair to say that today's high-tech world presents unique challenges to our brains, which just haven't had the luxury of time to evolve to meet them. The amount of information that we try to process is astronomical, and this is a recent phenomenon. Just consider the difference between how much information you dealt with daily before you had e-mail (and a cell phone) and the volume you shoulder now. Add to that the number of technologies at our fingertips and it's easy to see why many of us are lacking in focused attention. And while it's nice to think that we can create better habits around limiting those constant distractions, let's face it: It's a hard thing to do.

I have a friend who keeps a large water bottle on her desk as a reminder to herself about how much energy she has left to get through her day. She sees the bottle as a symbol of a limited supply, and as she drinks the water throughout the day it's emblematic of used brainpower. She can't get through half of it before noon or she'll run out of gas before the day is over. She has to allocate her resources wisely to deal with all that's on her plate and save room for unexpected responsibilities, too. Granted, the water bottle is more or less an analogy, because my friend will drink to her heart's desire if she's thirsty. But when she explained to me how she allocates her energy throughout the day with the help of her trusty water bottle on display as an example, it made perfect sense to me. Her brain can easily handle the 34 gigabytes of daily data.

If you're like most people, the idea of being a productive thinker is an enticing one. We all wish for this capability yet feel increasingly challenged by the realities of modern life. I don't know anyone who doesn't feel overwhelmed by information, stressed to the max, and physically and emotionally exhausted at least once during a "normal" week. But what if you could cultivate the habits of a productive thinker easily and quickly and dramatically lower your chances of feeling buried by your responsibilities? Is this possible? I'm going to prove to you in this chapter that this is indeed achievable, setting the groundwork for what's to come in your journey to becoming the smartest, sharpest brain in the room.

THE FACTS OF BRAIN MATTER

Productive thinkers are all around you. If we didn't have productive thinkers in the world, we'd be in serious trouble when it comes to innovation and just plain getting things done. And you don't have to be a CEO of a *Fortune* 500 company to qualify as someone who has an amazing ability to accomplish a lot and make excellent decisions at a moment's notice. Productive thinkers inhabit every facet of our world, from the corporate one to the home front, where they take charge and keep the proverbial trains running on time. They are the minds that drive the births of new ideas and flourishing companies as much as they are the force behind well-run families that enjoy more health and happiness than average.

Society has relied on productive thinkers for millennia, but I'm going to guess that you already knew that. You just want to know how to cultivate your inner "PT." But before I get to how exactly you'll do that, let's start with some basic facts about attention, productivity, and the culture of distraction.

ATTENTION IS A FINITE RESOURCE

There's a reason they call it "attention-deficit" disorder. When there's a shortage of anything, that generally means endless supplies of that particular thing just don't exist. And this is certainly true when it comes to mental attention. In fact, this is true for just about every biological transaction we force our bodies to make. One can only run so fast so far, sleep for so long, burn so many calories per hour, and think intently on a single subject for so many minutes or hours. Whether you're trying to complete a marathon or absorb Leo Tolstoy's *War and Peace* in a sitting, you have a limited supply of physical resources to complete the task—only so much glucose and other metabolic substances to get you through to the finish line. It's well documented that when you perform a task that requires focus and attention, the next task immediately following cannot possibly be done as effectively, since fewer resources are available. Of course, different tasks demand different levels of focus and attention. Taking the trash out is one thing, but engaging in high-energy undertakings— especially those that entail concentration, critical thinking, self-control, creativity, planning, decision making, and mental and/or physical exertion—is another thing. And distractions can really take their toll when demanding chores are in play.

DISTRACTIONS STEAL MORE THAN PRECIOUS TIME

How many seconds or minutes do you think it takes to return to a task that got interrupted? Twenty-five minutes. That's according to a study published in 2005, which also found that on average people spend a scant eleven minutes on a project before getting pulled away. Time is among the most precious commodities today. We all need more of it. As one *New York Times* journalist put it in an article summarizing the latest in the science of interruptions (and indeed, there is such a thing), "Information is no longer a scarce resource—attention is." If distractions weren't so tiring, then they probably wouldn't be so terrible. But distractions eat up time not just during the distraction itself but also afterward, when you're trying to get back to what you were originally doing. When you shift your focus from one task to another (or just mentally make a shift in thinking, for example, suddenly turning your attention from a project at work to weekend plans), your productive thinking time shrinks. All the while you're losing biological ammo in the form of glucose to sustain your attention, recover from distractions, be creative, tap memory, understand new information, and tackle the next task at hand.

THE HUMAN BRAIN LOVES TO WANDER

Distractions are appealing for a reason: The brain loves them. Our innate ability to rapidly turn our attention elsewhere probably had survival value long ago, when we had to escape the hungry jaws of a preying tiger or run away from a life-threating foe. But today those dangers are few and far between. We are more likely to victimize and handicap our brains with meaningless interruptions that have nothing to do with our survival. We are also increasingly at the mercy of our internal dialogue—the part of us that speaks to us all day and that some have called the "monkey mind." The brain, after all, works all the time, even during sleep.

In 2006, MIT neuroscientists Trey Hedden and John Gabrieli helped put this into perspective when they studied what happens in the brain when people are distracted by internal thoughts while doing difficult tasks. As Dr. David Rock, the author of *Your Brain at Work*, reported for *Psychology Today*, "They found that lapses in attention impair performance, independent of what the task is, and that these lapses in attention involve activating the medial prefrontal cortex. The medial prefrontal cortex is located within the prefrontal cortex itself, around the middle of your forehead. It activates when you think about yourself and other people. This region of the brain is also part of what is called the 'default' network. This network becomes active when you are not doing much at all, such as being in between activities while in a scanner." Put simply, he concludes, "when you lose external focus, this default brain network activates and your attention goes to more internal signals, such as being more aware of something that may be bothering you."

So we've got two baskets of potential distractions to contend with all day: those that arise from our outside world—via the Internet, colleagues, emergencies, and barking bosses—and those that originate from deep within—the silent chatter we hear in our heads that lures us in all different mental directions.

DIFFERENT BRAIN REGIONS RULE DISTRACTIONS AND CONCENTRATION

The part of the brain that keeps us alert and able to deal with a distraction is not the same part of the brain where we concentrate. In other words, when you learn how to drive a car in a classroom setting and study a book on the rules of the road, your brain is utilizing an entirely different region from the one you use when you're actually behind the wheel and avoiding an accident. Research in just the last decade has shown that our ability to willfully focus our attention is physically separate in the brain from our ability to deal with distracting things vying for our attention.

Earl Miller, a neuroscientist at MIT who led a 2007 study published in the journal *Science*, was among the first scientists to discover that willful concentration and unintentional attention (i.e., having to avert one's attention to an obvious, eye-grabbing distraction) are not one and the same and are not controlled by the same region of the brain. As beautifully described by Lauran Neergaard for the Associated Press when she reported on Miller's study, "There are two main ways the brain pays attention: 'top down' or willful, goal-oriented attention, such as when you focus to read, and 'bottom-up' or reflexive attention to sensory information—loud noises or bright colors or threatening animals. Likewise, there are different degrees of attention disorders. Some people have a harder time focusing, while others have a harder time filtering out distractions."

Miller performed his study on monkeys using painless electrodes to examine how these two key areas worked together when the brain was pressed to pay attention. Trained in taking attention tests on video screens, the monkeys were forced to alternately concentrate and deal with distractions. Meanwhile, Miller and his team could decipher which areas of the brain were lighting up depending on what the monkeys were trying to do. When the monkeys voluntarily concentrated (say, by picking out a left-leaning red rectangle from a field of red rectangles), Miller noticed that their brains' center for executive function was in charge. This is the "higher order" area of the brain, which handles advanced mental processes. We use our executive function to perform activities such as planning, organizing, strategizing, paying attention to and remembering details, and managing time and space—activities that characterize sophisticated thinking seen only in primates. But when something grabbed the monkeys' attention, their brains began signaling from another area found at the back called the parietal cortex. And then Miller observed electrical activity in both of these areas resonating together as they communicated. But their individual frequencies were not the same, suggesting that the "volume" of each signal was different. It turns out that sustaining focus and concentration entails lower-frequency neuronal activity, whereas sudden distractions involve higher frequencies. According to Debra Babcock, a neurologist at the National Institutes of Health, Miller's study offered our first look into how these physically distinct regions of the brain interact to govern our attention, or at least part of it.

When we zoom out to connect some dots here, it's easy to see how we evolved to compartmentalize the management of our attention. After all, reflexive attention—reacting to a charging bull, for instance—is a primitive survival tool. But the ability to concentrate for any length of time is a much more advanced skill. In Miller's words: "If something leaps out of the bush at me, that's going to be really important and I have to react to it right away. Your brain is equipped to notice things salient in the environment. It takes a truly intelligent creature to know what's important and focus."

The exact mechanics of how our brains make snap judgments to distinguish between truly life-threatening distractions and just plain nuisances is a popular area of study today. When the old parietal part of our brain identifies an attention grabber, how does it figure out what should be ignored and what's important enough to focus on and invite other, more advanced regions of the brain to chime in about? We don't have all the answers yet, but one thing is certain: We are innately equipped to handle both inconvenient interferences and high-concept ideas that require high-level thinking, often at the same time. And that, my friends, is probably what makes humans so unique and indeed intelligent. It's also what can create chaos in our brains when we're trying to process a confluence of ideas simultaneously. Conducting both high- and low-level thinking at the same time can generate a conflict of interest, so to speak, in the brain. Just recall the last time you meant to do something important, such as respond to a colleague's critical e-mail about a deadline, and realized after several minutes or even hours that you never tackled that chore because a series of diversions pulled you off task. We can have the best intentions of addressing certain responsibilities but then become easily and quickly thwarted by trivial pursuits as our brains try to juggle warring factions. Or consider a time when you were fully engaged in a creative endeavor, such as writing an article or brainstorming ideas for an upcoming meeting, and within seconds your train of thought was broken by a phone call or someone walking into your office. It takes you a long time to return to that same train of thought once the distraction is over, and for some, those insightful thoughts that were moving through the brain when the interruption occurred are impossible to retrieve. They are gone.

Later in this book, I'll discuss the notion of multitasking. Although we like to think we can manage multiple tasks at the same time, the brain doesn't do that. Instead, it handles tasks sequentially, switching between one task and another. But brains can juggle tasks very quickly, thus giving us the illusion that we can perform two things at once. In reality, though, the brain is switching attention between tasks, albeit fast enough for us to barely notice consciously.

THE HUMAN BRAIN HAS A BUILT-IN SYSTEM TO FOCUS!

So I just finished explaining how the brain can work as a unit to juggle competing demands that want our immediate attention and thinking processes that call on our advanced ability to focus intently. A good question: How do we stay focused? In other words, how can we prevent distractions from encroaching on the neural circuitry built to facilitate concentration? It depends on how well we can stop those distractions from gaining too much attention.

One of the most famous tests used to study the act of focusing is called the Stroop test, named after John Ridley Stroop, who published an article describing the "Stroop effect" in 1935. It has since become a widely used test in psychology circles to study how fast people can identify colors and words when those words and colors don't necessarily match up. For example, if you were given words printed in different colors and asked to say the color of the text—not the word itself—chances are you'd find it much harder to say the color than to read the word. In the simple example below, the brain has a strong desire to answer "gray" for option *c*, rather than "black." And that's the Stroop effect.

    a. Black
    b. Gray
    c. Gray
    d. Black

If you were to successfully say the word "black," then you would have inhibited an automatic response in your brain, which is not an easy thing to do. We know now from scans performed by neuroscientists that people who can block their natural responses are relying on one particular region of their brain to do so. It lies within the prefrontal cortex, tucked behind the right and left temples, and appears to be key to all types of restraints. (For those interested, it's called the right and left ventrolateral prefrontal cortex, or VLPFC.)

In everyday life, we intentionally foil a lot of our brain's natural, reflexive responses, and this ability rests chiefly on this little area in our prefrontal cortex. When we prevent our hand, for instance, from catching a dropping object, or inhibit mental or even emotional response, this tiny region becomes active. It helps to think of it as our internal braking system. Although the brain encompasses various accelerators to command myriad activities—from movement and language to emotions and memories—it apparently has only one centralized braking system. And our ability to utilize this braking system effectively seems to correlate closely to how well we can focus. Put simply, focus requires that we teach ourselves how to stop the brain from veering down the path of utter distraction, where braking becomes hard if not impossible. What's more, our internal braking system isn't as strong as we'd probably like it to be, especially given the forces we're dealing with today and the high level of distractions that can send any brain into overdrive. Because our internal braking system is housed in the prefrontal cortex, it's part of the most delicate, impatient, and energy-hungry region of the brain.

The good news, however, is that by virtue of our humanness, we can in fact gain control of this region and learn how to more effectively process incoming information so we can filter out the clutter and home in on the important. And I'm going to be helping you do just that with the help of my six skills.

TECHNOLOGY ISN'T ALWAYS OUR BRAIN'S BEST FRIEND

Technology makes our lives so much easier. We can communicate with people in a nanosecond using slick devices that we carry around in our pockets, and we can conduct extensive and comprehensive research today by letting our fingertips do the walking online as we use search engines like Google. But this wonderful accessibility engenders laziness. Computers do the work for us—and the thinking, too, in some cases. Our cell phones retain the phone numbers we need, so we don't have to remember them. Calculators cover most of our math, and apps on our smartphones tell us how much tip to leave at a restaurant. Even the art of longhand writing, which employs creative parts of the brain, is being lost to the keyboards.

There is a time and a place for all this technology, but there's also a time and a place for good old traditional problem solving—for letting your brain do all the work, which has benefits you wouldn't believe. One way for me to convey this to you is to offer the following analogies. Let's say you need to undergo serious heart surgery. Do you want the surgeon who learned all of his skills through an inanimate computer, or would you prefer the doctor who gained his expertise through hands-on training with real patients? My guess is that you'd pick the surgeon with the "real" experience. You want the one who has been challenged to use his brain in all sorts of ways to solve problems in the operating room. He's the one who has been doing what's called scaffolding for a long time. "Scaffolding" is a term used in educational circles to describe how we synthesize our experiences, pulling aspects from one experience into another in order to build our knowledge base and solve new problems using a combination of what we already know and what we're presently learning or confronted with.

In everyday problem solving, it helps to be book smart or to use technology to arrive at results, but the person who can cull from myriad lessons in life is often the one who will find a better or more precise and accurate answer. It's just like flying. You don't want the pilot who hasn't flown a real plane and who only recently graduated from flight-simulation school. You want the pilot who has successfully clocked thousands of real flying hours in a variety of circumstances.

So imagine this idea applied to the realm of productive thinking. Productive thinkers don't get to where they are in life by relying on technology or by being just book smart. They certainly take advantage of technology and textbooks, but they depend on their innate brainpower first and foremost, including the part that triggers them to ask questions, challenge the norm, and refuse to accept "I can't." They access and utilize "real" skills obtained from a combination of background knowledge and experience that allows them to stand out and make a difference in the world, to adapt and respond to new needs and circumstances.

PROOF OF CONCEPT

A couple of years ago, I hunted down kids I'd taught more than a decade earlier. I had trained them on many of the very lessons found in this book, all of which were intended to help them effortlessly learn anything that they'd encounter on their road to success in life.

I wanted to know what had happened to them. Did my tools help them sail through the rigors of developing bright, creative minds that could effortlessly tackle tough challenges? Did they mature into productive thinkers, excel in their academic pursuits, and graduate with honors from high school? Did they make it to college? To elite ones? Or did they fizzle out and mirror the average dropout rates nationwide?

Granted, this wasn't meant to be a scientific experiment, and the group of students was small, but I thought it would be worthwhile to see what had become of people I had encountered and trained early on. We managed to find a handful of those first students, and the outcomes astounded even me. All of them had not only graduated from high school but gone on to prestigious universities, from MIT to Berkeley. So I then had to ask myself: How much of their potential was innate and how much was shaped in those formative years? Could the lessons I taught them in how to become quick, efficient thinkers have had a tremendous impact on their overall success? Did I have anything to do with their achievements?

With much humility, I'm happy to report that these kids, who are now adults, had some very nice things to say about me and my strategies. Many of them attributed much of their success to those techniques, which helped them cruise through all sorts of different classes and subjects. One woman said she had to learn all of the bones in the body during a particularly tough college course, and she did so using the tactic she'd learned from me more than a decade before. Suffice it to say, I was very proud.

Now, you're probably assuming that I taught a highly gifted group of kids who were well on their way to grand futures regardless of my lessons. Perhaps that's true, though I will say that these were not kids enrolled in gifted programs, and I was not targeting private or prep schools. But for just a moment, let's consider what kind of impact I might have had on these students' developing brains.

It's long been known that brainpower is largely inherited. Experts believe that upward of 70 percent of our brain's processing speed is a factor of our genes, which leaves 30 percent to the environment.

But that 30 percent is much more significant than most people think. In fact, it can be the proverbial pièce de résistance—the whole heart of the matter.

For argument's sake, let's consider the following analogy, which may seem wildly unrelated, but bear with me. In
the general population, anyone's chance of becoming obese
is 33 percent based on the environment and 67 percent based
on genes. No one would disagree that genetics plays a role
in body type, size, metabolism, and propensity to gain or
lose weight. But doesn't it seem a little counterintuitive to
attribute just a relatively scant 33 percent of one's overall
risk of becoming obese to the environment? Don't exercise,
diet, and general lifestyle factors weigh into that equation a
bit more? After all, we hear plenty of success stories from
people who lose massive amounts of weight and escape the
fates of their overweight family members just by changing
how they live, what they eat, and how they move their bodies. For them, the percentages should be reversed—they may
be saddled with an unlucky set of genes that makes it harder
to maintain an ideal weight, but that doesn't render it impossible or prevent them from doing so. They defy the odds by
working on their bodies every day and making every percent
of that environmental factor count. Put simply, that 33 percent can be significant, really big (no pun intended).

I believe that the same holds true when it comes to the
brain's capacity. We tend to overestimate how much is determined by our genes and forget that a lot of our mental
processing power is a product of self-discipline, education,
and a commitment to training and using our minds to work a
certain way. It's like that old Thomas Edison saying: Genius
is 1 percent inspiration and 99 percent perspiration. Those
are percentages I can agree with!

Besides, if intelligence were so dominated by genetics,
then I probably wouldn't be so effective at helping to trans-

form the lives of thousands of students—and adults—every year. I don't say this to gloat or to toot my own horn. I say this because, in working with the general public, I encounter an enormous mix of talent and inherited intelligence across the spectrum, from those who struggle mightily with learning and performing math to highly gifted whizzes who are the envy of the average students.

And if there's one thing that my experience has demonstrated to me over and over again, it's that no matter what kind of brain you're born with, and regardless of genetic intelligence traits, the brain is highly pliable, much in the way a muscle can be made stronger with exercise. And neuroscientists agree. Let's take a quick tour of how the brain can biologically grow and change. It's yet more proof that you can develop into a productive thinker, because your brain function is far from fixed.

> The mind is truly the center of your life, processing and interpreting every moment of your experience. It is the main generator of the thoughts, emotions, and decisions that can affect you and your chance of success in big and subtle ways. When you learn to control its load and speed, you can maximize its power.

A SMALL LESSON ON YOUR BIG BRAIN'S BIOLOGY

When I say that I hold my brain to be the most important organ in my body, I really mean that—and I do all that I can to preserve its faculties. I baby my brain. You might argue that your heart or your "soul" holds the key to life, but I would pin the secret to life on my trusty old brain. And the fact that the brain is pliable at any age makes it even more important to train and preserve it every single day. Being able to change the brain is the foundation of my work.

If there's one defining feature to our brains that clearly sets us apart from all other species, it's got to be our amazing ability to think. Fish, amphibians, reptiles, and birds, for instance, don't do much "thinking." They instead concern themselves with the everyday business of gathering food, eating, drinking, sleeping, reproducing, and defending themselves. These tasks don't require cognitive thought at all. They are instinctual processes, so the animals' brains are dominated by the major centers that control these automatic functions. With our "reptilian" brains built into us, we also perform these functions, which are found in remarkably similar parts of the brain.

But additional regions in our brains have evolved that allow us to do so much more than a bug or a bird. We can think with purpose and intent, form language, plan our future, pass judgment, and analyze information and stimuli in uniquely sophisticated ways.

The amazing abilities of the human mind revolve around its capacity to bombard itself with millions of bits of diverse information every single day. It must also be able to store and convert these into intelligent thoughts. It achieves this by evaluating, sorting, figuring, and redirecting information based on sequences and relationships. It discards the irrelevant bits of information and fills the blanks with pieces of information from its stored files.

Each person has about the same number of brain cells at

birth as in adulthood, but those cells grow, reaching maximum size at about age six. A newborn's brain triples in size in the first year of life. (No wonder babies have such big heads!) After that first year, brain size doesn't increase very much as we learn more information and pack more into our roughly three-pound brains. But what does grow larger is the number of neurons—nerve cells—and the complexity of their network. The adult brain harbors between fifteen billion and two hundred billion neurons, and the fact that we can't know for sure exactly how many neurons the typical adult has goes to show how much we just don't know about our brains and their capacity. So much about our brains remains a mystery.

DID YOU KNOW?

10 to 23 = the number of watts of power your brain generates when you're awake (that's enough to turn on a lightbulb!)

20 = the percentage of oxygen and blood flow going to your brain

1,000 to 10,000 = the number of synapses for each neuron in your brain

100,000 = the number of miles of blood vessels in your brain

700,000 = the number of thoughts you have each day

10 billion encyclopedia pages = the amount of information your brain is capable of remembering

15 billion to 200 billion = the number of neurons in your brain

But one thing we do know: When we exercise our brains (as you're doing right now while concentrating on reading this), we stimulate the creation of new neurons. Every time we remember something or have a new thought—bam!— we've just created a new connection somewhere in our brain that boosts its overall power.

A great way to visualize this kind of activity and "growth" is to picture a brain and all of its squiggles and bits of data as represented by the stars and interconnecting lines to create networks:

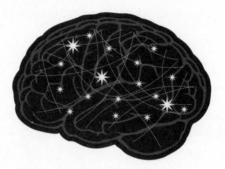

Let's pretend that this brain takes a history class. The brain then starts to look like this:

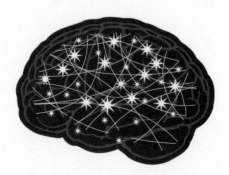

Notice that I've added a few more "stars" on the brain. These represent new facts or knowledge that the brain has had to retain during the class. Now look at what happens over time as more information comes in, some of which reinforces old knowledge and some of which is totally new:

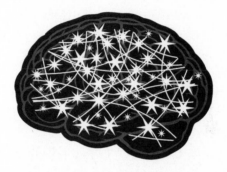

Here we have many more facts (stars) to accommodate—making a more complex network—and a much stronger brain working at a higher level of power. It's lit up with activity.

Granted, this description of how the brain works is merely a metaphor. It won't help you pass any medical tests or win you an easy A for explaining how the brain operates from a purely biological standpoint. But the metaphor is a good one. It shows that the brain has an immense capacity to accept incoming data, reinforce old files, and upload new ones by orchestrating a brilliant interplay among its millions of neurons. The brain remains capable throughout our lifetimes of creating new neurons and forming fresh connections among those neurons, and that's good news for us because it means that no one is stuck with a "bad" brain—anyone can improve his or her brain.

DID YOU KNOW?

- The brain is a lot more adaptable as it ages than you might think. Neurologists refer to the brain's ability to change as its "plasticity."
- Learning how to relax and rest your brain is as important as learning how to flex and work it. This explains why sleep is so essential to keeping the brain prepared to learn new information quickly. It's been shown that pulling an all-nighter decreases the ability to cram in new facts by nearly 40 percent! Apparently, sleep deprivation shuts down certain brain regions. (And for the record, I'm a master at sleeping. My brain won't quit during the day, but at night I can turn it off at a moment's notice.)
- One of the top ways to take care of your mind is to make sure your heart is performing at its best. In other words, when your body (and heart) are in good physical shape, so too is your brain, because exercise produces molecules in your body that help brain nerves stay healthy.
- Attending lectures and plays, enrolling in courses that expose you to new subjects and hobbies, and maintaining social connections are all excellent ways to nourish your brain.
- Certain foods, such as blueberries, almonds, and salmon, are "brain healthy."

THE SIX SKILLS IN BRIEF

At the heart of this book is learning to use the power of forgetting to effortlessly filter out the distractions and nonessential information to focus squarely on what's important and preserve your mental energy for all those high-energy functions. And this ability rests on developing six critical skills, which will allow you to "purify" massive amounts of data, triage your brain, and concentrate whenever and wherever you want to. This will ultimately allow you to work faster and smarter. Let's take a quick tour of these particular skills:

- **Focus and Concentration:** These two will be covered in chapter 3. Although they are similar, they are defined differently. Briefly, focusing relates to being able to stay in the moment, whereas concentration is about staying on task for as long as it takes to reach a certain destination or goal. The lessons I'll teach you in these two skills will help you to gain control of those distractions, "forget" intentionally, and strengthen your internal braking system, which in turn will streamline your brain's processing powers.
- **Increasing Mental Capacity:** Don't think you can retain massive amounts of information without old-school "memorizing"? Think again. In chapter 4 I'll show you how to create instant associations in just about everything in life to make the art of memorizing painless . . . and, to some degree, *mindless.*
- **Thinking Outside the Box:** Whether or not you'd call yourself creative or innovative, in chapter 5 you'll learn how to leverage your brain's inherent—and instinctive—

playful side, which will go a long way toward sharpening and honing your processing power. This will include exercises in thinking against conventional wisdom and contrary to how your brain really wants to calculate or process certain information. And you'll find, when you force yourself to take a totally different mental route from what you're used to, that you simultaneously open up new areas of your brain that fuel greater—faster—processing.

- **Organization**: You organize your physical spaces and weekly schedule all the time, but what about thoughts and incoming information? How do you organize all that? This is the purpose of chapter 6, which will equip you with tools to assemble and catalog your mental inbox. This will ultimately create more space for more information, as well as reinforce all the previous skills.

- **Forgetting**: Ah, now here is where I bring everything together and help you optimize this most important skill of all. In chapter 7 you'll see how the first five skills build on one another and help you to forget when you need to.

LEARNING WHAT NOT TO REMEMBER: HOW "MEMORY" FITS IN

One brain function that it is imperative to boost with the help of all these skills is memory. It is the cornerstone of all learning, and therefore maximizing it is a crucial part of my program. Memory is where we store knowledge and where we process knowledge. Unfortunately, many of us mistake memory for "memorizing." We view memory as a warehouse where we keep our knowledge when we are not using it, but that metaphor is not correct. Our memories are constantly changing as they take in fresh information and interpret it. Memory must decide what information is worth keeping and where it fits in relation to previous knowledge that is already stored. And what we store in our memories helps us process new situations. Without an active memory, you wouldn't be able to learn.

Consider what happens as you read an article in a magazine, in a newspaper, or online. As you digest the new information, you're no doubt utilizing information you've already got in your memory.

The new information can also evoke certain beliefs, values, and ideas that are unique to you and that help you interpret the information, make sense of it, and decide whether you choose to believe the new information while altering previously stored information and whether you'd like to retain this new info or just let it be forgotten. Thus, as you read the article, your memory changes by adding both new information and a new place to put that information.

At the same time, you're also giving yourself a different way to link that new information with older, now modified information.

Learning is therefore a memory process—the result of the attempt to understand new information. And every time you use your memory, you change it.

It's common knowledge that our memories work on two different levels: short-term memory and long-term memory. Short-term memory includes what you focus on in the moment, what holds your attention. Most people can hold only about seven items of information in short-term memory at any given time, such as a list of seven grocery items or a seven-digit phone number. To learn information so that you can retain and recall it, you must transfer it from short-term to long-term memory. Obviously, long-term memory includes all the information that you really know and can recall. In many ways, it becomes a part of you. Once information becomes a part of your long-term memory, you have access to it for a long time. The strategies in this book will help you make the most of both your short-term and long-term memories— and put you on the road to thinking productively—adept at optimizing both kinds of memory.

Now that I've given you a more technical view of the brain and the role of memory, let's turn back to the broader perspective and consider how you're going to go about tuning your brain to a channel where it can operate maximally. I'll preface this discussion by sharing one more misunderstood fact about the brain: It's not true that we use only 10 percent of our brains. Again, let's apply some logic here: If this were true, it would certainly make brain damage a lot less worrisome. The goal isn't so much to tap impenetrable areas of your brain as it is to use all that you've got access to at its fullest capacity—in much the same way you'd turn the volume up on your stereo. There certainly are parts of our brains that we can't ever reach or use, but that doesn't mean that we cannot develop those parts that we can in fact tap, including latent areas that need to be woken up. Igniting those undeveloped and underappreciated parts is what my exercises and lessons are all about.

Tapping into these parts of your brain is what will take you from average to awesome—and unleash your hidden productive thinker.

THE ROAD FROM AVERAGE TO AWESOME

Each part of the brain serves a special, defined purpose. Being able to wiggle our toes, make plans, dream, see, smell, talk, walk, solve complex problems, cry, know which way is up or down, remember our friends' birthdays, maintain balance, breathe, sweat, blink, flex our muscles, sense fear or danger, feel pain, and even keep our hearts beating are capacities that all originate in certain regions of the brain. We can do many of these tasks at the same time, too. Perhaps you're reading this book, drinking a beverage, digesting your lunch, thinking about your Saturday-night plans, and breathing, among many other things, all at the same time.

But you already know that I'm not here to teach you the exact biochemistry and topography of the brain. Rather than trying to understand the inner workings of your brain from a medical perspective, I want you instead to simply view it as a single room with certain compartments, as well as an entrance and an exit.

The secret to making this room power up and perform seemingly magical feats is to train it to operate like a computer—that is, to receive information, store it in the right compartment, and memorize all of the relevant information while ignoring the unnecessary information. In other words, to *forget* when it's appropriate so you can use your memory more effectively when necessary.

This last part is critical. Most people try to remember everything, and in doing so, remember little or nothing at all. The brain is ill equipped to handle an abundance of data all at once. It craves order and a streamlined flow, and that is exactly why optimizing its power entails training two different brain "regions" to work simultaneously yet independently of each other. One part absorbs information while another part is sorting and processing new information. Some of this sorting and processing no doubt entails a lot of "forgetting"—disregarding frivolous details immediately or discarding details once the brain has made quick use of them before moving on to the next important detail. These two processes are the heart and soul of memory—the foundation of all learning.

With the one-two punch of absorbing and processing—memory creation—your mind can then begin to work much more efficiently and become more powerful, giving you a huge advantage throughout your life. You can think of it as creating an assembly line for your brain. First, you compartmentalize the raw materials—the data—and then you input the data, one piece at a time, through a sequence of processes, sending the pieces onward to various places depending on how they need to be treated and whether they should be deposited in your short-term memory, put in your long-term storage tank, or entirely forgotten and tossed out to the junkyard.

Every chapter in this book is going to help you build and successfully run this assembly line like a well-oiled machine. It's not something you can do overnight, and it's also not something you can just build once and leave alone. Have you ever been amazed by a waiter's ability to take the orders of a table of six or more people without writing anything down? How does he or she get it right? It's even more impressive when people complicate their orders with personal requests—"Dressing on the side, please," "Can I substitute a baked potato for some fries?" "No cheese," and so on. How do they remember it all? Waiters are good at what they do because they do it a lot! Practice. Practice. Practice!

Knowing that brains require constant maintenance and the occasional repair, I work my brain every single day to keep it up to speed and stay ahead of the pack. My hope is that you will work your brain with the exercises in this book and that some of the strategies you learn here will become second nature. I don't expect you to become as obsessive about number and letter crunching as I am, but I do expect that you'll create new mental habits that will ultimately strengthen and expand your brain so that it can do incredible things. You'll find yourself in the car, for example, playing mind games with yourself or your passengers. You'll read street signs, license plates, and storefronts differently. You'll look at the whole world from a new perspective. And in doing so, you'll break away from your own pack.

Remember, I'm not here to make you just "average." This is not about trying to catch up. This is about blowing everyone else away. All of us enter school as youngsters and are surrounded by classmates with a variety of talents and strengths. That is when some of us find ourselves way ahead of others because we're mixed in with a wide range of ability levels. But as we grow older and mature into adults, we often find ourselves surrounded by peers—people who share our general characteristics, values, and intelligence. The pool of talent gets smaller and more similar to us in our particular environments, and that's when we can find ourselves fenced in by people who are just as sharp as we are—or even sharper. It becomes harder and harder to edge ahead of others and make ourselves stand out. We have to work so much harder to get that A, obtain that job or promotion, achieve that acceptance letter, succeed in the business world, or generally move forward in life the way we want to. And it's these moments that can come to define the rest of our lives.

Yet when we stop and focus on our brains, we have the potential to do just that—to leap ahead. You can accelerate your success whether you're in school, working a job, starting a business, or seeking a whole new career. You can get more done in less time, juggle competing demands with ease at work and in your personal life, and take multitasking to new heights that allow you to take care of true priorities effortlessly (and not feel guilty for letting a few things slide). You also can break out of your status quo and elevate your socioeconomic position to a loftier position. Imagine, for instance, being able to walk into a room and remember everyone's name. Or being a business owner or retail employee who can recall the name of every customer who has ever walked into your store (and thus keep them coming back). Or always adapting quickly to changes in your life that threaten your livelihood and ability to make a living.

Maybe you made a living fixing cameras over the past thirty years, but not the digital ones that now dominate the market. You might need to go back to school, become an apprentice, or take other steps to acquire a totally new skill set that will pay your bills.

In a world where it's increasingly difficult to find and maintain a good job, having an advantage and being able to reinvent yourself whenever necessary becomes all the more critical. Whether you like it or not, most everything in life is a competition. And it goes without saying that we need productive thinkers now more than ever. The good news, though, is that I promise to make this fun!

CHAPTER 2

The Power of Mental Habits

It's All About Patterns!

I never teach my pupils; I only attempt to provide the conditions in which they can learn.

—ALBERT EINSTEIN

When innovative people with clever minds are asked for their secrets to success, they often talk about the mental habits they keep. These include the ways in which they look at what's in front of them to generate new ideas and promote creativity. In addition to the obvious traits that help our imaginations, such as asking questions (e.g., What if? Why? How?) and performing experiments, an overarching theme in all things related to mental acuity is simply the ability to establish habits that help us to organize our thoughts and make breathing room for learning new things, which also entails a great deal of forgetting. Habits, after all, are nothing more than activities that we do repeatedly and that follow a certain pattern or rhythm. And habits are patterns of thought; the ones we keep in our thinking processes have everything to do with whether or not we can remember critical information, forget what's not important, tap creative areas in our brains, and free up mental energy to engage in complex thinking that requires a lot of focus and concentration.

This chapter is going to take you on what I hope will be a provocative tour of how habits relate to the brain's capacity and how we can use certain mental habits not only to sharpen our minds, and especially our memories, but also to look at things from totally different perspectives that can inspire insight, help us find new and better solutions to everyday problems, and spur innovative ideas. Our mental habits also play into our ability to forget when appropriate and maintain a clear, clutter-free brain ready to take on more. And at the heart of this lesson is an understanding of how patterns share a powerful relationship with habits.

WHAT'S IN A PATTERN?

First things first: What exactly is a pattern? It's simply a type of theme of recurring events or objects. Patterns exist everywhere we look. They are in numbers, in words, and even in nature. If you pick up any *National Geographic* magazine, for example, you'll see the most spectacular photographs of patterns found in animals, landscapes, flowers, stars, sand, and so on. Most of us don't notice patterns unless they scream out to us (as they do from a photograph) or we're challenged to find them or, like me, we become addicted to identifying patterns in everything.

If I were to ask you to give me an example of a pattern, you'd probably name one of those found visually in decorations, like stripes, zigzags, or polka dots, or on your bedroom's wallpaper, your favorite argyle socks, or your pinstriped suit. Or perhaps you'd think of the patterns heard in the rhythms and beats of a song, the striations that make up rock formations, the designs seen in architecture, the flow of traffic and signaling of streetlights, the predictable styles that are emblematic of certain car manufacturers, or the motifs found in artworks—you can detect patterns, for instance, in Monet's works, as well as in Van Gogh's and Rembrandt's. Patterns of hydrogen and carbon make up water, patterns of frozen ice crystals make up snowflakes, patterns of snowfall give us ski paths, and so on. We can consider the cycles of daytime and nighttime a type of pattern, just as our bodies follow biological patterns that mesh with the twenty-four-hour solar day. We often don't think of patterns existing on our insides, but these biological patterns actually dictate a lot about who we are and how we feel. Each one of us has a circadian rhythm—a biological clock—that maintains a steady, regular pattern twenty-four hours a day. We feel tired after the sun sets and charged when the sun comes up. These patterns often dictate the daily habits we keep. For example, most of us eat breakfast, lunch, and dinner in a predictable pattern. In addition to our consistent habits and behaviors that abide by patterns of sleep and wakefulness, our bodies release hormones at different times of the day to sustain our biochemical activities.

And of course patterns help give us computer programs, stories, and mathematics, which, as a matter of fact, is commonly described as the "science of pattern." Any sequence of numbers that can be modeled by a mathematical function is considered a pattern. These can be the most difficult patterns to identify, but they make for excellent mind sharpeners, as we'll see in part 2.

WHAT'S IN A HABIT?

You should know the answer to this already: patterns. Although we like to think we live exciting, ever-changing lives, we keep similar habits day in and day out from the time we get up to the people with interact with, the foods we gravitate toward, and the routes we use when we drive. As the old saying goes, humans are creatures of habit. But it's not just the activities we perform consciously that are driven by habits; our brains can somewhat unconsciously command certain repeat actions that help maintain our survival—governing basic processes such as breathing, digesting, and pumping blood without our having to think about it. When you consider all the tasks you do in a day, you soon realize that you can get a lot done without much mental effort. Your morning routine today was likely a carbon copy of yesterday's, and you probably managed to get ready for the day, eat breakfast, deal with trivial family stuff, and check off several to-dos quite effortlessly before 10:00 a.m. Most, if not all, of your mundane daily accomplishments are powered by habits—a systematic regimen that your brain is used to and can run pretty much on autopilot. Habits help us push through the day, and they become so ingrained in our lives that they are hard to break or change. They are as much shapers of our lives as we are shapers of our habits. As William James wrote in 1892, "All our life, so far as it has definite form, is but a mass of habits."

While it's natural to think that habits are all about the things we remember to do, they are as much about forgetting. The whole purpose of a habit—a repeated pattern or activity—is to be able to perform a task without much mental effort or thought. This allows you to then focus on other information that might enter the brain and that requires your undivided attention and concentration. In other words, we don't have to think about certain patterns in our lives that make up our habits. We can be "forgetful" in that department so we can save our mental bandwidth for other potential details that may need special treatment to get incorporated and remembered.

In his brilliant treatise *The Power of Habit*, Charles Duhigg writes: "Most of the choices we make each day may feel like the products of well-considered decision making, but they're not. They're habits. And though each habit means relatively little on its own, over time, the meals we order, what we say to our kids each night, whether we save or spend, how often we exercise, and the way we organize our thoughts and work routines have enormous impacts on our health, productivity, financial security, and happiness." He then cites a study from Duke University in 2006 that found that more than 40 percent of the actions we perform each day are not actual decisions—they are habits.

I couldn't agree more with Duhigg, but I will also add that, in my view, the actions we perform daily are also the product of "forgetfulness." The mere act of engaging in a habit means we're utilizing and repeating old information in our brains. None of this activity necessitates decision making. The ingrained habit takes over and our actions become based on the ability to forget more than on the ability to decide.

In his book Duhigg shows us how to harness habits for the better—from improving our willpower to turning failing products in business to runaway successes. In one particularly

interesting case study, Duhigg tells the story of Procter &
Gamble's crusade in the mid-1990s to make an odor-killing
spray that people could use on furniture and fabrics. Prior to
launching its marketing campaign, P&G assembled a team
of experts, including a former Wall Street mathematician
and several so-called habit specialists. Their job was to make
sure the ads for the product—Febreze—worked and could
generate strong sales. But after several false starts, including
ads that highlighted the product's power over smoky, stinky
clothes and couches that reeked of the family dog, Febreze
was on the path to becoming a total dud. It wasn't speaking
to consumers.

Not until a panicked marketing team visited the home
of a neat freak who also lived with nine cats did it dawn
on them where they had gone wrong. The cat lover could
not smell her home's stench anymore, so she didn't know she
needed a product like Febreze. And this scenario played out
in numerous other homes that P&G's marketing team visited. At this point, P&G hired another gun, this time a professor from Harvard Business School who was charged with
finding patterns in people's daily habits that could inform
the marketing of Febreze. After spending hours conducting
interviews and reviewing footage of people cleaning their
homes, the aha moment finally came when the team met a
mother of four in suburban Scottsdale, Arizona, who kept a
clean and tidy home and said she used Febreze as part of her
normal cleaning routine even though she didn't have to deal
with smoke or pets. For her, spraying a room that she'd just
finished cleaning was like "a little minicelebration."

No sooner had the P&G team taken note of this "little"
habit than they realized that they'd discovered the biggest

missing piece to the marketing campaign. Rather than trying to instill a whole new habit in people by adding the use of Febreze to their cleaning rituals, they simply needed to piggyback on the habits that were already established. In other words, P&G needed to position its product as something that finished the cleaning process and was part of the entire routine. Soon thereafter, the company rejiggered its ad strategy and added more perfume to the product's formula. TV ads featured women using Febreze to christen their freshly made beds, clutter-free rooms, and newly laundered clothes. The ads implied that Febreze finished the job and conferred a reward—a reminder that you'd done well and that your home was a pleasant place, not a stink joint. So rather than being sold as the ultimate antiodor spray, Febreze became an air freshener and symbol of a clean environment. It was used once things were already clean as the icing on the cake. Two months after P&G changed its marketing strategy, sales doubled. Today Febreze is one of the top-selling products in the world and has generated numerous spin-offs (and knockoffs).

I bring Duhigg's story of Febreze up for two good reasons: For one, it points to the power of habits in ways we often don't think about. And if we were to break this particular case study down further, we could identify an untold number of patterns—habits—that played into the journey that Febreze had to take before it became a marketing darling, including a few forgetful ones. P&G not only had to understand the cleaning habits of people but also had to mine the mental habits of its prospective customers while forgetting obsolete, useless assumptions about people's habits. What do people habitually think about when it comes to cleaning their homes today? What do they *not* think about or *forget* to think about? And how do those answers inform marketing strategies that can speak to the consumer? Only after considering these questions could P&G arrive at a best-selling campaign.

But the other lesson in this story is about how P&G's marketing team changed their approach to solve the problem, effectively forgetting old strategies. Relying on their usual marketing "habits" clearly wasn't working. They had to change the way they viewed the problem and accept a totally new perspective from which to derive their solution. This can be challenging when we're so used to doing things a certain way—and thinking a certain way. In addition to assessing consumers' habits to glean insight into their problem, the P&G team had to rethink their own problem-solving habits in the wake of failure to arrive at a marketing strategy that would strike a chord with their customers. This meant employing the power of forgetting on the level at which outdated models were forgotten to make room for an entirely new sales model.

Today, any company that hopes to reach the biggest audience possible spends a great portion of its marketing budget on seeking patterns in potential customers. And some have gone to great lengths to collect certain data for future marketing purposes. By spying on people's purchasing habits online or through traditional channels in brick-and-mortar stores, companies can tell who is expecting a baby or already has children, who is a fan of hockey, who is a runner, who favors organic foods, and even who will likely vote for candidate X in the next presidential election. In fact, President Obama's campaign once hired a habit specialist as its "chief scientist" to figure out how to trigger new voting patterns among different constituencies. (So the next time you receive a catalog in the mail addressed to you from a company you've never heard about but that seems to sell items that you'd like, you can thank your recorded buying habits.)

Before I bring this back to the realm of your brain's processing speed and mental acuity, let me share how Duhigg explains the brain's habit-creating methods. He writes:

> The process within our brains that creates habits is a three-step loop. First there is a cue, a trigger that tells your brain to go into automatic mode and which habit to use. Then there is the routine, which can be physical or mental or emotional. Finally there is a reward, which helps your brain figure out if this particular loop is worth remembering for the future. Over time, this loop—cue, routine, reward; cue, routine, reward—becomes more and more automatic. The cue and reward become neurologically intertwined until a sense of craving emerges. What's unique about cues and rewards, however, is how subtle they can be. . . . [S]ome cues span just milliseconds. And rewards can range from the obvious (like the sugar rush that a morning doughnut habit provides) to the infinitesimal (like the barely noticeable—but measurable—sense of relief the brain experiences after successfully navigating the driveway). Most cues and rewards, in fact, happen so quickly and are so slight that we are hardly aware of them at all. But our neural systems notice and use them to build automatic behaviors.

And that's the whole point of this book: to show you how to build automatic behaviors into your brain that support a fast-processing mind that has an infinite capacity to handle new information and know instantly what to do with it. This will indeed entail honoring your brain's inherent habit loops, which involve cues, routines, and rewards. At first you might not see how my exercises have direct connections to developing a more agile, nimble brain, but all of them reinforce the pattern recognition that lies at the center of streamlining your brain's operations. Even the ability to forget is itself a habit. You'll need to train your brain to rapidly decipher between valuable details and mere junk—or just temporary information—so you can keep your mind moving swiftly through incoming data while at the same time minimizing the amount of mental energy expended.

SEEING PATTERNS EVERYWHERE YOU LOOK

One of the best starting points for greasing your mind to find patterns in virtually every facet of life is to just consider the patterns in the world of language. I love to invent or identify patterns in my life using letters. I'll be driving down the street and looking for objects or other visuals whose names are long and don't have a repeat letter. Example: playground. Or I'll try to find things in passing that have double letters: Observing a man on a corner wearing glasses, I'll say to myself, *Guy with glasses* (double g's and, as a bonus, double s's!). I know, it's a weird habit to have. But it really gets my mind into pattern awareness like you wouldn't believe. Suddenly, I can find myself coming up with some wildly fun trivia, such as:

- "Stewardesses" is the longest word you can type using your left hand only.

- "Typewriter" is the longest common word that can be typed using only the top keys on a keyboard. (How cool is that?)
- "Strengths" is the longest one-syllable word and also the longest word that has only one vowel. ("Screeched" is just as long but has three vowels.)
- "Sequoia" is the shortest word that possesses all five vowels.
- "Uncopyrightable" is the longest word that does not repeat a letter.
- "Facetious" is one of only a few words that not only use all the vowels but also use them in the order they appear in the alphabet (*a-e-i-o-u*).
- "Four" is the only number that has the same number of letters (four) as its number value.
- "Forty" is the only number whose letters appear in alphabetical order.

On the surface, it may not seem that these admittedly arbitrary facts are rooted in patterns. But they are. By letting my mind think in terms of patterns, I managed to discover these strange oddities and, while doing so, work my brain in peculiar ways that brought my focus and attention to a much higher level. (Granted, others have probably found these fun facts, too.)

I recommend that you try it sometime—force your brain to seek patterns in things that don't seem to follow any pattern. Try to learn something without being taught. If you need a place to begin, look no further than your favorite Web sites and search for patterns in their design. Are company logos placed in similar spots? Do they advertise in roughly the same area? Why do you think this is the case?

• • •

You can learn a lot by studying patterns. Making a habit
of recognizing patterns can be a game changer in the real
world, because not only does the practice cultivate deep
levels of concentration, but it can unleash more creativity,
improve your logical thinking, and encourage you to think
outside the box, see things differently, and perhaps find some
solutions that work better than others.

Moreover, you'll bring fresh perspectives to conversations, you'll notice characteristics in other people that can
enhance your connections to and relationships with them,
and you'll be able to pay attention for longer periods of time
when you most need to do that.

In fact, being able to find patterns can ultimately help
you collect the information you need to make good decisions,
leverage your assets, and pave a pathway with fewer detours
and obstacles. All of this may seem too good to be true, but
what many people don't realize is that patterns shape who
we are and how we behave. There's a reason why it's said
that history repeats itself.

As humans, we reflect patterns in all that we do, and I
don't have to think hard to come up with an example from
my own life.

Back when I was a trader, I could sum up my whole job
as relying on my ability to find patterns. I made money by
seeking patterns in what other people did in their buying and
selling of commodities on the market. I also sought patterns
in the traders around me, predicting what they were buying so that I could accurately strategize my next move. It's
the same type of pattern recognition common among the top

Wall Street stock traders, who manage to buy low and sell high by "outsmarting" the market's wild vagaries.

You may not have any interest in playing the stock market or gambling, which also encompasses a lot of pattern recognition if you're good at it, but being able to read other people really well is a huge asset no matter what you're doing or trying to achieve. Most people are going to behave the same in every situation. Those who can detect the patterns in people's behavior can benefit from being able to predict how they will act and what they will respond to. You can understand your boss, your colleagues, your clients, your teachers, and your opponents in ways that allow you to maximize those relationships to your benefit. In fact, this ability is what separates amateur athletes from professional athletes. If you are acutely aware of patterns in your opponents, you can leverage your strengths and weaknesses against those patterns. Professional athletes don't depend on ability or physical strength alone—they need more than that to reach such a high level of success (and get paid for it!). It's the patterns they pick up from their opponents that ultimately help them plan their plays and achieve victories. For instance, batters know the patterns in the pitchers they face. Tennis players know the patterns in their opponents' serves, forehands, and backhands. Basketball and football players, and especially their coaches, know the patterns in the opposing teams' movements on the court and on the field. In his book, Duhigg covers how football coach Tony Dungy propelled one of the worst teams in the NFL to the Super Bowl by focusing on how his players habitually reacted to on-field cues.

In the business sphere, CEOs and business owners know the patterns in their industries' business cycles, as well as the

patterns in their own companies' internal rhythms throughout the year. This awareness allows companies to predict and
manage their cash flow in the best way and to weather the
storms that are inevitable from month to month. Much as a
weatherman predicts the weather from patterns in the sky,
clouds, barometric pressure, and temperature, so can business owners use their awareness of patterns to predict when
their businesses are going to suffer a serious revenue drought
or enjoy a windfall of revenues. The most successful leaders
and business owners are the ones who can make good pre-
dictions based on patterns and adjust their plans accordingly
to meet shifting needs and issues. And as we just saw, being
able to predict buying habits allows companies to maximize
their marketing strategies and capture more customers.

Clearly, being able to recognize patterns isn't just a
means to leverage your assets in a business setting or against
someone else's assets to outsmart them. As much as patterns
can give you an advantage in a competitive environment,
they can just as easily help you enrich your personal relationships. Most all of us behave in predictable, or patterned,
ways when it comes to what we like and don't like and our
general personality traits. It helps to surround ourselves with
people who take note of our patterns and respond to our
needs and preferences accordingly. By the same token, having an awareness of the patterns in others is what equips us
with the knowledge we need to best tend to their desires.
Awareness of patterns in others ultimately helps us become
better mentors, teachers, parents, caretakers, entrepreneurs,
colleagues, and leaders. It also inspires us to become the best,
most ideal version of ourselves.

Patterns uniquely tie into our habit forming, including the

habit of forgetting. When we find patterns in our thoughts, work, and daily duties, we can develop habits to streamline our lives and further shape and establish those patterns. And the more efficient habits we create, the more brain space we have on reserve to take on tough tasks and train our focus. The more we can leave to the automatic devices of our "forgetful," habituated minds, the more room we can reserve for higher levels of concentration on and thinking about new incoming information.

In the grand scheme, our relationship and interaction with patterns can essentially determine which direction we take in the world. Why? Our ability to recognize and capitalize on patterns ultimately heightens our awareness while revealing important insights that enhance our capacity to succeed.

Such a statement may sound obscure and somewhat philosophical, but not when we consider the fact that success itself follows a pattern.

Yes, there are patterns to success, whether it's building a successful business, working effectively with other people, or exploiting a trend for profit. Trends, after all, are patterns in themselves. Those who can predict trends make our brightest inventors, entrepreneurs, marketers, advertisers, fashion designers, Hollywood directors and producers, writers, Internet sensations, and trendsetters.

When *Big Brother* and *Survivor* became phenomena around the turn of the last century, reality television was born (and many old TV programming models were forgotten). Soon enough, dozens of imitators followed (surely you can name a few), each of which reflected a pattern—a formula—that had clearly worked and proved successful.

Not every reality show survived to live another season, but the overall lesson remains: Patterns can be great teachers as well as leading indicators of not only successful trends but also what's worthy of forgetting. Pay attention to them. The exercises later in this book will help you to do that.

MASTERING YOUR GUT INSTINCT: PERCEPTUAL INTUITION

Being able to see patterns—and making a habit of it—at a very early age is critical. Babies pick up on patterns quickly as parents follow the ritualistic patterns that are inherent in caring for a child. Pattern recognition explains why a baby can see a blanket and associate it with sleep or know that food is coming just by being placed in a high chair. It's astonishing to think that we humans create associations not only throughout our lives but starting the moment we are born, though we aren't always conscious of them. As we grow older, patterns become background noise that we ignore and "forget" for the most part, and yet those who notice and try to stay exceptionally attuned to patterns are typically the ones who get ahead more easily in life and find solutions to problems more quickly. They also are the ones who can take the most advantage of the power of forgetting. Coincidence? I don't think so.

In a later chapter, I'm going to teach you how to alphabetize the letters within a given word. It's arguably the best mental exercise to perform on a regular basis. Why? Because it entails some hard-core pattern recognition where you wouldn't think there would be a pattern. You'll take in bits of seemingly abstract information—in this case, a bunch of letters—and switch them around using a simple rule: alphabetical order. This is harder than it may seem, because most people don't know the alphabet as well as they think they do. So when they are told to spell "thought" in alphabetical order, they commonly spell it erroneously as "h-h-g-o-t-t-u," rather than correctly as "g-h-h-o-t-t-u." Why does this happen? It turns out that the mind often mixes up a few letters in the alphabet; it's difficult to know quickly, for instance, whether *g* comes before or after *h*. For this reason, it's much easier to spell "feedback" in alphabetical order than "knight." We'll explore why, and I'll reveal how to cement the alphabet in the brain for faster, more accurate recall.

Once you learn how to perform this skill, you'll find yourself doing it automatically all the time, since words are to be found everywhere—on the highway, in the mail, on television, in conversations with others, and in workplaces. It can be an addictive practice, but one that's incredibly fun and good exercise for the brain: It utilizes rarely worked areas of the brain whose "muscles," once trained, can strengthen the mind's capacity to retain information. It also fortifies the brain's ability to forget when necessary to handle more information quickly.

What you're essentially forcing yourself to do is to seek a different pattern by using all the information you're given and looking at it in a whole different way. We don't normally like to mentally juggle several pieces of a puzzle at once, but when we make a concerted effort to do so and use the power of forgetting as needed, we tap into greater brainpower. We also advance our perceptual learning skills.

Perceptual learning is a hot new field of study currently gaining momentum in psychological, educational, and scientific circles, and I think it helps explain why habitual pattern recognition is so powerful a factor in achieving greater success. In the simplest terms, perceptual learning is about being able to use your gut instinct to solve problems and "perceive" certain things. People with well-developed perceptual learning skills—such as the ballplayer who can detect pitches early, the art collector who can instantly spot a counterfeit painting, or the chess master who predicts the best move—have a great "third eye." This inner source of intuitive wisdom helps them make quick and, in many cases, accurate or correct decisions. It also helps them to organize their thoughts and instantly know, for example, what's important to remember without wasting precious mental energy and time. And all of this in turn allows them to forget petty details that can cloud their perceptual skills.

It's no surprise that some cognitive scientists are urging us to take far greater advantage of perceptual learning, especially in schools, where students should be taught how to learn. Benedict Carey wrote a marvelous piece on perceptual intuition for the *New York Times* in June 2011, aptly titled "Brain Calisthenics for Abstract Ideas." He explains the weakness in traditional schooling's so-called top-down instruction, especially for topics like math and science. He writes that we're taught to "learn the rules first—the theorems, the order of operations, the formulas and tables, Newton's laws, etc.—then make a run at the problem list at the end of the chapter. Yet recent research has found that true experts have something at least as valuable as a mastery of the rules: gut instinct, an instantaneous grasp of the type of problem they're up against."

According to cognitive scientists in this new area of study, gut instinct and perception are critical to success because they allow our brains to quickly deepen our grasp of a principle. They also allow us to make good decisions without really thinking about it—to arrive at conclusions effortlessly. One of the most exciting findings of recent research is that perceptual knowledge builds automatically, like a habit. To use the example provided by Carey in his article: "There's no reason someone with a good eye for fashion or wordplay cannot develop an intuition for classifying rocks or mammals or algebraic equations, given a little interest or motivation."

In other words, in subject areas that make us uncomfortable or whose ideas and rules are not easy for us to grasp, being able to rely on our perceptions can change everything. It can turn sciencephobes into scientists. It can help someone who could never before turn math equations into graphical interpretations become incredibly adept at this skill. And it can help anyone accomplish certain tasks more easily by relying more on intuition than on set rules and steps that require precise recall, thought, and consideration.

Carey brings up a good point in his reporting: When you think about it, perceptual learning is really just a way of looking at the world and asking yourself, *How can I solve this problem intuitively? Without really thinking about it, how can I arrive at an answer?* Although we're not always aware of it, in fact we ask ourselves these questions every single day, many times over. Whenever we're faced with a real-life problem, our first questions are always "What am I looking at? What's the problem? Where do I want to go with this? What should my solution or outcome be?" We then consider the facts, try to discern which ones are relevant and which we can forget, and figure out what to do next. All of this activity that our brain performs pretty much below our conscious radar is a perfect example of our perceptions at work helping us to solve problems. Our "perceptions at work" are what compose our habits. And by "problems" I'm referring to any number of situations, from decoding a serious math equation to deciding whether to turn right or left at a busy intersection. Put simply, our habits shape and hone our perceptions, which in turn streamline our daily duties and workload. The more we can effortlessly perceive throughout our day that's filled with decisions to make, the more we can save our mental energy.

Perceptual learning is rooted in the very fact that our ability to detect patterns, even the most subtle ones, happens subconsciously and well before we know we are learning. Carey cites a landmark 1997 experiment in which researchers at the University of Iowa found that some people playing a simple gambling game with decks of cards could unconsciously distinguish between the "good decks" (those that led to wins) and the "bad decks" (those that led to greater losses) after just ten cards. The study, which was published in the journal *Science*, proved that nonconscious biases can sometimes guide behavior before conscious knowledge does. In other words, you can perceive something different or special about a certain thing, such as a deck of cards, without any other knowledge or facts to consider.

Although some people, like me, develop sensitive perceptual radar the old-fashioned way through years of practice (and a self-inflicted obsession with recognizing patterns), there is growing evidence that a certain kind of training— "visual, fast-paced, often focused on classifying problems rather than solving them"—can build intuition quickly. For example, in another recent experiment cited by Carey, researchers found that people were better able to distinguish the painting styles of twelve unfamiliar artists after viewing mixed collections of works from all twelve than after viewing a dozen works from one artist and then moving on to the next painter. "The participants' brains began to pick up on differences before they could fully articulate them," Carey notes.

Steven Sloman, a cognitive scientist at Brown University, explains it beautifully in Carey's article: "Once the brain has a goal in mind, it tunes the perceptual system to search the environment for relevant clues." Or as Carey describes it, "In time the eyes, ears and nose learn to isolate those signs and dismiss irrelevant information, in turn sharpening thinking."

So how exactly is perceptual learning relevant to my ideas and exercises? The two are kissing cousins. The ability to take untraditional shortcuts in math, see equations and words in a whole new light, and generally manipulate and capitalize on pattern recognition in the ways I'm describing in this book is the very stuff of perceptual intuition. What I love about this concept is that it celebrates the art of guessing from an intuitive side of ourselves that we rarely tap but that can be incredibly resourceful when we nourish and utilize it. Said another way, perceptual learning pushes you to get creative where you never had permission to get creative before, and it turns tradition on its head. It forces you to cast aside—*forget*—facts and data in favor of pure intuition. With perceptual learning, the door is wide open for breaking old rules and discovering new ones that will work for you just as well—or even better. When it comes to memory strategies, you have to find what works for you and stick with that. There is no one-size-fits-all approach. And this is the soul of grooming the brain of a productive thinker who can become more effective by creating brain shortcuts that free up mental space.

Perceptual learning also helps to address one of the most widespread problems I see in people, adults and students alike: the "I give up" syndrome. All too often I watch individuals try to solve problems by doing only what they've always been told to do, and if that doesn't work they give up. They get stuck and refuse to think of other ways—kind of like hitting a wall in a maze and stopping right there rather than trying a different route. They also tune out their own inner gut instinct, which can be incredibly helpful and valuable. But with exercises and lessons based in perceptual learning, you're forced to try what makes sense to you and, if that doesn't work, to keep trying. You're compelled to seek another way out, another path to the answer.

Again, the brain is very good at sorting out patterns if you give it the chance and the right feedback. Sometimes it helps to remind yourself that the solution isn't always the first thing you think of.

So not only could there be multiple ways to solve a problem, but it may take time to find the best one that works for you. And in that regard, patience and determination become essential.

The actual science behind perceptual learning is quite stunning. Extensive research has demonstrated that, with practice, neurons in certain areas of the brain specialize to identify these signature patterns. And finding such patterns frees up mental resources for deductive reasoning, which can then be used to check answers or to move on to harder problems. Is this another way of saying that perceptual intuition is a new form of "cheating"? Not really. While it's true that creating brain shortcuts is like developing useful "cheats," they ultimately free up mental space, allowing you to reach a destination sooner. In other words, they let you tap the power of forgetting. Anything that enables you to forget the long road and take an effortless shortcut to a solution is a valuable tool in becoming an efficient thinker. Which is exactly why perceptual learning can be such an innovative, effective way of approaching problems and can outpace traditional problem-solving methods.

It's what a lot of highly successful people do, probably without even realizing it. Do professional basketball players really think through their steals and layups? Do doctors mentally thumb through their medical files and old textbooks when they diagnose a patient's illness? Do singers, actors, dramatists, and public speakers have to focus intently on every single word, phrase, sentence, or paragraph they utter to get through their song, act, or speech? No, they don't.

They forget all that previously recorded data rely instead on their intuition, which of course is developed over time and entails practice. To use an analogy I mentioned before, perceptual learning is like speaking a language intuitively. Anyone who has mastered a second language knows what it's like to go from thinking through every sentence and grammatical rule to letting the tongue just rattle off whole paragraphs in another language. At some point the brain takes off and knows how to navigate on its own. It hits cruise control, forgetting the nitty-gritty details. That's the power of intuition, which is also among the most underappreciated and underdeveloped skills in the learning sphere.

Perceptual training goes far beyond adding a layer of

practical context to abstract principles. It also prepares us to apply such principles in other situations, an ability known as transfer. This happens all the time when we're not even aware of it but can gain a huge advantage from increasing our ability to literally transfer knowledge—even if it's just a perception—from one subject area to another. You can, for instance, transfer a knack for cooking to a talent for improvising in a creative session at work during which you're ill prepared and asked on the spot to offer ideas. Or you may find yourself transferring an innate skill in understanding esoteric financial data to an ability to give practical advice to amateur investors who need your help in picking stocks. Indeed, most of today's entrepreneurs and business professionals owe their success to perceptual learning in some area. Their ability to leverage that skill through valuable products and services that others need is key.

Although it's argued that we don't know the best way to provide training in perceptual learning, I disagree. The six skills you're about to hone in these next chapters are not labeled "perceptual learning skills" per se, but I believe that if you practice them you'll simultaneously be developing your capacity to establish habits that reinforce perception and pattern recognition.

If you can make a habit of noticing and perceiving patterns everywhere you look and even in how you think, your success rate will be all the better for it. And for those of you who worry that you don't have the eye to identify patterns, try the following exercise. Pick two people you interact with on a regular basis and allocate some mental energy over the next week to pinpointing specific patterns in those individuals. These patterns can be anything—from what they wear to how they comb their hair, which foods they typically eat, how they walk, their habits, and so on. Make it a goal to come up with at least three patterns in each person, and if possible, find an additional two that are on the "unusual" side, such as your friend always twirling her hair in her fingers when she's bored or nervous or your brother routinely saying, "I'll let you go," when he's trying to end a conversation and hang up the phone. Maybe you've got a boss who leaves the office at precisely 5:20 most days but for some reason leaves at 5:45 on Thursdays.

People's behaviors are often a great starting point for noticing patterns in everyday life. We all communicate with other people on a daily basis, and being able to recognize and respect the patterns in our relationships is an essential first step toward having a constant awareness of and appreciation for all the patterns in our world, including those that are more subtle, obscure, irregular, and rare.

Once you're more naturally inclined to discern patterns, you'll soon find yourself picking out patterns that few others can see and that give you an advantage that will accelerate your success overall.

And that's what patterns really provide: access to greater understanding and greater success . . . for those who take notice!

Now that your brain is primed with a new understanding for patterns and habits, it's time to turn to the next part of the book, which will teach you to trust and tune your perceptual intuition using six important skills. This will ultimately help you develop the mental habits of a highly effective person. And as you can guess, one of these habits is all about forgetting on cue when necessary. Overall, the goal of the these six essential skills is to unleash your brain's full potential in ways that will help you to do the following:

- Strengthen your perceptual intuition and rely on gut instinct to solve complex problems, with an understanding that solutions come in many forms and that there is not only one "right" way to tackle a problem
- Improve your memory, concentration, and focus
- Apply mental multitasking to all areas of performance
- Make connections to math and the real world that can be transferred to other learning disciplines (such as reading or the social sciences) as well as to professional work and common personal tasks
- Continually clear out brain clutter and maintain a healthy volume of mental space for creativity and extra energy reserves
- Calculate facts and figures rapidly without pencil and paper, calculators, or computer apps
- Think for yourself
- Find your own shortcuts
- Live life as an active learner, regardless of your age, and accept new challenges

That's my ultimate wish for you. Now, with that possibility in mind, let's turn to the heart of the matter.

PART II

Mastering the Six Skills of a Productive Thinker

CHAPTER 3

Skills 1 and 2: Focus and Concentration

Can You Focus on Your Concentration?

I hear and I forget. I see and I remember.
I do and I understand.

—CONFUCIUS

Focus and concentration are two separate skills, but they are uniquely tied together. For myself, I've come to define focus as the ability to stay in the moment—to remain on target and attentive to whatever is before you in that moment without getting distracted.

Concentration, on the other hand, encompasses the bigger picture; concentration is being able to look at what's in front of you as a whole. When you're driving an unfamiliar route to a new destination, for instance, concentration accomplishes the overall goal of getting you to your end location, but focusing gets you there without an accident. Focus is the point-by-point, stoplight-by-stoplight attention that moves you along without incident. Although one can define focus and concentration separately, since for our purposes they are so inextricably interwoven, we're going to deal with them together in this chapter. You need both to streamline your mental faculties. And you need to form habits that help you to employ focus and concentration at the right time to handle incoming information smartly.

Take a moment to think about the types of jobs that require high levels of focus and concentration for extended periods of time. Surgeon. Test pilot. Race car driver. Member of the special forces in the military. Champion chess player. People who go into these lines of work or who take up hobbies that demand intense precision and rigor must train their brains to achieve exceptional levels of concentration. They have to be able to combat potentially distracting threats in the form of interfering thoughts—ranging from annoying songs that are "stuck in your head" to recurrent reflections on personal stresses or family problems, and even positive thoughts that can bombard the brain unexpectedly like a kamikaze.

Unfortunately, just telling yourself not to think about incoming thoughts doesn't always work so well (and science has actually proved that the attempt is usually futile). If something is preying on your mind, it's not going to go away so easily.

Aside from being able to deal with intrusive thoughts that take your mind and eye away from the task at hand while you're trying to focus and concentrate, there's the other side of the coin to consider: being able to conjure focus and concentration at a moment's notice and sustain them at a high level. Think about the last time you forced yourself to focus or concentrate really hard. You were probably under pressure, maybe taking a test, maneuvering in traffic to avoid an accident, preparing for a presentation, or figuring out your next move in a game or an ongoing problem at work.

Sometimes we have to will ourselves to focus and concentrate, to virtually and silently chant, *Concentrate! Pay attention!* in our heads. In this regard, a certain level of self-control and willpower is involved in keeping your attention on a single thing.

I've known for a long time that my brain—and everyone else's—uses a lot of energy when it's fully engaged in solving a complex problem (or just trying to get me safely across a busy street). Thinking hard is mental exercise. So is navigating daily activities, from the mundane to the unanticipated things that must be taken care of at a moment's notice. And when we're tired, it's difficult to stay focused on a single task for a long time and much easier to let intrusive thoughts steal precious mental energy and thwart our focus. For this very reason, learning how to preserve mental energy and habitually shun distractions has allowed me to "outfocus" most other people. But you, too, can master this skill and, in turn, achieve a level of willpower that makes prolonged focus and concentration virtually as instinctual as they are for me.

Luckily, now we can turn to science to understand what's going on from a biochemical standpoint. Roy Baumeister, the author of *Willpower: Rediscovering the Greatest Human Strength*, wrote about this in an article for *Bloomberg Businessweek*. He explains that the chemicals that enable our brain cells to fire are made from the glucose in our bloodstream and that all manner of self-control—including control of our focus and concentration—draws on the same stock of energy. When we think hard, calculate through problems, and make decisions, we're depleting that glucose in our bodies and at the same time eroding our willpower.

This explains why it becomes more difficult to concentrate or resist the temptation of intruding thoughts the longer you've been in a focused mode. But what about being able to lengthen the time it takes for your focus and concentration to wane? More important, what if you could naturally have the ability to focus and concentrate all the time without having to tell yourself to do so—and without relying on a steady stream of energy from your bloodstream? If you could have a mind that automatically kept competing thoughts at bay and important thoughts in the forefront, you'd be able to accomplish so much more—and so much more effortlessly!

Certainly that's what separates the best surgeons, test pilots, and chess players from the rest of us. It's not so much that they can inherently concentrate better, the way an Olympic sprinter can run faster by virtue of genetics. Much to the contrary, experts in concentration simply know how to get rid of extraneous thoughts and focus on the task at hand, no matter what. They can forget inane, distracting details and mentally disregard information that isn't helpful or informative. This isn't rocket science. It's just having the patience and expending the effort to develop this important skill so it becomes a habit. And that's exactly what I'm going to help you do in this chapter.

First, however, I want to share one of the more underrated aspects of this skill, which may seem to have nothing to do with focus and concentration. Believe it or not, self-confidence can be one of the most essential ingredients of focus and concentration. Self-confidence and the self-control vital to focus and concentration go hand in hand. To really get a true understanding of this, we're going to turn to baseball.

SELF-DOUBT CAN BE A DISEASE

If you ever feel the urge to read a few good stories about talented men who fell to a strange and unexplainable performance bug, then I recommend logging on to the Internet and searching for "Steve Blass Disease." In 1971 the Pittsburgh Pirates' Steve Blass was regarded as the best pitcher in Major League Baseball. Two years later, he could not even throw the ball to the catcher. He'd step on top of the mound, TV cameras all on him, and he'd freeze.

Unfortunately, this sudden and inexplicable loss of control after the 1972 season would become Blass's most famous and enduring legacy. He walked eighty-four batters in eighty-eight innings and struck out only twenty-seven. Blass suffered through the 1973 season, then spent most of 1974 in the minor leagues. He retired from baseball in March 1975 and today enjoys the game as a broadcast announcer for the Pirates.

"Steve Blass Disease" has become a part of the baseball lexicon. The "diagnosis" is applied to talented players who mysteriously and permanently seem to lose their ability to accurately throw a baseball. It's as if they suffer a serious breakdown of basic mechanics from which they cannot recover.

Worse yet, this incompetence emerges only during actual games. Their pitching is dead on during practice, but then they struggle (or completely fall apart) when it really counts. The fielder's variant of Steve Blass Disease is sometimes referred to in baseball terminology as "Steve Sax Syndrome." Sax's story is equally head scratching, though it has a better ending.

Steve Sax was a much-celebrated second baseman and right-handed batter for the Los Angeles Dodgers (1981–1988), New York Yankees (1989–1991), Chicago White Sox (1992–1993), and Oakland Athletics (1994). Though never regarded as one of the top-fielding second basemen in the league, Steve Sax became incapable of making routine throws to first base in 1983, committing thirty errors that season. As his accuracy suffered, fans sitting behind the first-base dugout began wearing batting helmets as mock protection. (Teammate Pedro Guerrero, an outfielder pressed into service at third base in 1983, reportedly once stated that his first thought whenever he was on third was "I hope they don't hit it to me," while his second thought was "I hope they don't hit it to Sax.") Luckily, however, Sax seemed to be completely "cured" by 1989, when he led the American League in both fielding percentage and double plays.

And then we have the story of Chuck Knoblauch, who became victim of a similarly career-ending condition. Knoblauch played all or part of twelve seasons in the majors, from 1991 until 2002, for the Minnesota Twins (1991–1997), New York Yankees (1998–2001), and Kansas City Royals (2002). He played mostly as a second baseman before moving to left field for his last two seasons.

Though he was once considered one of the game's best fielders (in fact, ESPN personalities nicknamed him "Fundamentally Sound" Chuck Knoblauch), Knoblauch's play deteriorated shortly into his Yankee career.

In 1999 he began to have difficulty making accurate throws to first base, and the labeling soon started. People began to refer to him as having "the yips," Steve Blass Disease, or Steve Sax Syndrome.

By 2000 the problem had grown serious enough that he began seeing more playing time as a designated hitter.

Knoblauch tried various solutions to his problem, but his throwing would not improve. He made an unprecedented number of throwing errors, routinely making abnormal throws out of the reach of the first baseman. During one game, an errant throw sailed into the crowd and hit sportscaster Keith Olbermann's mother in the face. Stumping commentators, fans, and himself, Knoblauch never fully recovered his throwing accuracy. He was reassigned to left field by manager Joe Torre, never to return to his old position.

OVERCOMING MENTAL BLOCKS

I share these stories not just because I love baseball and am well versed in these players' stories (and trust me, there are more MLB victims that I could talk about, such as Rick Ankiel and Dontrelle Willis, not to mention countless other professionals in other sports) but also because they illustrate a universal experience to the extreme: failing—or in more unrefined terms, "choking"—when you least expect it or when the stakes are unusually high. Not all of us are in the limelight like a professional athlete, celebrity, or public figure is, but all of us have choked at one time or another when it cost us more than we bargained for. Perhaps it was a big test. Maybe it was a job interview or a project that ran aground at work and took us down with it.

Of all the skills you're going to learn and sharpen in this part of the book, there's one in particular that needs to be growing right alongside the others—and that's confidence. Self-doubt is a big thing. As your confidence wanes, so does your ability to focus and concentrate. I don't know anyone who hasn't suffered a mental block or two in life. Take my friend Larry, for instance, who shared with me his own frustrating story. It happened a few years ago while he was interviewing for a coveted job in the tech industry. As a software developer applying for a highly competitive spot in a new firm, he had to undergo a computer test proving his technical skills and programming savvy. He studied long and hard prior to the exam but worried that he'd encounter something unexpected and beyond his expertise. He knew that he was among dozens of candidates vying for the same position and that some of his competitors were better at certain programming techniques. Given the volume of potential skills that could be tested, Larry didn't know what to expect and hoped for the best.

Minutes before the HR person at the company gave Larry, alongside others sitting in a room filled with computers, the green light to begin, Larry reminded himself of the formulas he'd memorized, running his eyes across his notes, then tucking them away. He felt ready. But he also felt overwhelmingly stressed and under pressure. Looking around, he could sense the tension and anxiety in the room, swirling like an invisible storm. The clock ticked high noon, and the HR rep announced that the candidates could commence. The sound of furious typing on keyboards began.

And then the unthinkable happened. Larry forgot some of the most basic programming rules of all. They had vanished from his brain.

He tried to "see" in his mind the notes that he'd just reviewed a few seconds earlier. But everything was blank—his mind, the mental picture of his notes, and the pages of the test on the desk before him. Immediately, Larry began to rummage through all the horrific scenarios in his imagination—the biggest of which was failing the test, losing this great opportunity to advance in his career, and disappointing himself and his family.

He took a few deep breaths and tried to relax, but the anxiety continued to mount. The clock ticked.

Eventually, Larry managed to tackle many of the problems on the test, but he used the wrong programming concepts for some of them, which cost him several points. He didn't fail the test, but suffice it to say it wasn't a shining moment for him either—he didn't get the job. Had he not stumbled in those first few minutes—had he not experienced such a profound mental block—Larry could have aced the test and accelerated his career path. But alas, that was not to be on that particular day.

Luckily, things went better for Larry at his next opportunity. Six months later, he interviewed for another job, equally prestigious, and breezed through the qualifying test. When I asked him his secret to success, he said that learning to relax helped him to take the next test in stride and be less stressed out about the end result.

What Larry described so well to me was the same experience I hear about from so many others. People lament that they cannot understand why they can perform so well in everyday work but then fall to pieces when they are put to the test somehow, either literally with an exam or by being asked to present, lead a group, or represent the company at a conference. One of the first things I tell people is that the brain works so much better when it's not under pressure. This may seem obvious, but I have to remind people all the time about the value of being comfortable and relaxed when you're put to the test. I've had my own experiences with this simple truism. Back in my trading days, I noticed a pattern in my success. On the days I felt calm and collected, I performed so much better. It took me a long time to learn how to calm myself down and gain the confidence I needed. I won't sugarcoat the truth: getting comfortable with yourself and your abilities takes time and practice, but it's arguably one of the most essential and fundamental skills to develop.

Every January 1 my New Year's resolution was the same: "Mike, don't be nervous!" It took eight or so years for that to really click, though. I had to eventually let logic take over, stop beating myself up, and say, *I'll be okay. And if I screw up, I'll get back on my feet.*

I see people kill themselves (figuratively speaking) over one bad review or one disheartening comment from a colleague or other adult. But if you can tell yourself that you'll be okay no matter what—even if you falter a few times first—then you'll pull ahead of the pack and achieve success at some point. Sure, what I call the "law of compounding errors" will always exist, which dictates that a single, huge error tends to be greater than the sum of its individual parts—the little errors that add to one another and build up to that big mistake. But when you try really hard, those errors will become fewer and farther between. The law of compounding errors looms large over people who don't try to avoid mistakes or who commit "unforced errors" because they lose focus and concentration. But those who genuinely put their best foot forward with resolve and faith in themselves are the ones who leap forward (all the while making it look easy).

The Law of Compounding Errors: We all make mistakes. We're human. But sometimes we make stupid little mistakes from a lack of focus that can end up costing us big-time down the road. One mistake leads to the next mistake, and then another one . . . and five misses in a row can veer you so far off track that you can't win or succeed. Productive thinkers know about the law of compounding errors, and they work hard at avoiding this trap.

I wholeheartedly believe that the only thing that can hurt any of us is not having confidence in ourselves. What often happens is that when we lose confidence, we also lose our logic. As happened with Larry, our minds can sense "danger" or imminent failure and quickly spur catastrophic thoughts (*I'm gonna fail! I'm a loser! I'm never gonna succeed! I'm never gonna be good enough! I'm gonna die!*). How illogical are those statements?!

I'll admit, I wasn't perfect at performing shows when I first got started. I wasn't used to the setting, the format of being on a stage or in front of a large audience and pressured to impress people with my math skills. So I made mistakes, and sometimes my mistakes were big enough to really bother me. Occasionally my wife reminds me that in those very early days, after a show rife with mishaps and errors on my part, she once heard me say something to the effect of "I feel like going home and blowing my brains out—I'm gonna kill myself!" She yanked me aside after the show to tell me that I hadn't said that statement to just myself—I'd actually unwittingly shared that out loud with my entire audience of youngsters and their adult supervisors, teachers, and parents.

That experience alone taught me a lot. Granted, it took me time to realize that it was okay to make a mistake. But now I turn my mistakes into some of the most teachable moments in my shows.

When people realize that someone with a brain like mine can falter once in a while, I sense a palpable exhalation from them, because they finally register that there is no such thing as "me" versus "them." We are all the same. Even when we're good at something, we can have a bad day. And what separates those who endure those bad days (or bad seasons) from those who never get back up again is confidence. If you lose a job over a poor performance, you just have to tell yourself that you can get another job and have another opportunity. You have to sustain this confidence within yourself because no one else is going to do it for you. By the same token, don't expect anyone to give you confidence. It must come from within.

I don't know anyone who doesn't fear failing when they're under the weight of serious pressure or stress. What I want you to keep in mind as we move forward here is that it's okay to feel uncomfortable when you're put to the test. But here's your assignment: Work on using your brain where the consequences aren't so terrible.

I can't express in words how transformative it can be to flex the brain where it's weak and to build skills that haven't been substantively addressed in formal education. Then one day when you're asked for real to use your brain in some innovative way while under pressure, you'll be able to meet the challenge. You'll rise to the occasion and wow your peers. People tend to practice what they're good at rather than working on skills they aren't good at. So let's change that, and we'll start with the most fundamental skills of all: F&C—focus and concentration.

FOCUS ON YOUR CONCENTRATION AND CONCENTRATE ON YOUR FOCUS

Focus and concentration are the keys to keeping your confidence intact, to thinking logically, to avoiding those catastrophic "I can't do it" thoughts, to combating anxiety, to beating the pressure, to quelling any burgeoning insecurities, to learning to relax, and to hitting your own balls out of the park. Sadly, though, within the past ten years alone I've witnessed a dramatic shift in people's ability to focus and concentrate. We used to have to focus and concentrate a lot just to survive. We'd have to watch our step as we—and tigers— roamed the savannas in search of food. We'd have to conduct lots of math and science on our own in navigating new territories and exploring the world; think of early pioneers and sailors during the days before GPS. And just a few years ago, we'd have to think about where to find a public telephone if we were caught in an emergency away from home.

Today, however, our modern culture is bursting at the seams with distractions. We have an enormous wealth of technology and media at our fingertips to make life way more convenient and easier to navigate. This same technology and media, however, can steal our attention and prevent us from using the kind of focus and concentration that we still need—skills we must actively preserve and practice. Which is why the problems I often see in classrooms and among adults have nothing to do with people's inability to actually do math or read. The problem lies in their inability to simply follow directions.

Many of the games I play with students are all about following directions—obeying five or six sequential steps that involve punching numbers into a calculator. But rarely do I have a session with kids where at least half a dozen don't arrive at wrong answers because they missed a step in the instructions. It only takes a fraction of a second to be distracted, fumble a critical piece of information, and then go down the wrong road. I'll make students aware of this, show them where they went wrong, and then encourage them to try again until they get it right. But in the real world, we don't always get second chances. Daydreaming or momentarily losing focus is usually what triggers accidents and mishaps that can cascade into serious problems. People who've been in car wrecks after taking their mind or eyes off the road for a mere millisecond know how easy it is to lose your focus, and the consequences can be huge. In the grander scheme, little mistakes here and there can accumulate, affecting your performance at work or your personal reputation.

We're all aware of how our modern society presents challenges to maintaining focus and concentration. We've fallen victim to absentmindedness and being scatterbrained thanks to that errant e-mail or phone call. Or we've made mistakes due to interruptions and distractions while we try to complete a task. Rather than center on the negative here, let's turn this into a positive and dive right into strengthening your focus and concentration no matter how weak and distractible they are. This means reinforcing your "forgetting" muscles so you can train your precious mental energy on important tasks at hand. Being able to forget nonessentials is a critical part of maximizing focus and concentration. I will ask that you avoid all other interferences as you read forward. Turn your cell phone off. Get comfortable in a room and see if you can spend just a few minutes now bringing all of your attention to the upcoming pages. What we're going to do is (1) test the strength of your focus and concentration, (2) make you more aware of when you lose your focus and concentration, and (3) develop ways to build your ability to focus and concentrate. Ready?

TESTING, TESTING, ONE-TWO-THREE

Below is a sentence. I want you to read it once and concentrate on what it says while counting the number of *f*'s. (Alert: This exercise is meant to be done only once—right now—and that's it!)

A scientific study of fossils was conducted in the laboratory of Jonathan Frank.

Now look away from this page and recall how many *f*'s you counted. One? Two? Three? Four?

The purpose of this exercise is to show how hard it can be to force the brain to perform two different tasks at the same time: comprehend and count. If you're like most people, you may have found two or three *f*'s. Maybe you culled four. But there are actually a total of five. It's common to miss a few of these *f*'s, especially to skip ones in the small words, such as "of." The mind is naturally inclined to skip the small words and focus on the large words.

We know that the larger words will tell us the important part of the sentence—they are what provides the key thought, whereas the little words are the links, the trivial connectors. Additionally, it's human nature to think of the "of" as an "uv" rather than a word with a sharp-sounding *f.* When we say "of" in our minds it sounds like we're saying "uv." So we hear a *v* and forget that it's in fact an *f*!

But there's something else going on here that I want you to notice: Did you find it hard to focus on the meaning of the sentence while counting the *f*'s? Right now, can you explain what the sentence conveyed? Or are you having to go back and reread the sentence, this time without counting anything?

Many of us multitask all day long. So why can't we multitask at this level? Why can't we count the *f*'s and soak up the meaning of the information? As it turns out, these two tasks start to compete with each other when we simultaneously count and comprehend. It's hard to do both at the same time. Molecular biologist and University of Washington professor John Medina explains the reason why in his book *Brain Rules*:

> *Multitasking, when it comes to paying attention, is a myth. The brain naturally focuses on concepts sequentially, one at a time. At first that might sound confusing; at one level the brain does multitask. You can walk and talk at the same time. Your brain controls your heartbeat while you read a book. Pianists can play a piece with the left hand and right hand simultaneously. Surely this is multitasking. But I am talking about the brain's ability to pay attention. It is the resource you forcibly deploy while trying to listen to a boring lecture at school. It is the activity that collapses as your brain wanders during a tedious presentation at work. This attentional ability is not capable of multitasking.*

I love how Dr. Medina describes the crux of the problem: being able to pay attention, which he calls "attentional ability." And therein lies the secret to peak performance: being able to pay attention one "sequence" at a time. Sometimes, however, we can have trouble just paying attention at all, with focusing and concentrating on just the one task at hand before moving on to the next. Which is why I've designed the following exercises to help you do just that.

First I'll showcase a math shortcut that demands focus and concentration; then I'll move on to a word game that requires even more intense focus and concentration because you have to be aware of what you're doing every step of the way. And finally I'll round out this chapter with a test that illuminates your mind's natural ability not only to focus and concentrate on the spot but also to notice patterns and heighten your "attentional" capacity.

DIVIDING ANY NUMBER BETWEEN 10 AND 90 BY 91

The following exercise forces you to place different information in your brain in sequence and then retrieve certain information at different times in order to arrive at your answer. First, however, I want you to take note of the pattern involved with the solutions to all of these types of equations. Below are four different solutions to the problem of dividing any number between 10 and 90 by 91. Can you figure out what these four solutions have in common?

Can you find the pattern? (Note: I'm giving only the first six decimal places.)

$$72 \div 91 = 0.791208$$
$$84 \div 91 = 0.923076$$
$$31 \div 91 = 0.340659$$
$$56 \div 91 = 0.615384$$

When I first designed this shortcut for dividing any two-digit number by 91, I did so by finding patterns in numbers that relate to the number 1,001. For example, 91 times 11 equals 1,001, and 13 times 77 equals 1,001. Now, before you start trying to figure out how I went from seeing that pattern to arriving at a trusty new formula for working with the number 91 as a denominator, don't ask. I'll save you from having to hear the very long story of how I finally reached my shortcut. But it's worth emphasizing that my shortcut invention wasn't arbitrary. It was possible due to my pattern awareness. (For those who want to spend time thinking it out, by all means, have at it! You can go online at www.MikeByster.com to share your step-by-step approach and see if it syncs up with my formula or offers a whole new approach.)

So, with that in mind, let's turn back to these equations. In all six digits of the answers, patterns exist in relation to each equation.

Did you find some of them? Here they are.

The six digits of each answer always add up to 27. Hence, in our first answer, 0.791208, if you were to add those individual numbers up, 7 plus 9 plus 1 plus 2 plus 0 plus 8, you'd get 27. The same is true of 0.923076 (9 plus 2 plus 3 plus 0 plus 7 plus 6 equals 27), and so on.

In each answer, there will be three even digits and three odd digits. (Zero is considered an even digit.)

The first and fourth digits of each answer add up to 9, the second and fifth digits of each answer add up to 9, and the third and sixth digits of each answer add up to 9.

Spend time admiring and looking at these patterns if they didn't jump out at you initially. The next time you're asked to find a pattern, maybe it'll emerge in your mind's eye a lot faster. Okay, so let me take you through figuring out how to divide any number between 10 and 90 by 91. Note that this shortcut only works for numbers between 10 and 90, and the number cannot end in 0. (Did you catch that? I said between 10 and 90, so you can't use either 10 or 90. Are you paying close attention? You need full processing power to get really good at this.)

Alert: In many of the exercises I will use language like "tens digit number" and "ones digit number" as I explain the steps. This helps me to identify the numbers. If you need a brush-up on this language, here's a cheat sheet just in case:

In the number 123, the 3 is called the ones digit number, the 2 is referred to as the tens digit number, and the 1 is the hundreds digit number.

Let's take 72 divided by 91. Here are the sequential steps to take:

- Step 1: Take the numerator, which in this case is 72, and add it to the tens digit of that number, which is the number 7. So 72 plus 7 equals 79. Put a decimal point in front. So now we have 0.79. (In case you didn't notice, this first step means that every time you divide a number between 10 and 90 by 91, your answer will be a number less than 1. All answers will have a decimal point in front of them.)

- Step 2: Next, take the ones digit of the numerator, subtract 1, and tack that onto what we have so far. Hence, 2 minus 1 equals 1. Tack that number 1 onto what we have so far: 0.791.

- Step 3: Ask yourself: How far is the first digit of the answer (7) from the number 9? Seven is 2 away from 9. Tack on the 2 to get 0.7912.

- Step 4: Ask yourself: How far is the second digit of the answer (9) from 9? Nine is 0 away from 9. Tack on the 0 to get 0.79120.

- Step 5: Ask yourself: How far is the third digit of the answer (1) from 9? One is 8 away from 9. Tack on the 8 to get 0.791208.

- Step 6: Since the calculator repeats or carries out to show more numbers, you have to say it like the calculator, so to add one more number, just repeat the first digit after the decimal point. Tack on the 7 (or repeat the entire pattern, "791208"). And there you have your answer: 0.7912087 (or the longer version: 0.7912087912087).

Try three more on your own:

$28 \div 91 =$ _____

$35 \div 91 =$ _____

$19 \div 91 =$ _____

HOW MUCH?

I recommend that you attempt problems like these on a monthly basis at a minimum. Every last Sunday of the month, for instance, remind yourself of the secret formula and then work your brain through these problems. See if you can recall the shortcut without having to study it first!

If you're feeling ambitious, you can attempt these on a biweekly or weekly basis. For a more advanced version of this shortcut, try doing this exercise without writing down the numbers and without giving or saying the answer until you have the entire six-digit answer. Here's a hint: Once you have the first three digits of the answer using steps 1 and 2, start talking out the answer to find the last three digits using the final four steps. Don't try to pack the entire answer in your head before speaking it. Let your brain flow through arriving at the remaining three digits as you think it through sequentially.

Remember, every number divided by 91 will go on forever, but after six digits it repeats itself. So, 72 divided by 91 equals 0.791208791208791208 . . . and so on.

JOTTO

This second exercise works your logic skills. It's a two-person game, and you'll need a pen and paper. It can be played as many times as you like. As with physical exercise, your body can't ever get enough, so long as you rest between sessions! The more you play, the more your brain benefits from a serious workout. Try playing at least once a month to start and then more frequently once you have the basic rules down and find yourself going through the motions of this game relatively quickly and easily.

How to Play

Each player thinks of a five-letter word and writes it down, keeping their word to themselves. These words must contain five different letters. Each player then writes out the alphabet, *A* to *Z*, at the top of their page. It's up to each player to guess the other's word. They do this by saying other five-letter words to their opponent. It's the opponent's job to say how many letters this word has in common with the chosen word but not to say what those letters are.

Jotto can get busy: You'll find yourselves volleying back and forth, suggesting words while keeping an eye on your own word.

And remember to write down your guesses so you don't repeat yourself. Once you find a letter that you feel isn't in your opponent's word, cross it off your alphabet at the top. When you think you've found a letter in your opponent's word, circle it. Jotto is a process of elimination.

Let's take an example:

Player 1's word is "brain." Player 2's first guess is "shirt." Player 1 now says how many letters in "shirt" are also in the word "brain." In this example, those letters are *i* and *r*, so Player 1 says, "Two letters." Player 1 doesn't have to state which letters the two words have in common—this is what keeps Jotto fun. Player 2's second guess is "short." Player 1's response is "One," because *r* is the only common letter. Now Player 2, having learned that *i* is in the secret word, circles it on his alphabet list and crosses off *o*, having also learned that *o* is not in Player 1's word. Meanwhile, both players are writing down each word they guess so they won't use them again. That would waste a turn.

On Player 2's next turn, he guesses "those," to which Player 1 answers, "Zero." Now Player 2 crosses *t*, *h*, *s*, and *e* off his list (he's already eliminated *o*). He's eliminating letters to arrive at the correct word. And he's circled *i* and *r* because he also knows from his first guess that those two letters are part of the word. Two letters down; three to go!

Play continues until Player 2 guesses Player 1's word. But while this is going on, the opposite has been happening as well—Player 1 has been trying to guess Player 2's word. Both players have been very busy.

Jotto has a few other rules:

- The word must be common and found in the dictionary.
- No foreign words, proper nouns, or contractions are allowed (plurals are okay).
- If someone says a letter is in his word when it actually isn't, he loses that round.

Tip: It's good to guess words that are close to your previous guesses so that they use some of the same letters as these other words.

If you guess more matching letters, you're headed down the right path.

IN THE MIND'S EYE

Now let's get a little playful and test your "attentional capacity." I want to show you the power of your mind's inherent ability to detect certain patterns automatically. This will also play into your mind's adeptness at automatically focusing, concentrating, and—yes—*forgetting* when necessary.

Look quickly at the following word and see if you can figure out what it would spell if the letters were arranged differently: salttre.

Can't "see" it? Don't stare at this word for more than a few seconds, and avoid trying to unscramble it. Just look at it as a whole.

If you've got the answer, pat yourself on the back. But don't beat yourself up if you haven't decoded it yet. Before I reveal the answer, let's move on to one more exercise. Take a look at the following box and begin reading:

Aoccdrnig to a rcheeraser at Cmabrigde Uinervtisy, it deosn't mttaer in waht oredr the ltteers in a wrod are; the olny iprmoatnt tihng is taht the frist and lsat ltteer be at the rghit pclae. The rset can be a toatl mses and you can sitll raed it wouthit porbelm. Tihs is bcuseae the huamn mnid deos not raed ervey lteter by istlef, but the wrod as a wlohe.

Or rather . . .

According to a researcher at Cambridge University, it doesn't matter in what order the letters in a word are; the only important thing is that the first and last letter be at the right place. The rest can be a total mess and you can still read it without problem. This is because the human mind does not read every letter by itself but the word as a whole.

Like some of the other exercises in this chapter, the content in these boxes may not seem to have anything to do with patterns, but in fact the ability to read the first paragraph—where the words are scrambled (with the exception of the first and last letter in each word)—has everything to do with patterns and, more specifically, associations that the mind can make in an instant. (And for the record, this text circulated through the Internet—and many people's e-mail in-boxes—in the fall of 2003. Although some have suggested that the original research may not have come from Cambridge University, it's nonetheless intriguing. Because this text has been passed on so many times, it has mutated along the way. What you see here is merely one version.) The first scrambled word on page 100, by the way, is "startle." Or maybe you saw "rattles" or "starlet." Why was it easier to decipher a whole paragraph than a single word?

As the next chapter will illustrate in rich detail, all memory, whether trained or untrained, is based on association.

When you see the single word mixed up, it's much harder to make an association in your mind than it is to see a pattern amid the medley of mixed-up words in an entire paragraph. The pattern in the paragraph reflects a series of associations. There's a hidden system to the way the letters are scrambled in each word, and the brain can start to pick up on that system by looking at a whole batch of words that follow its rules. Another thing to note is that the brain has an enormous capacity to adapt quickly. Once it sees a few words scrambled a certain way, it can adapt to seeing those words as it picks up on the concealed pattern. At the same time, the mind is "forgetting" the details in the scrambled words (i.e., the individual letters) and instead focusing just on the overall pattern to decipher the meaning of the paragraph.

To really understand how easy it is for the brain to suddenly "click" and dial into a certain pattern or way of looking at something while forgetting the nonessentials, try playing any classic video game such as Pac-Man, Tetris, or Minesweeper. Surely you'll recall the first time you played such games and found yourself working hard to remember which keys matched which actions. Then at some point, quite instinctively, your fingers could find the keys when they needed to without your really "thinking" about it. As your mind adapted to the game's intrinsic patterns, you were able to play the game much faster and allocate less brainpower to paying full attention to what your fingers were doing. After much practice, you could probably play any of these games while performing other tasks, such as talking on the phone or with another person in the room—or any other task that didn't require the use of your playing hand!

You don't need to play video games to appreciate this mental experience. If you've ever driven yourself to work, the grocery store, a friend's house, etc., and arrived without really remembering the drive, then you know that your brain tuned in to the usual patterns of that habitual drive to get you there. You've experienced the same phenomenon if you've cooked up a meal almost subconsciously while talking on the phone or engaging in conversation with family members nearby: mental cruise control driven by known patterns ingrained in your brain.

In all of these scenarios, it's as if the mind takes over, in much the same way you can speak English without thinking through every word as you create a sentence. And in fact, you experience a similar process when you learn a new language: In the beginning it's hard and requires lots of practice, but after a while, as your mind adapts to the new language and learns its structural patterns (yes, all languages have patterns that reflect sets of rules that we call "linguistics" or "grammar"), you begin to speak the language without having to think so intently about how to compose each sentence. You "forget" the nitpicky rules and let your brain work on autopilot, which focuses on the overall task.

Because associations are so key to memory building, providing the foundation for all mental skills, they are essential when you're trying to remember abstract ideas, which we encounter a lot in real life. Perhaps, for example, it's linking the year when World War II ended (1945) with the pass code to get into your garage at work. Even when we create bizarre associations between two different things, all associations are about relationships—establishing connections between numbers, words, concepts, images, or pictures. Sometimes these associations are nothing more than substitutions—a method of association that has given us cryptograms, secret codes, and ciphers that date back thousands of years. These are prime examples of patterns in action.

PRACTICE, PRACTICE, PRACTICE

Your ability to focus and concentrate, which in turn helps you to automatically identify patterns, will require routine practice.

As we go through the other skills in the upcoming chapters, you'll find your focus and concentration tested over and over again.

Every time you're challenged to learn something new you'll be simultaneously cultivating, developing, and maintaining your focus and concentration faculties. What I want you to be extra vigilant about as you move forward is to notice any moment when your focus and concentration wane or falter. See if you can stop yourself and ask: *What happened? Why did it happen?* Then center yourself again and bring your focus and concentration back up to speed. Although I have described focus and concentration as two separate skills, we don't really keep track of when we're focusing versus when we're concentrating; often we're performing these two skills at the same time. This is because we need to enlist both skills to achieve a given goal, such as driving to a destination or cooking a soufflé.

I have a habit—a ritual—of looking a certain way when I intently focus and concentrate at the same time. If you ever watched me solve a really hard equation or rapidly rattle off a series of solutions to difficult problems, you might get the idea that I've got a massive headache. That's because when I'm put to the test, I keep my eyes tightly closed and pinch the bridge of my nose with my fingers.

I look like I'm in pain, but what I'm really doing is forcing myself to go inward—to access the mental file I need and "download" it to the front of my mind so I can answer the questions. This habit of mine isn't meant for show, and I didn't develop it on purpose. This is just my own natural way of becoming very aware of the task at hand so I can retrieve and hold the important information in my brain to then work with it. My point in telling you this is to encourage you to do what's necessary to focus and concentrate as best you can, especially when you need to focus and concentrate for a brief but critical moment of time. This may mean closing your eyes, as I do, or taking a deep breath to distance yourself from any distractions and summon up a razor-sharp awareness for what your brain is tackling.

One of the chief reasons I wrote this book was to help readers bring a level of consciousness and awareness to their lives that they might not have had before. We have a natural inclination to let our minds lie dormant until we have to use them to do something, and even then we tend to minimize how much we use our brains. We draw from them only what we need to get by, rather than deploying the full extent of their potential. My goal is to make you activate your brain as much as you can and as often as you can. So the next time you're driving from point A to point B—and I mean this figuratively as well as literally—don't just drive "subconsciously."

Instead, make the most of your journey and engage your mind in ways that will make you smarter and sharper by the time you reach your destination.

Chapter Guide

The exercises in this chapter are designed to be done more than once, and preferably as many times as your schedule allows. This is a great chapter to save for a Saturday or Sunday afternoon when you have twenty minutes or perhaps a whole hour to play with these mental activities. See if you can go through every exercise in this chapter at least once a month, and more frequently if possible. Pull out your trusty math trick for friends at social events. Remember, the more you practice, the better your brain becomes.

SOLUTIONS TO THE PROBLEMS IN THIS CHAPTER

$28 \div 91 = 0.307692307692$

$35 \div 91 = 0.384615384615$

$19 \div 91 = 0.208791208791$

Skill 3: Retaining Massive Amounts of Information Without "Memorizing"

Increasing Mental Capacity Through the Fine Art of Association

The aim of education should be to teach us rather how to think, than what to think—rather to improve our minds, so as to enable us to think for ourselves, than to load the memory with the thoughts of other men.

—JOHN DEWEY

When I was seven or eight years old, I had an incredibly difficult time distinguishing my left boot from my right boot during those long Chicago winters. I often ended up with my boots on the wrong feet. My teacher at the time wasn't the nicest of people, and she'd terrorize me over my boots being mixed up. My mother had an idea: She suggested that we put an *L* in the left boot and an *R* in the right boot. But I told her that it would be embarrassing if anyone saw that, because everyone else could tell their left boot from their right boot (and I knew that my teacher would continue to be mean about it). So my amazing mom then came up with a better solution.

She wrote my entire name, Michael Byster, in each boot, which was fine because a lot of kids had their names in their boots.

However, in the left boot my mom underlined "Michael" because it ended in *L*, and in the right boot she underlined "Byster" because it ended in *R*.

This experience taught me at a very young age that there are many different ways to tackle a problem, and it gave me the confidence to know that it's okay to try another path to a solution.

It also marked one of the first times that I really understood the power of association. Making a connection between my name and my boots (and my feet) that made sense to me proved to be another pivotal point in my life. Of course, I would come to adapt a lot of things in life to my personal challenges, and just knowing that adaptation was how to get things done would also become a huge confidence builder. But the art of association has become one of my strongest skills in keeping my brain efficient and clutter free—able to focus on the spot and immediately distinguish between what's important and what's not so I can store only the information I really need.

In the last chapter, I covered a lot of ground about focusing and concentrating. These will be recurring themes throughout the book, as they provide the foundation for all the strategies that build a better brain.

Now let's develop the third essential skill for igniting your brain's potential. I call it increasing mental capacity, or expanding how much information you can retain. I'm not talking about traditional memorization here. Much to the contrary, I'm going to show you how to activate your memory skills in ways that allow you to develop a faster mind—literally. Remember, memory is the basis of mental capacity and of learning itself. In the past you may have equated memory with memorization, but as you should know by now, memory goes much further than that. Memory is also more than "a good memory"—it is the means by which we perform the largest share of our mental work and ultimately solve problems big and small. It's also the means by which we become productive thinkers.

From the moment we get out of bed each morning, we use our trained memory to solve problems—from deciding how to drive to work (and navigate through traffic) or how to handle a difficult business or personal call with someone who isn't happy with us, to simply planning out the week in advance given our responsibilities, our obligations, and the competing demands of work and home. The inability to problem solve is what characterizes illnesses like Alzheimer's disease and other forms of dementia. People who suffer from these afflictions have lost their ability to reason, think, and remember the way a healthy brain can by recalling certain information to use in making critical decisions. Thus, they lose their capacity to perform the complex tasks of daily living. One of the more fascinating revelations of studies on dementia is that brain diseases are more about learning problems than about memory problems.

Those who have symptoms of Alzheimer's find it hard to absorb information, so when they seem forgetful, it's not that they don't remember the facts—it's that they never stitched them into their brains to begin with!

I bring up the case of dementia because examining

extreme conditions under which mental faculties have declined or vanished helps us come to a better understanding of how we can keep our minds sharp. And you don't have to have a brain disease to lack the ability to problem-solve effectively. Unless you learn how to optimize your memory, you won't be able to make good decisions in life—and life is, after all, a series of important choices to consider: "What should I say yes to?" "What jobs should I try or start?" "What career path should I take?" "Whom should I marry?" "Where should I live?" "What should I do with my life?" "How can I get ahead faster?" These choices force you to consider multiple options; mentally organize streams of competing and sometimes conflicting data; navigate hard-to-understand ideas for which you don't have the benefit of hindsight; differentiate between key information and that which is immaterial, irrelevant, or even nonsensical; weigh pros and cons; employ logic where necessary; sort out competing agendas; tease out details you may need to help you decide while ignoring the rest; and generally evaluate, examine, and handle information smartly to arrive at an answer or a positive outcome of some sort that helps you live a better, more successful, more fulfilling life. Which is really all any of us wants.

And then we have the other types of problems to solve that do indeed feel problematic when we struggle with them. You could be faced with the challenge of recalling someone's name or phone number, remembering where you put your keys, storing difficult words or other random pieces of information, or learning a new language or hobby that requires lots of tugs and pulls on your rusty memory. Now, some of you might argue that no one needs to memorize things like phone numbers anymore because we have high-tech gadgets that store all that data. Similarly, you might be thinking that practicing such a skill is worthless when we have technology at our fingertips to do the work for us. But remember what I said earlier about relying too much on technology: Such dependency can weaken your mind in the same way an unused muscle can atrophy. When we don't actively engage our memories in ways that help us quickly and effortlessly retain information, we impair our minds. So while it may seem impractical to memorize people's phone numbers today, when you do you're actually strengthening the parts of the brain that can help you solve much bigger, more profound problems—from figuring out how to get home when the subway strands you in an unexpected and unfamiliar part of town to choosing a profession, deciding between two acceptance letters, or going with plan A over plan B. In short, there is a direct connection between being able to commit mundane facts to memory and becoming an expert decision maker in all areas of life. The more quickly your memory functions, the better off you'll be, because you'll make fewer mistakes and rarely veer off track.

When we work specifically on memory strategies, we're creating new neural connections and growing a more extensive network in the brain to stretch its current boundaries. But I'm going to make good on my promise and avoid teaching anything close to rote memorization. Instead, what you're going to do is learn how the fine art of association can increase your memory—and more important, your capacity to "forget" when it's essential to being a productive thinker who isn't easily distracted and can stay fully attuned to just the vital facts and data (no matter how voluminous those facts and data are).

MEMORY SYSTEMS DISPLACE MEMORIZATION

Virtually everyone has experienced the difficulty of trying to memorize disconnected and seemingly arbitrary facts. At one time or another, everyone has also had trouble recalling things they once had memorized. And most everyone has struggled to remember something they actually do know but in a different context.

If you grew up in the United States, you probably spent a lot of time as a child memorizing the state capitals and the names of the presidents. Can you now write down all of the capitals? How about all of the presidents' names—in order? Can you remember who was president when the nation's capital moved to Washington, D.C. (hint: 1800)? Unless you are a serious history buff, the answer is probably no. Learning these facts is perhaps a rite of passage through middle school, but does that effort really pay off?

Such knowledge rarely sticks very well and doesn't make itself available when it would be useful. Sure, we can memorize random facts, but we are notoriously bad at it. Why else would we have so many devices for taking notes and making reminders?

And yet it's hard to argue with the notion that our value or success in everyday activities, including our chosen business, profession, trade, or other occupation, depends to a great extent on the degree of memory we've developed. Our memory of faces, names, facts, events, circumstances, and other aspects of our everyday work affects our ability to accomplish our goals and tasks. In our social circles, having a retentive memory—chock-full of available facts—helps us become well-respected members of society. It can even help us achieve upward mobility, leaving behind lower socioeco-nomic levels. In the words of Lactantius, who was an adviser to the Roman emperor Constantine I in the third century, "Memory tempers prosperity, mitigates adversity, controls youth, and delights old age."

Memory systems have been around for as long as humans have tramped across the earth. In much the same way we've always known somewhere deep down that sleep is good for the brain, we've always known that memory systems exist, that there are in fact "secrets" to optimizing our brain's stor-age capacity and processing speed and that it pays to develop them. Think about how valuable it must have been to have a good memory back when there were no practical ways to take notes, store information digitally, or keep a journal. It was memory techniques that enabled people to remember their stories, poems, and songs or the need to avoid a certain path because the local rodents had made it their home. If someone walked in a forest and picked up poison oak, how would they be able to remember what it looked like so as to avoid it in the future?

They'd have to find a way to firmly "implant" that image in their mind and be able to recall it the next time. And to make sure that image wouldn't be crowded out by too many other competing images, they'd also have to find a way to forget and disregard the multitude of innocuous, harmless plants. In other words, they'd have to "forget" in order to re-member. Indeed, one of the linchpins of an awesome memory is the ability to forget.

During the days of ancient Greece and Rome, orators

who delivered long speeches no doubt relied on memory systems to accurately recall every thought without skipping a
beat or missing important information. Simonides of Ceos
(c. 556–468 BC), a poet famous for his public performances,
is probably best known as the father of all memory techniques. But scraps of paper dating back even a thousand years
or so before his time have been found that indicate memory
techniques were an integral part of an orator's equipment.
Mind you, oratory was an important career during ancient
times, and to this day the ability to deliver a compelling
speech is a critical skill for anyone who seeks public office or
hopes to share their ideas with the masses.

During the Middle Ages, philosophers and theologians
depended on memory systems to broadcast their ideas. They
may have been the only people of their time who knew about
applied trained-memory techniques. I can imagine that being
able to memorize was on par with being able to read and
write. All three skills were necessary to gain people's trust,
attention, and loyalty.

DID YOU KNOW?

Centuries ago, some philosophers and priests taught
that memory systems showed people how to gain
entry into heaven and avoid hell. In other words,
memory systems were a tool for proselytizing, teaching religion, and conveying ideas.

Despite the early history of memory systems, it took thousands of years for books to appear that shared the secrets to training the mind. One of the best-known early memory-training books was *The Phoenix*, published in Latin by Peter of Ravenna in 1491. It's amazing to think that of all the topics written about in those early printing days, a book on memory was among the first to be distributed to the lay public—proof of the importance placed on having a well-trained mind. During the fifteenth and sixteenth centuries, many other books were written on the subject.

I would venture to guess that virtually all the great leaders and rulers of the world used memory systems, whether their own or those learned from others. The same goes for all the great teachers, storytellers, philosophers, physicians, writers, lawyers, judges, inventors, orators, scholars, academics, mathematicians, entrepreneurs, and business owners. Shakespeare's Globe Theatre wasn't called the "memory theatre" for nothing. It was a center for grand performances in the art of memory itself, for his actors would have to recall lots of lines in performing his plays.

WHERE DID I PUT THAT?

Memory systems are part of who we are, and the mind's ability—need, really—to patternize the world and create associations all the time is what ultimately ensures our survival. Each one of us has the built-in "technology" to have an amazing memory. We just have to learn how to train our memory systems to optimize their functionality. We also need to train those same systems to forget when appropriate.

Let's assume that you're a pretty good sleeper, which helps you to nourish your mental faculties and in particular your memory bank. Let's also assume that you do the other things typical of a "brain-healthy" way of life. You take your vitamins, you eat pretty well, and you solve crossword puzzles to keep your brain agile. You also have already begun (let's be optimistic here!) to engage your mind in the ways I've been suggesting in this book. But today you misplaced your keys. What's up with that?

Don't panic. Forgetting where you put your keys stems from one of the most widespread "afflictions" and annoyances: absentmindedness.

When we find ourselves misplacing items that we "just put down" or worrying about whether or not we turned off the oven, locked the door, unplugged the iron, sent that important e-mail, or left something valuable on the train, on the bus, or at our friend's house, we can become frustrated, question our intelligence, or even begin to wonder if this is the sign of a cognitive decline toward full-blown dementia.

The good news is that absentmindedness is not a factor of intelligence. Occasionally forgetting critical information isn't due to lack of inherent brainpower. After all, we all know people with high IQs who lose their keys, forget where they parked their car, or leave the oven on. And there are just as many people who have fantastic memories but whom we wouldn't call smart. But what does it mean then when we do things unconsciously—without thinking?

Earlier we discussed that one of the hallmarks of mental decline isn't so much the inability to remember as the inability to create a memory—to take in a new piece of information and store it somewhere so it's retrievable at a later date. When people say, "I forgot," what really happened is that they never stored the memory in the first place. Hence the solution to remembering: Lock it in initially and you can never forget it!

How is this possible? After all, this entire book is about having a better, faster, bigger brain, so is there a single way to do this? A magic bullet? In short, yes. I've already been emphasizing the importance of creating associations in your mind, and the longer answer to this question entails a quick tour of how we typically lose our mindfulness in everyday activities. Rather than making conscious connections between two disparate things in our minds, we tend to skip over this essential step, and then later we find ourselves missing an important piece of information, such as where we placed our keys or what time our kids told us to pick them up.

In their seminal work *The Memory Book*, Harry Lorayne and Jerry Lucas eloquently describe this very process of what they call establishing "original awareness." It's a brilliant term, so I am going to use it as well. It explains precisely the issue: Anything of which you are originally aware cannot be forgotten. But awareness isn't something we routinely maintain. A classic example would be the act of driving. When you operate a car, you're not really "aware" that you're driving. You do it quite subconsciously, especially if you've been driving for a very long time. You can get from point A to point B while talking with passengers or thinking about other things besides when to press on the gas pedal and when to brake. Or take the experience of "mindless eating" while watching television or a movie. It's not called mindless eating for nothing! Anyone can find themselves downing an entire bag of chips or popcorn without thinking about every bite.

So what do Lorayne and Lucas mean by "original awareness"? They use the term simply to refer to the "first time"— as in the first time you see or do something that you want to remember. When you set your keys down on a table, in order to remember that you put them there you need to have an original awareness when you initially set them down. You need to actively observe what you're doing. In fact, observation is essential to original awareness, and it's not the same as just "seeing."

As Lorayne and Lucas compellingly detail in their book, there is a difference between what the eyes "see" and what the mind "observes." If your mind is "absent" when you perform an action, there can be no observation; more important, there can be no awareness of the action (learning) and subsequent creation of the memory. But how, you ask, do you create original awareness, especially when it comes to random events and abstract or intangible things? Using associations takes care of this, but the key to making memorable associations is to construct associations in your mind that are meaningful to you. Let me repeat that: You must manufacture associations in your mind that have personal significance to you. This is a fundamental fact of trained memory.

It is always easier to remember things that have meaning to you than it is to remember things that do not. And because it's possible to make any intangible or abstract thing in your mind meaningful to yourself, there's really no such thing as abstraction! Being able to make an oddity personally relevant transforms the oddity into something real, concrete, and unforgettable. Once you've mastered the art of creating associations everywhere you go, all remembering—and thus all learning—will be easier for you for the rest of your life.

Back when we discussed patterns, I mentioned that we as human beings seek patterns all day long even when we don't realize it. And we've been doing so since birth—for example, as a baby associating a bottle with food and the satisfaction of hunger or as a child hearing the familiar bells of the ice cream truck rolling down the street and beginning to crave a treat. We are instinctively attuned to patterns in our routines, habits, and daily activities. But patterns are themselves associations. When we recognize a certain pattern, we are in fact making an association somewhere in our mind, and usually it's very relevant to us.

Take, for another example, the repeated pattern of hearing a car pull into the driveway at night. Hearing the same car every evening, the same sound of the car door closing, alerts family members that someone, perhaps Mom or Dad, is finally home. This experience is rich in sensations for those family members who are attuned to it—the feeling that a loved one has arrived home safely and the emotional satisfaction of that arrival. While it's just the sound of a car parking, it's not just any car—it's one that is filled with associations for certain people.

Anyone who has ever heard a certain song and been cast back in time to a specific memory conjured by that song can understand the power of association. Have you ever smelled something that instantly reminded you of someone or a place from the past? For example, a whiff of a certain type of perfume may call your grandmother to mind, or the smell of disinfectant may remind you of your dad, who worked in a hospital. How many times have you heard or seen something that made you snap your fingers and say, "Oh, that reminds me!" Usually, the thing that reminded you of something had absolutely nothing to do with what it reminded you of. Somewhere in the back of your mind—in your subconscious—a random or absurd association was made, but not as a fluke or a coincidence. Our senses hold big keys to our memories, and they often provide the "glue" that cements an association in our minds. Everything we see, hear, touch, smell, and taste can factor hugely into our ability to make associations.

So you've used associations all your life, but probably without even being aware of it. Anything you clearly associated with something significant to you, even if subconsciously, is sure to be something that is now easily remembered. But since you have no control over your subconscious, associations have been hit-or-miss most of your life. Let's change that.

THE ART OF ASSOCIATION

Many of us try to remember things by rote memorization— repeatedly saying the information in our heads and hoping that it eventually sticks. Sometimes this method works for short-term recall, but the information fades away over time. Occasionally it disappears quickly once we've used the information—the proverbial "in one ear and out the other," or cramming for an exam and forgetting all the information when you walk out of the exam room!

Unlike associations, which demand a certain level of awareness to create the link and make it relevant to us personally, rote memorization doesn't include awareness. When we memorize something by rote, we're not really "aware" of what it is we're memorizing, and it often remains an abstract construct. Anything that stays abstract and intangible to us cannot reach the areas of our brains where the information can sink in for future use.

So here's a basic rule to all memory training that all memory trainers, such as Lorayne and Lucas and countless others (myself included!), teach: You can remember any new piece of information if you can associate it with something you already know or remember.

One of the most abstract things we're trained to memorize very early on is the alphabet. And how do we recall it? By associating it with a song. Right now, you can probably hear the alphabet song playing in your head. The alphabet comes naturally to anyone who has the alphabet song down, but when you think about it, the order of letters is fairly arbitrary.

If you ever took music lessons, then surely someone told you that the ideal way to remember the notes that ascend the lines of the treble clef—E, G, B, D, and F—is to think of the sentence "Every good boy deserves fudge." The first letters of the words correspond to the notes. The ascending notes for the spaces between the lines are F, A, C, and E, which can easily be remembered, since they spell the word "face." The notes that fall on the lines of the bass clef in ascending order are G, B, D, F, and A, which can easily be remembered by the sentence "Good boys deserve fudge always." The ascending notes in the spaces are A, C, E, and G, which correspond to the sentence "All cows eat grass." Your music teacher wasn't making this stuff up. These sentences have been used for a long time to teach abstract information, and they follow the basic memory rule: Associate the information with something you already know or at least understand—in this case, a simple sentence—and the information will stick.

A mnemonic ("mindful") device uses advanced patterns to remember things. "Spring forward, fall back" helps us remember which way the clocks move at the beginning and end of Daylight Savings Time. "Every good boy deserves fudge" is another example of a mnemonic device.

Associations come in all shapes and sizes. In other words, there's an infinite number of ways you can create associations. All of us can instantly picture Italy in our heads because we were told it's the shape of a boot. But what about Germany? That's not so easy, is it? You probably haven't created an association for that one. (As an aside, anytime you need to memorize something about Germany, try thinking about the actress Meg Ryan. Her name shares the exact same letters as "Germany"; maybe that association will help you.) To remember how to spell "Ohio," many of us were told to break it into O (as in "Oh!"), then *hi* (picturing someone from Ohio waving hello), and finally *o* ("Oh") again. Or to spell a word like "piece," some of us were told to think of a "piece of pie." "Pie" is pretty easy to spell, so the hard part of spelling "piece" (knowing the *i* comes before the *e*) is already taken care of just by associating the word with the phrase "a piece of pie." And anyone who has had to memorize the Great Lakes might have used the word "homes," as in "homes on a great lake." The letters correspond to the first letter of each of the Great Lakes' names: Huron, Ontario, Michigan, Erie, and Superior. Similarly, the four voices in a quartet can be recalled by picturing a quartet being stabbed, because "stab" gives us soprano, tenor, alto, and bass.

Despite the value in these specific examples, they will

only work if you can make them relevant to you. "Homes" might not be the word you want to use to remember the Great Lakes. You might have to come up with another word or sentence that has more meaning to you personally. If there's one great thing about memory systems, it's that if you're willing to employ them there really are no limits. If you know how to consciously associate anything you want to remember with something you already know (ahem: create that original awareness), you'll have a trained memory. Associations needn't be logical or commonsensical, either. In fact, later on we're going to see that bringing a level of absurdity and silliness to your associations can be an incredibly powerful tool. Anytime you use your imagination in establishing original awareness you maximize your memory building because you're forcing yourself to concentrate and form associations.

Let's take a quick example. Say you're told to remember the following items in this order: T-shirt, milk, sand, boat, and clock.

How will you commit this list to memory and not fumble the sequence? Start by making an association between the first two words, T-shirt and milk. There are a number of ways to do this, one of which is to first picture a T-shirt stained with milk. Then find a way to tell a story through the rest of the words, or at least picture something that encompasses all of the words. Maybe you see a kid in a T-shirt drinking milk while he sits in the sand on the beach. He looks out to the boats on the water and then turns to his mother and asks, "What time is it?" This last part is a tad absurd, but it's exactly the kind of storytelling that helps commit things to memory. The crazier it gets, the stickier it will be.

But isn't logic important? Why am I confusing you with

talk about making things as illogical and weird as possible? There's definitely a role for logic in all things mind related, particularly with regard to using your brain, thinking through problems, and not letting external influences hijack your sensibility. But when it comes to memorizing per se, it helps to recruit your quirky side—that part of you that yearns to be funny, strange, different, and sometimes even ridiculous. When you bring your creativity to the table, you're in fact making things more logical for you. So it's not as contradictory as you think. Anytime you fuse your imagination, artistry, and originality with facts, data, and information in a way that retains the integrity of the data, you essentially enhance your personal logic.

Centuries ago, Aristotle began one of his books with this sentence: "It is impossible even to think without a mental picture." How true that is. Einstein himself confirmed this when he stated, "If I can't picture it, I can't understand it." Our minds tell stories all the time. We mentally see pictures and images all day long, as if we're running a movie in our heads. Try it right now: If you read the words "baby," "truck," and "rhinoceros," you cannot think of any of those things without "seeing" a picture of them, if only for a split second. The same is true of actions, or things in motion.

When you read the words "skiing," "mountain climbing," and "surfing," what does your mind do? It briefly pictures those actions. It is the image-making part of the brain that facilitates higher thought processes. We never think without making a mental picture, for the thinking faculty thinks of its forms in pictures.

Even blind people think, and in turn "see," in their own world of imaginary pictures. In fact, we'd never learn or understand anything if we didn't have the ability to perceive

pictures. When we're forced to think about abstract or spec-
ulative ideas, our minds try hard to create some mental pictures with which to think about the ideas. Those who invent
trained-memory techniques teach us to construct images in
much the same way Aristotle had in mind when he said that
it's possible to put things before our eyes.

Because we are picture-oriented creatures, nearly all
memory techniques rely on some form of imagery, especially
when it comes to objects and intangible things like people's
names or places. When you hear or see a word or phrase
that seems abstract to you, think of something that sounds
like it or that reminds you of the abstract material and can
be pictured in your mind. We'll see how this works in the
sections coming up that cover how to remember names and
faces, but for now let's take a quick example. Say you want to
remember a street named Kelton. You can't easily "picture"
that in your mind, but the word sounds pretty darn close to
"Celtic," so you could picture a Celtic tribe, or something
else symbolic of Ireland, in your head. When you need to recall the street's name, you could say to yourself, "I'm going to
Ireland," and maybe the association would be strong enough
for you to remember the link to "Kelton." Of course, it helps
to strengthen the association with other details. Perhaps your
friend who lives on this street has red hair and freckles, making the reference to Ireland all the more vivid and memorable.
The key, though, is to create associations that work for you.
Personalize them to your expérience, knowledge, and sense
of humor. And don't overly complicate your associations or
spend too long trying to force them. They should be easy and
quick to create; if they're not, find another association that
works better.

The art of personal moviemaking is what also allows us

to recall certain information in a sequence. If you want to remember a list of items, an exercise I'm going to take you through shortly, having a story that moves from one scene to the next can help you recall that information correctly.

So there you have it. The combination of creating original awareness and employing the power of association, imagination, and storytelling (moviemaking) in our minds is the ticket to training our memories to be the best they can be. We're going to see all of these tasks in action to a much greater degree throughout the rest of the book. I think it's quite telling that we know now that absentmindedness, which routinely affects the vast majority of the elderly, is not necessarily a sign of illness. It's also highly preventable.

What's more, a growing number of studies have shown not only that mental exercises are a powerful preventive measure but also that they can slow down, halt, or even help to reverse disease. Some studies have proved that staying mentally active can slash the risk of developing Alzheimer's disease by half! And you're never too old—or young—to start boosting your brainpower to stave off that kind of decline.

But here's the catch: Although people think they are sharpening their thinking skills and mental acuity by playing Scrabble, completing crossword puzzles, or getting immersed in Sudoku, these games are very limited in how they challenge the brain; they don't really recruit the parts of the brain that enhance its imagination, concentration, and observation. They are not going to help you when you need it most, such as in remembering where you placed your keys, remembering faces and names (particularly when you meet a roomful of people at once, which happens a lot at gatherings and parties), recalling phone numbers or other many-digit numbers, mentally storing difficult words whose meanings are hard to remember, or picking up a foreign language. Which is where we're going to next: I'm going to teach you my strategies for tackling these things, and those lessons will call upon all the ideas I've just described—namely, the beauty of awareness and association.

THE CURE FOR ABSENTMINDEDNESS

Absentmindedness means exactly what it says: You are absentminded when your mind is absent—when you perform actions without thinking. I've already pointed out that there's a difference between what you see and what you observe. Our eyes do the seeing, but it's our minds that do the observing, which entails a more complex process. Our minds have to go through a few steps in order to take in a new piece of information, organize it, and then place it somewhere. If the mind is not made aware that it's supposed to notice the incoming information that the eyes are seeing, then it cannot complete its mission. Put simply, if your mind is neglected or is absent when you're performing an action and seeing new information, then it cannot observe. It cannot create the all-important original awareness.

The remedy for absentmindedness should be obvious: making sure you generate original awareness when you're in the middle of your action. You have to think of what you're doing at a very conscious and active level. This means forcing yourself to generate an association on the spot. Otherwise, how else will you make yourself think of a minor action at the moment you're doing it? It's very easy to fall into the trap of doing things almost unconsciously, so you have to push the envelope here by coercing your mind into finding an association, however bizarre or imaginative. After all, original awareness compels you to register something in your mind in the first place—when the moment occurs. The mere act of establishing original awareness via association should free you from absentmindedness, or at least help prevent as much of it as possible.

Let's take an example. You're at your desk tending to e-mails. You're just about to respond to an important message marked "high priority (!)" when the phone rings. During your conversation, you minimize your e-mail program on the computer screen so you can open a file in another program and deal with the call, which becomes a long one. After the call is over and you hang up, you totally forget to return to that e-mail message. When the phone rings several hours later, it's the person who sent you the message marked high priority, asking for an explanation. You had promised to reply right away, so what happened? How could you have forgotten? You're deeply embarrassed and have to come up with an excuse. You'd love to avoid doing this kind of thing in the future, as it happens a lot.

Here's what you need to do: The next time you're pulled in another direction and want to remember what you were doing once that interrupting task or emergency is resolved, momentarily find a way to create a fast mental picture in your mind before you switch directions. If the e-mail you were about to write is going to your colleague Sally, then before you pick up the phone, "see" Sally with an angry look on her face because you've put her on hold. Or perhaps you could visualize Sally standing in front of your desk—frozen in time—with a stamped letter duct-taped to her forehead, symbolizing the e-mail. She won't come back to life until you get back to that e-mail. These ideas may sound silly, but they will force you to think of what you were doing at the time you were interrupted.

I'll be honest: Making a habit of forming associations like this every time you want to remember something while shifting gears or performing an action takes practice. You'll probably have to force yourself to make associations in your daily activities for a little while until you establish the habit, at which point it becomes relatively automatic.

When you do make these associations, it helps to make them as absurd and visual as possible. For example, if you drop your keys on your dining room table (where you usually never leave them) because you're dashing to pick up a ringing phone in the kitchen, you'd do well to drum up a wild image, such as your keys being thrown into a fruit salad and taking on the appearance of a piece of fruit. Or "see" your keys hanging from the chandelier and dripping with ketchup or barbecue sauce. This association, by the way, can be made in a fraction of a second—you don't even have to break your stride. While the mere act of consciously thinking about your keys as you put them down likely will help you remember where they are, the association you've made with the contents of the dining room (chandelier and food) definitely will help you remember where you put them.

How many of us have put a treasured item in a "safe" spot—a really good hiding place—and then torn our hair out trying to find it again? Or never seen it again? It doesn't have to be that way. All you have to do is generate a weird and vivid association in your head as you tuck your special item away. For instance, say you want to keep five hundred dollars in cash for emergency purposes, so you put it in a box that is destined to sit atop a bookcase for a very long time. As you place the box on top of the bookcase, take a second to "see" the box becoming attached to the bookcase as if it were a big button that opens a secret passageway behind the bookcase, which, in your mind's eye, leads to a safe with your money in it. Absurd? Yes.

Memorable? Yes. The next time you think of that box, no matter how long after you've placed it on top of your bookcase, you'll know exactly where it is.

Tired of leaving items at friends' houses? Or leaving your house and forgetting to bring something with you? Association solves all of these problems. Just be sure to create an association that leads you from one thing to another. If you don't want to leave behind the serving tray for your contribution to a potluck dinner at your friend's house, then while you're entering your friend's foyer at the start of the evening, picture the platter on the front steps and imagine that you're stepping on it as you leave the house, smashing it into pieces. This picture will associate the platter with the moment of leaving. Add one more helpful image by associating the platter with your car if you traveled to your friend's dinner party by car. Imagine the platter as replacing your windshield. When you get back into your car after dinner, if you don't have your platter with you, you might remember to go get it if you just look at the windshield.

When making these kinds of associations, it helps to associate items with the last thing you normally see or do as you're leaving a place. If you don't want to leave your cell phone at work (again), then, as you're putting your cell phone down for the day, see yourself using it to call the elevator up to your eleventh-floor office. Most of us leave our homes and lock them with a key. Find ways of associating any items that you don't want to leave behind with locking the front door. Picture your rent check, which needs to be mailed, as the actual key to lock the door when you write out your check and seal the envelope.

As you can see, it's all about making associations and generating ones that reflect the very things you're trying to remember. This isn't the same as just tying a string around your finger, scribbling a note to yourself, or setting the alarm clock to remember to take the roast out of the oven. Often we fail to create effective reminders for ourselves because we make no relevant associations. So what happens is that we're alerted to recall something but don't remember what that something was (unless we really did write it down in detail)! The whole point of creating associations is to achieve two important goals: (1) to generate the reminder, that is, to create original awareness, and (2) to clue yourself in to what it is that you need to be reminded of. The next time you're baking and want to go catch a thirty-minute television show as your cake bakes in the oven, go ahead and set an alarm in the kitchen, but also bring a spatula with you to the den and place it on top of the television or in the middle of the coffee table before you.

Just think of all the frustration you'll now avoid by applying the simple rule of association. You'll never have to turn back home and check to see that you turned the oven off, unplugged the iron, or locked the front door. You'll never lose time searching for your "misplaced" keys, cell phone, or wallet. (And hopefully you'll never call yourself "forgetful" in a negative manner; being unable to remember important things isn't about being forgetful in a traditional sense.) You'll have seen your keys scratching your television screen as you placed them on top of the TV; you'll have seen your cell phone calling your dog as you dropped it on the table by Fido's favorite spot in the living room; and you'll have pictured yourself getting folded into your wallet as you tossed it into the top drawer of your desk. Don't spend too much time coming up with the perfect image to make the association. The image you choose isn't as important as the fact that you're forcing yourself to think of the act in the moment you're doing it. It's like "grabbing your mind by the scruff of the neck and forcing it to think of a specific thing at a specific moment," as Lorayne and Lucas so perfectly describe it. The first time you try this technique it will feel strange and perhaps ridiculous. But over time you'll become accustomed to it and it will become a ritual—a habit that you won't want to break because it'll save your day in more ways than one.

Dr. Seuss's perennial bestseller *Oh, the Places You'll Go!* is a much-beloved classic. It's become the perfect send-off gift for people entering a new phase in their life. If there's one thing Dr. Seuss was an absolute genius at, it was creating memorable stories through the art of absurdity, comedy, rhythm, and silliness. His works continue to engage the imaginations and can-do spirits of millions of readers, young and old alike. If you, too, can mimic just a small slice of Dr. Seuss's talent and transport yourself to wild and crazy places in your mind, you can harness the most effective and enduring strategies in all memory systems.

DRUMMING UP NUMBERS

When my son was seven years old, he asked me one day during our drive home what the numbers on his water bottle meant: 120507. I told him that it was probably a code for the date when the bottle would expire: December 5, 2007. We usually play games with letters and numbers during our drives, so for fun I told him to remember that number and that I'd ask him to recall it the next day. The next day he remembered the number, and then I added the number 3 to it. Again, I told him to recite this new number the next day, which he did. This went on for quite some time. I gave him a new number to add to the sequence every day by posting it on his bedroom door at night. Josh would review the sequence every night once he had the new number to add. After several months, he had a two-hundred-digit number written into his brain. How did he do it? What strategy did he use?

To memorize a long number like that, you can't rely on repetition or rote memorization. That just won't work for such a confusing array of arbitrary numbers. I didn't give Josh any clues to memorizing this sequence of numbers as new ones were added, but when I asked him later on how he managed to achieve such a feat, I was proud of his ingenuity.

Josh employed a few techniques. First he'd break the numbers up into sections that seemed to have natural breaks. Different numbers come out of the mouth at different speeds—for instance, the word "seven" takes longer to say than "two." Then he'd create a song in his head to help him get the numbers out. He'd hear drums playing and group the numbers by certain rhythmic patterns, chiefly in groups of three and four. Because Josh was taking piano lessons at the time and was already musically inclined, this was what came easily to him. In other words, hearing drums playing to the tune of his numbers came pretty naturally, and it was familiar. As I've been emphasizing, any form of memorization that you can relate to is key.

Josh is now a teenager, and even today he can still recite much of that long number just by bringing his drum-filled song to mind. I realize that the thought probably crossed your mind: What was the point of his memorizing such a long and random number? What did he really gain from doing so? First of all, one of the most important lessons that this experience taught him was to know in his heart that he could memorize anything. When students have an overwhelming amount of information to memorize, they can easily feel psychologically overwhelmed and lose confidence in their abilities. Josh, however, can always fall back on his two-hundred-digit experience to remind himself that there's nothing he can't do. If he could commit a two-hundred-digit number to memory at the age of seven, he knows he can do practically anything now. He has a certain level of confidence gained from that single feat.

Second, Josh's mental stunt tapped more storage capacity and power in his brain. It's practically unfathomable how much we can pack into our brains, and we take their capacity for granted. Theoretically, our brains have the room to hold a lot more information than we realize—upward of ten billion encyclopedia pages' worth. But in order to do so optimally, we have to continue to work the brain in ways that compel it to absorb, sort, organize, and file away information properly. This includes utilizing the brain's internal trash compactor, where we throw away the nonessentials we intend to forget in order to make room for the important stuff. Obviously, the number Josh memorized wasn't important in and of itself. It was meaningless. But the task of committing that number to his memory was indeed important. And it was a very meaningful lesson.

Most of us have to remember lots of information in life, some that's important, some that's not important, and some that we'd like to avoid. With the help of fun memory systems, it's possible to make anything that we need to retain, from the most boring and tedious details to the critical information, really stick. To navigate the basics of the world requires remembering lots of information—information that can further be used to solve any problem.

Now I'm going to take you through a few ideas on committing phone numbers to memory. On the surface, this may not appeal to you at all, since we have nifty devices called computers and smartphones today to remember our contacts for us. But the overall lesson is an important one, because these strategies can have an impact on how your brain rewires itself to retain other types of information, especially the kind that you cannot rely on anything or anyone but yourself to remember. This exercise also sharpens your ability to forget where appropriate to make your brain stickier for the salient points you need to commit to memory. So I encourage you to try all of these techniques and to find ways of applying them to other types of memory challenges in everyday life. For instance, perhaps the skills you acquire here to instantly memorize a series of numbers will ultimately help you pick up all the engrossing facts embedded in a magazine or newspaper article, thus making you the center of an enthralling conversation at your next social event (perhaps with your boss, who no doubt would be impressed!).

PHONE NUMBERS

Have you ever lost your cell phone only to realize that you don't have or know anyone's number? Many of us today rely on technology completely to be our substitute memory banks. Cell phones can store so much data now that we don't have to remember numbers anymore as we used to. We simply choose a person from our contacts list and hit "send." In fact, smart phones can be programmed to include people's faces and names, so we don't even see phone numbers anymore on the screen when the phone is dialing. What we see are photos of our friends and family or just a name.

For old-fashioned folks like me, it's easy to recall the alignment of the alphabet with the numbers on a phone's keypad. The number 2 could also be *A*, *B*, or *C*; the number 9 covers *W*, *X*, *Y*, and *Z*. The 0 is "OPER"—the direct code for "operator." But even younger generations today should be pretty familiar with the letters on a keypad by virtue of their texting experience. Those who don't have a newer cell phone might still be using the letters of the keypad to punch in words. I marvel at how fast some teens can text by single-handedly punching in words via a rapid-fire strike of dozens if not hundreds of numbers.

There are four ways to put phone numbers into memory in an instant. Obviously, the first option is to create a word or sentence from the number itself. The key, though, is for this word to be significant to you and to be linked to the person whose phone number it is. For example, let's say your friend Joe's number is 563-7622. When you look at the keypad in reference to this number, you'll see that I've made this one super easy. The numbers 563 could spell "Joe." To find an appropriate word for 7622, we can apply something about Joe to the number. What I didn't tell you is that Joe graduated from the University of Southern California, otherwise known as USC and sometimes referred to as "SoCal." You could definitely remember 7622 just by thinking of the word SoCa. Every time you have to drum up Joe's number, you just think "Joe SoCa," and you'll be able to spell it out using the numbers.

Don't know how to deal with the numbers 1 and 0, which don't have any letters attached to them? It's totally up to you how you treat these numbers. One way would be to move the *A* over to the number 1 so that the number 2 is just *B* and *C*. Since it's natural to associate 1 and *A*—the first letter in the alphabet—this is an easy designation to make. You could do the same for the 0 by assigning the *Z* to it, but you could also just make the 0 equivalent to the letter *O*, since 0 looks like the letter *O* anyhow. This means you lose the *O* from the number 6 on the keypad. However you create your mental keypad, just make sure that it makes sense to you so that you can not only recall it but also use it. That's all that really matters.

Another option is to look at the pattern created on the keypad as you dial the number. In the example we just used, 563-7622, we start in the center with 5, go right to 6, then up to 3. The 7622, however, is not so easy to spot. It gets a little messy. This number might not be the best one to memorize using pattern recognition. But other numbers might be ideal for this way of thinking. Take, for instance, a number such as 456-1379: The 456 is easy because these are the three numbers in the second row on the keypad; 1379 constitutes the four "corners" of the main keypad. So if you refer to this pattern when you need to recall this number by heart, you could picture the keypad in your head and find the numbers.

The third tactic is to look at the mathematics of a number, especially the patterns. Say you have the number 475-1288. The first three numbers are quarters in the sense that 4 could be seen as ¼, and 75 could be seen as ¾. With 1288, some people might instantly see that the number 88 is 12 less than 100. This may not seem so intuitive at first, but once you start to search for patterns in numbers, you'll be able to pick up this skill rather quickly.

Finally, the fourth strategy for remembering numbers is to attach a story or facts to them. Let's say you're trying to remember 4561, the pass code you need at work to get into the garage. The pattern this number creates on the keypad doesn't do much for you, and you can't seem to find a good, memorable word to make out of it. You also don't instinctually see an obvious math equation or numerical trend in the set of numbers. Instead, what pops into your head are two facts: World War II ended in 1945, and your spouse was born in 1961. There you have it. Remembering just the last two digits from each of those facts—45 and 61—you'll be able to recall this code. Whether or not you can link World War II to your spouse is another story! Or perhaps you can find an event and date more appropriate to your personal story and match up the numbers. This is a prime example of thinking outside the box.

Of course, you can always use any combination of these strategies. Because I know a lot about sports figures, I use athletes' names and uniform numbers a lot, making up little sentences. Do what works for you and is relevant to your life. Just break the numbers down and try to see them differently.

I always know that when I see the number 843 it's the word "the." Seeing words through the lens of numbers takes practice, but everyone can work on this skill and get good at it. Like memorizing strings of numbers, this skill taps more mental storage power and helps ignite networks in your brain to facilitate quick processing. An added bonus is that when you're calling an automated answering machine from your cell phone and it asks you to dial the person you want by the numbers on your keypad, you'll be able to do it! Try some for yourself. What do these "words" mean?

82253
27323
7428873
24453736
2886662453

Here's an added challenge. It's hard to do this when you don't know where one word ends and another begins. See if you can decode the following short sentence or statements. What is being said here?

4277924784329!
47328646378446525453

AND YOU ARE...

Names tend to be pretty abstract on the surface. For many people, it's easier to recognize faces than to remember names, which is why the secret to mastering name recall is to apply a strategy whereby a feature of that person tells you his or her name.

Being able to remember names comes in handy when you're in a business setting or want to impress someone. Let's say you're attending a cocktail party for work and have a meeting with your boss the next day. Imagine being able to engage in an engrossing conversation with your boss just because you were able to remember certain people's names from the night before. Or let's say that you've represented your company at an important convention and need to re-port back to the CEO. Adding people's names to the stories you share not only gives your stories more life but also shows that you paid attention. It indicates that you've got an amaz-ing memory, which is a serious asset in the eyes of a boss. It's also a serious asset to small-business owners who want to remember the name of every single client or customer. If you own a store, being able to call people by their names when they enter could be the secret to keeping them coming back again and again. The same holds true even for doctors who maintain small practices and want to retain their patients over the long term. Those who can establish that immediate rapport with people upon greeting them enhance these important relationships and increase their success.

Obviously, there are names that have built-in reminders. Meaningful words can be substituted for names like Goldman, Payne, and Fanning. We can picture a "gold man," someone who is always in a lot of "pain," and a person who is "fanning" herself. Then we have names that hold meaning via an association with an object or place we can picture in our minds. The name Summer reminds you of a season, the name Dole reminds you of the pineapple brand (or the former senator), and the name Casey reminds you of the musical group KC and the Sunshine Band. But what about other names that don't mean much of anything to us when we first hear them? What about names like Byster, Asderaki, and Karasek? We're more likely to encounter names like these than the easy ones. And they rarely have meaning, but they do have lots of sounds to them. They might as well be a foreign language.

I like to use three strategies to commit a name to memory. The first strategy is simply hearing the name to begin with! So many of us fail to establish original awareness of a name when we first hear it. So it's not that we forget names; it's that we never hear them clearly at the start and end up with only gobbledygook to remember.

I think it's human nature not to want to ask someone

to repeat his or her name. We don't want to look stupid. To that I say, get over it! If you don't catch a name clearly when you're introduced to someone, ask again. And if it's not an easy or common name, ask the person to spell it. That's not rude, and there's nothing to be embarrassed about. If anything, the person will be flattered that you're interested enough to want to remember their name. Even if you don't think that you'll ever see this person again in your life, get the name right the first time so that you won't be caught off guard when you do meet again after all.

Once you've gotten the name through your eardrums, the second tactic is to see if you can create a similar-sounding word or sentence using the sounds of the name. For instance, Karasek could sound like "carrot on a stick." My name, Byster, could sound like "by the stairs." In each case, you'd picture the individual embodying the phrase. So you'd picture Mr. Karasek holding a carrot on a stick, and you'd picture me standing by a staircase. As with any association you make when you want to remember something, it's important to create the link in the moment—the very instant you're first hearing the name (and perhaps shaking hands). And like most anything else, it will become easier and easier to apply this tactic as you practice it. Soon enough, you'll be able to turn names like Kraszynski (pronounced "kra-zin-ski") into phrases such as "crazy zin on skis" ("zin" for a bottle of zinfandel), or make the zin a "sin"; Djokovic (pronounced "joke-a-vich") becomes "joke and fetch," and Gutierrez becomes "gut in tiara." If you're familiar with more advanced vocabulary or the romance languages in particular, you might have noticed that the second part of Gutierrez contains sounds that are close to the word *tierra*, which means earth or land. So alternatively, you could associate this name with "gut in the earth." As you can see, absurdity is allowed here, and the phrase you create needn't contain every sound or syllable in the name. You just need to have enough sounds to give you the gist of it—then you can figure it out. Your memory will fill in the blanks.

The third strategy is to identify a feature or characteristic about the person and link it to their name. The mere act of seeking an outstanding feature will force you to be aware of the person in a conscious manner, creating original awareness. Such a unique feature can be any number of things—crooked teeth, ears that stick out, a high forehead, a puggish nose, a mole on the cheek, acne, freckles. First impressions count! That is to say, first impressions tend to be lasting ones, so try to make your association the moment you meet. Use the first thing that comes to mind. The feature you choose doesn't necessarily have to be something permanent. Let's say you meet someone named Barry who happens to be wearing a blue shirt. Say to yourself, "Blueberry." This word will trigger your memory the next time you see him and need to recall his name. Or let's say you meet a Tamara who has a toothy grin. It's not a name you've heard before, and it's not easy to pronounce; you're not sure if it's closer to the word "tomorrow" or "tomato." Assuming that it sounds more like "tomorrow," with the second *a* sounding like the *a* in "car," you could come up with "going to the dentist tomorrow" or something similar. The point is to single out a specific feature to which you can link a word or phrase and instantly associate that person with it. Even if it's challenging to find a link that's good and strong enough to permanently interlock a name and face in your memory, just trying will improve your memory. Face it: You're doing what so few people do when they meet someone—and that's paying attention!

I should add here that you do not need to know everyone's name and face. Focus on just the ones you need or want to recall and forget the others. Practice these strategies in situations where you're not feeling the pressure to remember. I started connecting names with features when I was twelve or thirteen years old so I could memorize the people on my Little League team. There was Richie Lieberman, the big kid who was taller than all of us. I associated his last name with "taller than the rest of us when he lies down," and the "lie" part gave me enough clues to retrieve "Lieberman" from my memory. Richie was also a funny guy whose behavior was very liberating. The word "liberating" was another code word I'd use to remember the name Lieberman. Then we had Mark Mendelson, who had a habit of whistling all the time. He was such a musical sensation on the field that I'd associate his last name with Felix Mendelssohn, the nineteenth-century German composer. Larry Axelrod, another Little League teammate of mine, had the misfortune of possessing an unbelievably scratchy throat, as if he'd smoked two packs of cigarettes a day since birth. His name suited him perfectly: "axe in throat" signaled "Axelrod" anytime I needed to recall it. I'll give you one more: Steve Kost, who happens to still be a good friend of mine, was the only guy among my friends who had any money back then. He earned money doing odd jobs in the neighborhood and liked to spend it on nice things. His last name to me meant "cost" because money was no object to him. For a twelve-year-old, Steve was probably ahead of all of us when it came to the notion of "cost." But he did well for himself, ending up owning his own business.

TAKE THE CHALLENGE

Over the course of the next month, make a commitment to create associations every time you meet someone new. Find a feature—such as the way the person dresses or looks or talks—and make it a goal to come up with a crafty way to remember his or her name. Remember, you're the only one who needs to know what your secret strategy is, so don't be afraid to get very imaginative—or even gross, grim, weird, or wacky!

If you practice making associations as much as possible, then when you're meeting a roomful of people and are under pressure to remember them all, the method will come to you naturally. Don't give up if the first couple of times you try this technique it doesn't work. This can be a challenging strategy to apply in everyday life, and it takes practice. Remember, we're trying to change habits here. Habits aren't just hard to break—they're hard to establish! Just recall the day you were learning how to type. Now it comes automatically to you, but not that first time. Back then it was tedious, overwhelming, and far from automatic. But look at you today: You don't even have to think about it anymore, whether you're typing in Word or firing off a text message. The mind is an incredible machine if you let tasks become natural. Then they stay with you forever.

STORYTELLING

You're at the grocery store and realize that you forgot your list. Or you've just driven out of your driveway for a long day of running errands and realize that you left your list on the kitchen counter. Do you go back for it?

At the beginning of the book, I asked you to take a quiz that tested your ability to remember ten items (see page 14). How well did you do? If you scored a perfect ten, then my bet is you employed a memory trick of some sort; otherwise, my guess is you were able to recall about six or seven of the things listed. Don't panic: This is the average for most people. During my presentations to both adults and kids, I give people the same list aloud and ask them to sit and listen to the list. They are not allowed to write anything down. Then, after a few seconds, I ask audience members to get out a piece of paper and try to recall all ten items. The vast majority of people get at least half of the items, but few can recall eight or nine. Once in a blue moon someone manages to come up with all ten. But that's a rare moment, and as I said, when it happens it's usually because that person applied some kind of strategy. Would you like to learn a reliable strategy for achieving such a feat and scoring a flawless ten?

I sometimes hesitate to teach how I memorize specific things because I feel that every person is different. What works best for me may not work for you. So what I'm going to do is illustrate the main concept by sharing how I would remember these ten items. But you will have to modify this tactic so it makes sense to you and, most important, has meaning to you.

The main technique to use here is storytelling. It helps to make up a story as you hear the words, and if you can fabricate a funny and eccentric story, that's all the better. I'll share with you the story that I've fashioned out of these words as an example. First let's review the list again:

silver tray
six crystal glasses
bar of soap
banana
chocolate pudding
laundry detergent
dental floss
loaf of bread
red rose
tomato

In my brain, the story I like to tell goes like this:

*I had a dream last night in which I was working at a restaurant and thinking about my date later that evening. While walking to a table, I carried a **silver tray** on which I balanced **six crystal glasses**. I took a step and landed on a **bar of soap**. I didn't want to break the glasses, so I rebalanced myself quickly with my other foot and stepped on a **banana**. I then fell down and into a gigantic bathtub filled with **chocolate pudding**. I panicked. I ran home as fast as I could and put my clothes in the washer, adding a box of **laundry detergent**. Later I retrieved my pants and shirt from the dryer and prepared to go to the store. But the only store that was open was on top of a* *huge hill. So I pulled myself up the hill using a big roll of* **dental floss.** *I went into the store and bought a* **loaf of bread.** *(Yes, I am a cheap date!) As I was leaving the store, I figured my date was a special lady, so I decided to buy her a* **red rose.** *I went to the flower-shop window, stuck my hand in, and pulled out what I thought was a red rose, but it was a red* **tomato.**

This story is totally wacky and ridiculous, but it's memorable for the person who made it up. Whenever I tell this story and then have my audience members try to recall those ten items a few minutes later, guess what? The vast majority of them can get all ten. Their minds finally have a few scenes they can mentally flip through like a movie to retrieve the words. The words have context—and that's exactly what you can do with any list you're given, no matter how random it is. What you're essentially doing is concretizing the words, making them less abstract, and adding meaning to them to make them memorable. At the same time, you're essentially *forgetting* the list and turning the items into thematic vignettes that you can remember. Your perceptual intuition is also at work here. As you transform the words into mini scenes, you're drawing on your brain's ability to intuitively perceive (and retrieve) the actual words without your having to really think about it too much.

I first figured out that storytelling could be a powerful tool for memorizing long lists when my mom used to put the onus on me to remember forty or so things to buy at the supermarket. It took me a while to get used to telling stories in my head based on a random list of items, but eventually I was able to take her long list of groceries, commit the items to memory while still at home, and then go with her to the market—leaving the list behind. At first I could only deal with ten things. Then, as I got better at creating stories to accommodate an entire list, I was able to pack more items into my brain and make room for longer and longer lists. You, too, will need to practice this technique on your own over time, and you may have to start with a few short lists until you get used to the task of quickly crafting stories and linking words to items that you want to remember. So don't get frustrated. Just continue to practice, which in and of itself will speed up your brain and make room for more information.

ALL THE PRESIDENTS' NAMES

The following set of sentences, each of which reflects a bizarre statement, is how I remember all the presidents of the United States. Remember, this is my way of doing it, but it doesn't have to be your way. Use this as an example—a model. See what you can come up with in your own wild imagination. I encourage you to go online and post your ideas there; let's see who can come up with the best, most vivid mental pictures!

1. George and Jeff made money.
   - George = George Washington
   - and = John Adams
   - Jeff = Thomas Jefferson
   - made = James Madison
   - money = James Monroe

2. Quickly, Jack drove the van to Harry's tie shop.
- Quickly = John Quincy Adams
- Jack = Andrew Jackson
- van = Martin Van Buren
- Harry's = William Henry Harrison
- tie = John Tyler

3. He poked Zack and said, "Fill up the pair of cannons!"
- poked = James Polk
- Zack = Zachary Taylor
- Fill = Millard Fillmore
- pair = Franklin Pierce
- cannons = James Buchanan

4. Abe and John were granted a hay field.
- Abe = Abraham Lincoln
- John = Andrew Johnson
- granted = Ulysses S. Grant
- hay = Rutherford B. Hayes
- field = James Garfield

5. Arthur went to Cleveland with Harry. Cleveland, no kidding!
- Arthur = Chester A. Arthur
- Cleveland = Grover Cleveland
- Harry = Benjamin Harrison
- Cleveland = Grover Cleveland
- kidding = William McKinley

6. Teddy ate taffy with Will. Hardly cool.
   - Teddy = Teddy Roosevelt
   - taffy = William H. Taft
   - Will = Woodrow Wilson
   - Hardly = Warren G. Harding
   - cool = Calvin Coolidge

7. Who did Frank tell the truth to? Howard and Kenny.
   - Who = Herbert Hoover
   - Frank = Franklin D. Roosevelt
   - truth = Harry S. Truman
   - Howard = Dwight D. Eisenhower
   - Kenny = John F. Kennedy

8. John nicked the Ford car again.
   - John = Lyndon B. Johnson
   - nicked = Richard Nixon
   - Ford = Gerald Ford
   - car = Jimmy Carter
   - again = Ronald Reagan

The next three presidents are easy to remember: George H. W. Bush, Bill Clinton, and George W. Bush. Few people have a tough time with these because they are so recent (and I'm assuming you can name the current president).

Remembering the thirteen colonies is a much easier task. You just have to remember the following three sentences:

> **George** and **Mary** were on the **verge** of **cutting** a **deal**.
> He received **three new road maps**.
> She received **two cars** and a **pen**.
>
> From these sentences can you guess the connection to all thirteen colonies? I'll list them here, and I bet you'll "see" them soon enough: Georgia, Maryland, Virginia, Connecticut, Delaware, New Hampshire, New Jersey, New York, Rhode Island, Massachusetts, North Carolina, South Carolina, and Pennsylvania.

FOREIGN SUBJECTS AND CALENDAR DATES

Whether you're trying to pick up a new language; gain more knowledge of art, literature, world history, or politics; learn a new hobby such as cooking or playing the piano; manage your stock portfolio; or play a sport better by knowing the top strategies ("plays") by heart, the art of association again reigns king. Being able to create associations on the spot when you receive new information also helps you commit to memory seemingly random things like appointment dates, anniversaries, birthdays, and historical data.

By now you should realize the benefits of retaining information. And as you've learned, the solution to most memory problems is to break things down into two steps: (1) stop and think about what it is you want to remember, which helps create that original awareness, and (2) figure out a creative way to associate that thing you're trying to remember with your own life, or at least with something that's memorable to you. The second step can entail using substitute words

or phrases and conjuring mental pictures in your mind's eye
that are outrageous enough to be unforgettable. Here are a
few more examples:

- You want to remember that most tech companies trade
  on the NASDAQ. Let's say that you're a big fan of Apple
  computer products and you follow that stock closely.
  The word "NASDAQ" sounds close enough to "nice
  daiquiri," and you can picture an apple daiquiri in your
  mind's eye. This immediately associates Apple Inc. with
  the NASDAQ, and you can easily tell yourself that, like
  Apple, other tech companies trade on the NASDAQ.
- You want to remember that, as a general rule of thumb,
  the ideal cooking time for fresh fish is ten minutes per
  inch of thickness. When the fishmonger tells you this in
  the supermarket, you say to yourself: "Ten finches in a
  pear tree." Clearly, the two key pieces of information to
  remember are "ten minutes" and "one inch." The word
  "finch" popped into your head because it rhymes with
  "inch," and "ten finches in a pear tree" brings to mind
  that holiday tune "The Twelve Days of Christmas," even
  though you've substituted finches for partridges, and
  there are ten of them rather than just one. Assuming the
  jingle works for you, you won't be asking yourself later
  on, when you're in the kitchen cooking the fish, whether
  it was twenty minutes or ten. If you need a way to remember that it's ten minutes per one inch and not per
  two, then you can add another image, such as a baby
  finch that is just one inch tall.
- You need to remember that the first breakthrough in
  antibiotics came with the discovery of penicillin by Al-
  exander Fleming in 1928. The key pieces of information

are "antibiotics," "Fleming," and "1928." You drum up
the following: "My phlegm in February is awful." This
somewhat disgusting phrase gives you a mental picture
of suffering from a cold in winter and dealing with congestion. The word "Fleming" sounds close enough to
"phlegm," and since February has twenty-eight days
in it (excluding leap years), you can figure out "1928."
From the word "awful," which begins with the letter *a*,
you can get "antibiotics." Or you could come up with
another word, such as "antisocial"—which would make
the statement even funnier! Now, what if you want to
remember that vaccines predated antibiotics? (Although
the earliest reports of vaccines seem to have originated
from India and China in the seventeenth century, as recorded in ayurvedic texts, they were more officially developed by Louis Pasteur during the nineteenth century
to combat anthrax and rabies.) People sometimes mix
up which came first, vaccines or antibiotics. And unfortunately it doesn't help that the letter *a* for "antibiotics"
is the first letter in the alphabet but is not the first letter of the first invention here (vaccines). While you can
mentally try to tell yourself that the order is reversed,
another possible strategy is to say to yourself something
like "Vaccines have a vast history" or "Antibiotics are a
newer invention."

• You cannot forget that your boss's birthday is on September 30. His name is Seth, and you can associate "September" with "Seth" easily, as the two words share the
same first two letters. But to implant this particular date
in your mind, you need to go further. September 30 is the
last day of the month, and you can't stand the fact that
your boss is always late to staff meetings. He's always the

last one to show up, so when you're trying to commit this date to memory, picture your boss being late to his own birthday party—as well as the last one to leave.

As I hope these examples demonstrate, anything is possible! This is just a tiny sampling from hundreds if not thousands of ways to make facts stick to your brain. And these examples represent only three areas where you can apply this strategy. I've used them simply to show you one way to make an association. They are examples for you to use to test yourself; I hope you go on to create your own associations in any subject area where you need to retain factual material. Include any information you like, and don't limit yourself to the obvious. A tree has nothing to do with cooking, but in the context of an association it can work. It doesn't matter how difficult or abstruse the content or information seems to be. I can't reiterate this enough: So long as you can construct a meaningful association, anything goes!

Now, it's one thing to extinguish absentmindedness, memorize phone numbers and faces, and think for yourself along the way. But what about seriously more complex tasks? What if your son is told to memorize the periodic table of elements, every single capital in the Union, or all of the Constitution's amendments (including the Bill of Rights)? What if your boss tells you to present the same speech that he gave at last year's company retreat to a new group of hires? How will you get in front of a podium and rattle off his words of wisdom without a Teleprompter (and without relying on reading)? Now that we've covered the fine art of association—creating sentences and stories to help you recall lots of information—you need a booster shot, because sometimes you need a little more than that to retain complex, in-depth information—knowledge, really. The lessons you've learned in this chapter provide a strong foundation for being able to accomplish these tasks effortlessly, but the skills you'll gain in the next chapters will really help you accomplish more than you ever thought possible. To start, you need to push yourself outside of your box. Then you'll need more tools to organize your thoughts and occasionally forget. But before we move on, one last word . . .

TO THINE OWN SELF BE TRUE

In the play *Hamlet*, Polonius prepares his son, Laertes, for travel abroad with a speech (act I, scene 3, lines 55–81) in which he directs Laertes to commit a "few precepts to memory." Among these precepts is the now-familiar adage "Neither a borrower nor a lender be" (line 75) and the dictum "This above all: to thine own self be true" (line 78).

This is a useful dictum to bear in mind throughout life, whether you're a fictional character in a play or a real person in the flesh. Everyone learns differently, and I hope by now I've impressed upon you the importance of making everything you encounter in the world relevant to yourself somehow. Experiment with what works for you and don't feel like you have to use what's given to you. How you use the strategies has to be up to you. And if I had to create a bottom line here, it would simply be this: Think for yourself! Only then can you maximize your mental capacity, find the associations that will work for you, solve problems quickly and effectively, and turn on your sharpest, smartest you.

Chapter Guide

This chapter presented a lot of strategies rather than straightforward exercises and games. See if you can apply these techniques starting today, including the challenge of avoiding the use of devices and forms of technology to remember names, faces, phone numbers, and so on. Tap your imagination and engage your inner storytelling ability; try to create your own mnemonics, sentences, and phrases to retain and recall information. I encourage you to reread this chapter whenever absentmindedness finds its way back.

I may have implied that there's a permanent "cure" for absentmindedness, but it requires booster shots on occasion! This might be a chapter you'll want to reread every couple of months to refresh your memory on its numerous strategies.

SOLUTIONS TO THE PROBLEMS IN THIS CHAPTER

Numbers and words

82253 (table)
27323 (bread)
7428873 (picture)
24453736 (children)
2886662453 (automobile)
4277924784329! (Happy birthday!)
47328646378446525453 (Great minds think alike.)

CHAPTER 5

Skill 4:

Thinking Outside the Box

What Hitler and Mother-in-Law Have in Common

It's what you learn after you know it all that counts.

—HARRY S. TRUMAN

In chapter 4 I mentioned that I had a hard time distinguishing my right boot from my left boot as a kid. The story doesn't end there. Between first and second grade, it was determined (officially, by no less than a licensed psychologist who tested me outside of school) that I was developmentally delayed in what are called gross motor and motor planning skills, which means I had a hard time understanding the space around me. No wonder I'd repeatedly break my pencil pressing down on paper, strain to tie my shoelaces, button my sweater all wrong, and be totally uncoordinated and clumsy on the playground. To this day I have problems with spatial stuff, which also explains why I can struggle with some IQ tests that are filled with too many questions about visual geometry and spatial patterns. On a more practical level, I'm not very handy around the house, and my wife won't ask me to screw in a lightbulb.

I like to tell people, kids especially, about my "developmental challenges" because my own life proves that such a label doesn't necessarily affect one's ability to adapt and succeed. Success also doesn't necessarily have anything to do with whether or not you can develop a fast and furious brain to rival the best and brightest minds.

Full disclosure: The following is an excerpt from my "report card" from a psychologist who tested my developmental skills when I was seven years old. Check out the note about my ability to teach myself ways around my "handicap."

Like many capable children, Michael has done an amazing job of getting around his handicap (visual-perception and motor scores), but it is essential that parents and teachers should realize the fine job he is doing and give him full praise and recognition for his truly remarkable accomplishment. Unless he has had individual teaching of which we are not aware, Michael is, in many important respects, really "self-taught."

That said, official diagnoses like that can be hard on parents. Sure, I was gifted in some areas, but to learn that I was "way below grade level" in other important developmental areas could not have been easy for my parents to swallow. Luckily, they took the news in stride and decided against taking any specific action. They decided to keep me right where I was and to find ways to make up for my "delay" until my body caught up. They wanted to make sure that I felt like a typical kid, that I was "normal"—whatever that is!—rather than send me to a special school.

It took me ten times longer than any of my friends to learn how to ride a bicycle. For a week I would arrive home all bloody and bruised from my determined attempts. But I kept trying. Just as my mother helped me with my boots, she was good at helping me adapt and find different ways to do other things. When I wanted to play ice hockey, she encouraged me to stick with playing goalie, knowing that I'd be much better equipped to guard that small space than to have an entire rink in which to maneuver. She's the one who also taught me to pull my sweaters down and match the bottoms together so I could see how all the holes and buttons aligned.

Play to your strengths and work on your weaknesses. Don't do yourself an injustice by abandoning areas you find challenging. Learn as much as you can and know that you can improve in every area—and this book will help you gain the confidence and capabilities to do so. If you struggled in formal schooling and think you're a bad learner today as an adult, with no hope of improving your brain's mental capacity, think again. Traditional schooling often forces us to learn within the same box as everyone else, but once we begin thinking and solving problems outside that box (especially if it's not working for us), we can experience unprecedented success. We also can take maximum advantage of the power of forgetting.

My developmental delays made it essential for me to do things a tad differently and approach problems or tasks from an unusual angle or perspective. From the time I was a young child, my mother always encouraged me to think "outside the box" and offered me new ways to tackle daily problems. Since my father was good with numbers, everyone assumed I was most like him. Actually, I was a product of both of them, and I couldn't have gotten to where I am today without that perfect combination. Although my dad could calculate 53 times 7 in his head in seconds, he had no understanding of the mental process involved in the calculation. My mother, who was not naturally gifted with numbers, taught me to take my innate ability with numbers and discover easier ways to do things. She always looked for shortcuts or simpler approaches. She also had a very good sense of humor, so she was able to make learning enjoyable. I think my ability today to blend my dad's "science" of numbers with my mom's "art" of making it enjoyable to learn and work the brain is what has allowed me to be so successful.

Constantly thinking outside the box was an important skill I mastered out of necessity when I was young, but it's never too late to start thinking in this manner. If you've never been pressured to think too far out of your box, and you're an adult hoping to make the most of your life and get further ahead, then there's no time like the present to pick up this skill and make it a habit. The ability to think outside the box will increasingly become a highly valued asset that separates the people who don't excel from those who achieve enormous success—that is, those who are prepared to change the world and excited about doing it. These are the people who also happen to find life more fulfilling on a deeply personal level because their minds think in ways that keep them entertained and resourceful when they least expect it. In other words, they rarely get bored.

Thinking outside the box has everything to do with being a productive thinker. The skill allows you to discover novel solutions, become more efficient in everyday tasks, problem-solve more quickly, and ultimately maximize the development of all the other skills outlined in this book. Even your capacity to forget when you need to will depend on your ability to think outside the box. Once this skill becomes second nature, you'll find that identifying and labeling incoming content to your brain as either important ("retain and remember") or destined for the trash can is much easier. Which ultimately helps you to make room for more information and have more mental bandwidth to think creatively.

In this chapter I'm going to nudge you to think outside the box in the hope that you can take these mental exercises and open up areas in your mind that encourage you to be more creative. More resourceful. *Different*. What I love about this skill is that it compels you to integrate all of your talents and abilities at the same time. You'll blend logic with creativity, unite reason with imagination, and mix rationality with absurdity. The whole point of being able to think outside the box is to honor discovery, playfulness, invention, independence, and adaptation. No sooner will you be thinking further outside your box in all that you do than you'll transform your brain into a sweeping source of ideas, fresh insights, and intuitive wisdom. You'll also be stimulating its processing speed, power, and capacity. In short, you'll be edging it toward that place where you optimize your mind's productive output.

THE NINE DOTS PUZZLE

Let's start with a classic puzzle: the Nine Dots. See if you can find a way to link all nine of the following dots using four straight lines or fewer, without lifting your pen and without tracing the same line more than once.

Here is just one way to solve this (indeed, there's more than one solution to this puzzle):

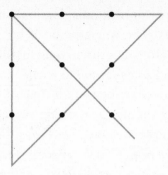

How difficult did you find this now-famous puzzle? The Nine Dots—which originated in the early twentieth century and actually predates the slogan "outside the box"—has come to signify the concept of thinking outside the box because it literally shows an invisible "box" and how you have to go beyond the boundaries to link all the dots in four straight lines.

It's well documented that people who consistently think outside the box tend to be more inventive, more creative, and often more successful overall in life. But what does thinking outside the box really mean—and how can you develop this skill?

This chapter is filled with games that will help you look at things differently. That's all that thinking outside the box really is. I'm going to take you on a wild ride through fresh and innovative ways to solve traditional yet complex math problems whose shortcut solutions using my techniques are surprisingly simple (easier than the traditional route!). The goal is not so much to learn how to perform these math tricks but to train you to empower your mind in ways that go against traditional or ingrained modes of thinking. These methods can spur new ideas and tap a deeper level of creative genius that will serve you well in every area of life. And who doesn't want to be more creative and inventive?

In my everyday work, I'm constantly encouraging and training kids to think outside the box. What I'm up against, though, are the "rules" that they've learned and resolutely stick to. Although the very nature of education is supposed to foster their creativity and teach them how to use their own independent minds to arrive at solutions, I frequently find that the very nature of education also encompasses customs and habits that inhibit the creative spirit. Rather than being encouraged to think differently and break tradition by coming up with their own solutions to problems, they are instead taught that if they don't follow certain rules they will fail.

Take, for example, the how-tos of squaring numbers. When asked to square a number, the kids I work with cannot do it in their heads very easily. They write it out, move from right to left, carry the one, and so on (or resort to a calculator). They don't even try to do it any other way—because they are trained to believe that there *is* no other way! Or, as I've already discussed, if given the task of memorizing a long list—say, reciting the presidents in order starting with George Washington—they will approach the task by trying to drill the facts into their heads using rote memorization. That rarely works well.

So let's see how far you can flex your mind and how much permission you can give yourself to seek different pathways to solve problems. The exercises in this chapter will call upon lessons you've already learned from previous chapters and challenge you to go further in stretching your mind's muscles. The Nine Dots puzzle should have helped to loosen up those latent areas of the mind that rarely get the attention they deserve. Now let's take it up a notch!

TWENTY-FOUR

The game of Twenty-Four is great for revving up your brain and getting creative. (It's especially fun to play while driving.) Here's how to play:

The object is to turn four random numbers into a mathematical combination that equals 24. You can use addition, subtraction, multiplication, and division. While on your trip, keep an eye out for any signs that contain numbers in a row (such as a roadside assistance sign with a phone number), license plate numbers, or even the numerals at the bottom of a dollar bill. Write down the last four digits of that number and use basic math to create an equation that equals 24. Use parentheses if you like. The first one to come up with a solution wins. For example, let's say you see the following numbers:

| 3 | 7 | 9 | 10 |

Here are some potential ways to play with these numbers using basic math to arrive at the number 24:

$[(9 \times 3) + 7] - 10 = 24$

or

$[(10 - 7) \times 9] - 3 = 24$

or

$[(10 - 9) + 7] \times 3 = 24$

I'll give you one more example:

2   4   5   8

Possible solutions include:

$[(8 \div 2) \times 5] + 4 = 24$

or

$[(8 - 5) \times 4] \times 2 = 24$

or

$[(5 + 2) - 4)] \times 8 = 24$

REBUSES

A rebus is a pictorial representation of a name, work, or phrase. Each rebus puzzle box below portrays a common word or phrase. Can you guess what each one says?

1.
┌─────────────────┐
│   │
│   MAN   │
│   BOARD   │
│   │
│   │
└─────────────────┘

2. economy

3. WINEEEE

4. PumPkinPie

5. JOBINJOB

6. L
   O
     V
       E

7. NINE
  CUMULUS

8. DOCTOR DOCTOR

9. MCE MCE MCE

10. BAN ANA

11. ABCDEFGHJMOPQRSTUVWXYZ

12. CAN CAN

13. 9S2A5F4E1T8Y6

14. BillED

15.   E
      K
      A
      M

Did you notice that as you moved through these games, your mind got better—faster—at picking up the answers? That's some serious mind sharpening in action! Rebuses call on imagination, focus and concentration, pattern recognition, problem-solving ability, thinking outside the box—just about all the skills of a quick mind. You can find hundreds more of these rebus games online by searching for "rebus puzzles." Better yet, try to come up with some of your own rebus puzzles, using this list of phrases and words.

- Bird on a wire
- Bad influence
- *Alice in Wonderland*

- Well-balanced meal
- Camping overnight
- Take a step backward
- Many are called but few are chosen
- Three strikes you're out!

Remember, there are likely to be several ways to design these rebuses. For an added challenge, see if you can devise at least two representations for each phrase!

TRIPPY TRIANGLES

Here's another visual game that forces your brain to fire on multiple cylinders, utilizing different areas to see the image (and images) from different perspectives. This requires lots of focus and concentration, among other skills.

How many triangles can you find in the following figure?

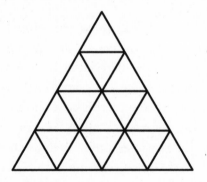

Here's one more:

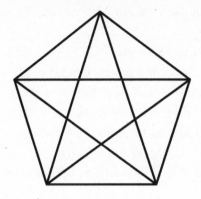

WHAT'S THE CONNECTION?

Each question below is made up of a number followed by some initials—there's a connection! Can you work these out?

1 = H on a U
1 = GL for M
52 = C in a D
88 = PK

For more of these types of games, go to http://intelligence-test.net/part1.

MENTAL MATH SHORTCUTS

Seeing patterns in geometric shapes and strings of letters is one thing, but what about seeing patterns in traditional math equations? I've already given you a few math shortcuts in this book, but the ones here were designed specifically to help you think outside the box. How? They break all the rules that you've probably been taught when it comes to these types of equations.

I'll give you nine shortcuts in this section. By following the directions and doing a little mental math, you should be able to solve some seemingly complex problems rather easily. The challenge will come when you know all of the shortcuts and then are asked to solve problems using one of the patterns and must first figure out which one to use, then apply it quickly. (You can use notes or work from memory.)

PATTERN 1: SQUARING NUMBERS IN THE FIFTIES

Example: 57 × 57

Step 1: Always start with the number 25. Now add the ones digit (7) to it (25 + 7 = 32).

Step 2: Square the ones digit (7 × 7 = 49). Tack that number onto the answer from step 1.

Answer: 57 × 57 = 3,249

If the number from step 2 is less than 10, you have to put a 0 in front of it.

Example: 53 × 53

Step 1: 25 + 3 = 28

Step 2: 3 × 3 = 09 (Since 9 is less than 10, put a 0 in front of it.)

Answer: 53 × 53 = 2,809

PATTERN 2: SQUARING NUMBERS THAT END IN FIVE

Example: 65 × 65

Step 1: Take the tens digit (6) and multiply it by the number one greater than it (7) (6 × 7 = 42).

Step 2: Tack 25 onto the end of the number from step 1.

Answer: 65 × 65 = 4,225

PATTERN 3: MULTIPLYING TWO NUMBERS THAT END IN FIVE AND ARE EXACTLY TEN APART

Example: 75 × 85

Step 1: Take the smaller tens digit (7) and multiply it by the number that is one greater than the larger tens digit (8) (8 + 1 = 9; 7 × 9 = 63).

Step 2: Tack 75 onto the end of the number from step 1.

Answer: 75 × 85 = 6,375

PATTERN 4: MULTIPLYING TWO NUMBERS THAT END IN FIVE AND ARE TWENTY APART

Example: 65 × 85

Step 1: Take the smaller tens digit (6) and multiply it by the number one greater than the larger tens digit (8) (8 + 1 = 9; 6 × 9 = 54).

Step 2: Add 1 to the number from step 1 (54 + 1 = 55).

Step 3: Tack 25 onto the end of the number from step 2.

Answer: 65 × 85 = 5,525

PATTERN 5: MULTIPLYING TWO NUMBERS IN THE NINETIES

When you multiply two numbers in the nineties, in parentheses next to each number put how far away that number is from 100. Since 93 is 7 away from 100, and 96 is 4 away from 100, the problem 93 × 96 would be written like this: 93(7) × 96(4).

> *Example:* 93(7) × 96(4)
>
> *Step 1:* Add up the numbers in parentheses (7 + 4 = 11) and subtract that number from 100 (100 − 11 = 89).
>
> *Step 2:* Multiply the two numbers in parentheses and tack that product onto the end of the number from step 1 (7 × 4 = 28).
>
> *Answer:* 93 × 96 = 8,928

If the number from step 2 is less than 10, put a 0 in front of it.

> *Example:* 97(3) × 98(2)
>
> *Step 1:* 3 + 2 = 5; 100 − 5 = 95
>
> *Step 2:* 3 × 2 = 06
>
> *Answer:* 97 × 98 = 9,506

PATTERN 6: SQUARING NUMBERS IN THE FORTIES

> *Example:* 43 × 43
>
> *Step 1:* Start out with 15 and add the ones digit to it (15 + 3 = 18).
>
> *Step 2:* Figure out by how much the number you

are squaring (43) is less than 50 (50 − 43 = 7) and square that number (7 × 7 = 49). Tack that number onto the end of the number from step 1.
Answer: 43 × 43 = 1,849

If the number from step 2 is less than 10, put a 0 in front of it.

Example: 48 × 48
Step 1: 15 + 8 = 23
Step 2: 50 − 48 = 2; 2 × 2 = 04
Answer: 48 × 48 = 2,304

PATTERN 7: MULTIPLYING TWO NUMBERS THAT ARE BETWEEN 100 AND 109

Example: 106 × 108
Step 1: The first digit of the answer is always 1.
Step 2: To get the next two digits, add the ones digits (6 + 8 = 14).
Step 3: To get the final two digits, multiply the ones digits (6 × 8 = 48).
Answer: 106 × 108 = 11,448

If the number in either step 2 or step 3 is less than 10, put a 0 in front of it.

Example: 102 × 104
Step 1: The first digit of the answer is always 1.
Step 2: Add the ones digits together (2 + 4 = 06).
Step 3: Multiply the ones digits (2 × 4 = 08).
Answer: 102 × 104 = 10,608

PATTERN 8: MULTIPLYING TWO NUMBERS THAT ARE BETWEEN 200 AND 209

Example: 204 × 209

Step 1: The first digit of the answer is always 4.

Step 2: To get the next two digits, add the ones digits and double the product (4 + 9 = 13; 13 × 2 = 26).

Step 3: To get the final two digits, multiply the ones digits (4 × 9 = 36).

Answer: 204 × 209 = 42,636

If a number from either step 2 or step 3 is less than 10, put a 0 in front of it.

Example: 207 × 201

Step 1: The first digit of the answer is always 4.

Step 2: 7 + 1 = 8; 8 × 2 = 16

Step 3: 7 × 1 = 07

Answer: 207 × 201 = 41,607

PATTERN 9: MULTIPLYING TWO TWO-DIGIT NUMBERS THAT END IN ONE

Example: 71 × 51

Step 1: Multiply the tens digits (7 × 5 = 35) and tack a 0 onto the end of that product (350).

Step 2: Add the tens digits (7 + 5 = 12) and add that number to the number from step 1 (350 + 12 = 362).

Step 3: Tack a 1 onto the end of the number from step 2.

Answer: 71 × 51 = 3,621

Example: 31 × 41

Step 1: 3 × 4 = 12. Tack on a 0 and you get 120.

Step 2: 3 + 4 = 7; 120 + 7 = 127

Step 3: Tack a 1 onto the end.

Answer: 31 × 41 = 1,271

ON YOUR OWN

Can you perform a few more on your own? And without looking back at the steps I've given you for each type of pattern? I encourage you to go back one more time to each of the above steps. Aim to commit each pattern's shortcut to memory, as this will force you to think outside the box and forget about traditional rules. Then, once you feel like you're ready to tackle a few more on your own and no longer need to revisit the steps, turn to this section and see how fast you can solve the following problems.

54 × 54 =	59 × 59 =
85 × 85 =	35 × 35 =
55 × 65 =	25 × 35 =
25 × 45 =	55 × 75 =
95 × 94 =	96 × 92 =
46 × 46 =	42 × 42 =
103 × 105 =	104 × 109 =
206 × 205 =	208 × 202 =
41 × 61 =	91 × 31 =

You'll find the answers to these equations at the end of the chapter.

THE BOX IN THE INTERSECTION

I can't reiterate enough the value of being able to think differently from the mainstream. While productive thinkers may be varied, they all have one feature in common: creativity. You might not think that playing a rebus game or learning a shortcut in math is going to help you in real-life situations where you want to access your creativity, but in fact practicing these types of brainteasers opens up areas of the brain that support inventiveness. We owe some of our most beloved inventions today to people who thought outside the box and took "accidents" in their daily work to the next level by asking themselves "outside" questions.

Take, for example, the microwave oven, which is now a standard appliance in most American households. When you Google the history of the microwave oven, you find a great story about how this now-ubiquitous machine came to be. In 1945 Percy Spencer was experimenting with a new vacuum tube called a magnetron while doing research for Raytheon Company. When his candy bar melted in his pocket, he took note of it and stopped to ask himself how this phenomenon could be applied elsewhere. Thinking outside the box, he tried another experiment with popcorn, and when the kernels began to pop, Spencer immediately saw the potential in this revolutionary process. In 1947 Raytheon built the first microwave oven, the Radarange, which weighed 750 pounds, was five and a half feet tall, and cost about $5,000. When the Radarange first became available for home use in the early 1950s, its bulky size and expensive price tag made it unpopular with consumers. But in 1967 a much more popular hundred-volt, countertop version was introduced at a price of $495. Today you can buy a microwave oven for under $100.

I'll admit that I'm a big consumer of diet soda—much to my doctor's chagrin. I don't drink alcohol, and I don't gamble, but I do drink a lot of diet soda pop. And I have a famous accident to thank. Saccharin, the oldest artificial sweetener, was accidentally discovered in 1879 by researcher Constantin Fahlberg, who was working at Johns Hopkins University in the laboratory of professor Ira Remsen. Fahlberg's discovery came after he forgot to wash his hands before lunch. He had spilled a chemical on his hands, and it caused the bread he ate to taste unusually sweet. Had he not been thinking outside the box when he took that fateful bite, he might have missed the discovery entirely. In 1880 the two scientists jointly published the finding, but in 1884 Fahlberg obtained a patent and began mass-producing saccharin without Remsen. The use of saccharin became widespread when sugar was rationed during World War I, and its popularity increased during the 1960s and 1970s with the manufacture of Sweet'N Low and diet soft drinks. Today I'm among the millions who keep Fahlberg's patent valuable. (To clarify: Several other artificial sweeteners have been developed since saccharin was discovered. Saccharin got a bad rap in the 1970s owing to exaggerated claims that it causes cancer, and it's now outpaced by aspartame and sucralose in the market. Tab may be the only soda left that's based on saccharin.)

I'll give you one more example, well detailed by the folks at www.HowStuffWorks.com. In 1943 naval engineer Richard James was trying to develop a spring that would support and stabilize sensitive equipment on ships. When one of the springs accidentally fell off a shelf, it continued moving—and a lightbulb turned on over James's head. He climbed out of his "box" and got an idea for a toy. His wife, Betty, came up with the name. When the Slinky made its debut in late

1945, James sold four hundred of the bouncy toys in ninety minutes. Today more than 250 million Slinkys have been sold worldwide.

The point I want to make is that no matter where you are or what you're doing—whether you're a cook, a CEO, a midlevel manager hoping to advance and land the corner office, or a stay-at-home parent with a part-time job as a blogger—things tend to happen that can result in surprising opportunities. People don't necessarily stumble upon good fortune or luck. They come to situations and circumstances with a mind-set that prepares them to "get lucky." As that old saying goes, success happens at the intersection of preparation and opportunity. And being able to think outside the box—to stop and ask yourself *why* or *how* as often as you can—is key to that preparation.

I should also point out that while few of us are going to invent the next big thing on par with the microwave or sliced bread, all of us will be faced with problems to solve that demand we think outside the box. This is true no matter what kind of job we have, where we live, or what resources we possess. When we take this skill to work or employ it at home in even the most mundane of habits and daily tasks, we can make life a whole lot easier. Don't for a minute believe that thinking outside the box is reserved for the super artsy types who work in highly creative or technical jobs. I wish that this skill weren't always so linked to innovation and creativity. I see it more as a necessary tool equal in importance to being able to read, write, and even *think* at all!

Only those who can routinely think outside the box go on to achieve what they set out to do in life. And sometimes those people's goals have nothing to do with invention per se. So the next time you're wondering how thinking outside the box will help you, remember: This skill provides the foundation for all kinds of problem solving in virtually any type of setting. It also facilitates new opportunities that present themselves (often when you least expect it) and help you to take advantage of those possibilities. While I may have outlined historical examples of thinking outside the box in action, plenty of newer examples abound. Popular social-media technology, for instance, owes its origins to productive thinkers who took note of an opportunity and capitalized on it. Just look around you to see the fruits of someone else's productive thinking outside the box at work. Every time you visit a Web site; buy a product; respond to an advertisement; read an engaging article, blog, or book; or compliment a co-worker for a job well done, chances are you're recognizing the upshot of thinking outside the box. Pure and simple.

> When the creative part of the brain begins to churn, it can be hard to stop it! And the rewards are limitless.

ANAGRAMS AND PALINDROMES

It may seem odd to end this chapter with a few anagram and palindrome exercises. These are not problems to solve as you would solve a math equation or a rebus puzzle. But they are helpful in tapping those areas of the mind that are eager to take an uncharted path and get creative. They also help turn on the productive thinker in you. Just having an awareness of what these devices are will help you see words and numbers differently in the world and reinforce the whole purpose of this chapter: to get outside of your box!

An anagram is a word or phrase that is formed by re-arranging the letters of another word or phrase, such as "teacher" and "cheater" or "woman Hitler" and "mother-in-law" (hence, what mother-in-law and Hitler have in common). The word "anagrams" is an anagram itself of *ars magna*, Latin for "great art." As someone once said, "All the life's wisdom can be found in anagrams. Anagrams never lie." It's also been said that the right to lampoon royalty and politicians using anagrams was enshrined in English law when King John signed the Magna Carta ("Anagram Act") in 1215.

Clever anagrams are all around us—if you stop to notice them. Japan's former capital city (Kyoto) and present capital city (Tokyo) are anagrams of each other. The name of the synthetic fiber "spandex" is an anagram of "expands." The Toyota Camry is an anagram of "my car."

Here's a list of the most famous anagrams in English. Can you figure out their counterparts in a crafty rearrangement?

    postmaster = _____
    Elvis = _____
    the eyes = _____
    Clint Eastwood = _____
    a decimal point = _____
    a gentleman = ____ _____
    no cigar = _____

Anagrams are great for bending the mind. I once saw an anagram made from a few paragraphs of Lincoln's Gettysburg Address. Now, that's thinking outside the box! Seriously, it's not that you need to "know" anagrams or memorize the examples given here. It's all about training your mind to look at words differently. Once you begin to switch letters around and create new meanings, you're engaging your brain in exactly the way that makes you the most productive thinker you can be. You're igniting new neuronal pathways. You're working the "muscles" of your mind that, when strong, will allow you to advance profoundly in life because you're forcing yourself to flex them when most people aren't exercising their brain that way.

I should also point out that playing with anagrams improves logical thinking. You can think of them as similar to geometry proofs: You don't need to *know* a geometry proof to get along in life, but working through such proofs helps to improve your logic skills. And anything that enhances your logic skills boosts brainpower. Logic is how we ultimately make sense of the world, solve problems effectively and quickly, organize our thoughts, maximize our memories, and intertwine our imaginations with reasoning to come up with new ways of doing things or arriving at answers. When we improve our logic skills, we in turn enhance all of our skills, because logic plays a role in each one of them. Logic skills can even give a boost to your focus and concentration. Don't for a second think that just because you're tapping the wildest or silliest side of your imagination or forcing yourself to think as far outside the box as possible you are not using your logic. Logic is always an undercurrent. It in fact *informs* your imagination, intuition, and ability to think outside the box.

For those looking for a more practical application for anagrams, consider using them for the sole purpose of generating your various passwords. It's a good idea to have a different password for each e-mail account, online account, and so on. What's difficult is having to remember all those passwords. Try using various anagrams of your favorite words or phrases as passwords.

KEEP THINKING!

Life is filled with "games" you can play, so long as you notice them and engage your mind. You don't need pencil and paper or an iPad to play hundreds of games, no matter where you are. Just look around you and see where your mind takes you. When I'm in a car, for example, I love searching for vanity plates and deciphering their messages, such as the one I saw recently: TJQKA, I figured out, stands for "ten, jack, queen, king, ace." Which of course inspires me to make up a story about the driver (he must be a gambler!).

Another game I like to play is challenging myself to figure out the exact time it will be when I pull into the driveway. Based on the percentage of lights I hope to make, my average speed, and the miles I must cover to get home, I mentally calculate the duration of the drive and aim to be accurate within two or three minutes (and I usually am). Try it yourself! Do anything to keep your mind moving.

Palindromes, which date back to at least AD 79, are words or phrases that read the same way forward and backward. The most familiar palindromes, in English at least, are character-by-character ones: The written characters read the same backward and forward. Here are some examples of common palindromic words: civic, radar, level, rotor, kayak, reviver, race car, redder, madam, toot, pop, and noon. Some well-known palindromic phrases and sentences are:

Able was I ere I saw Elba.
A man, a plan, a canal: Panama.
Madam, I'm Adam.
Madam in Eden, I'm Adam.
Doc, note: I dissent. A fast never prevents a fatness.
    I diet on cod.
Never odd or even.

And "Rise to vote, sir" was once featured in an episode of *The Simpsons*.

Some palindromes use words as units rather than letters. For example: "Fall leaves after leaves fall," "You can cage a swallow, can't you, but you can't swallow a cage, can you?" "First Ladies rule the State and state the rule: ladies first," and "Girl, bathing on Bikini, eyeing boy, sees boy eyeing bikini on bathing girl." The command "Level, madam, level!" composed only of words that are themselves palindromes, is both a character-by-character and a word-by-word palindrome.

Even though many palindromes seem like nonsense, some people have written entire palindromic passages thousands of words long! Very cool, but hard to figure out. Here are some shorter ones to decode:

No way, a papaya won!
Some men interpret nine memos.
Too bad I hid a boot.
Was it a car or a cat I saw?
A Santa at NASA.

Again, you're probably wondering why you'd ever want to play with palindromes. Like anagrams, they are an excellent way to give your brain a workout that draws from both your logical brain and your imaginative, outside-the-box brain. Having to think about and manipulate words and letters exercises areas of your mind that strengthen and support your problem-solving skills. Try to come up with a few on your own.

Palindromes needn't be restricted to words and letters. They can be found in a variety of places where you'd least expect them, such as in numbers, dates, acoustics, music, and even molecular biology and classical music. Joseph Haydn's Symphony no. 47 in G is nicknamed "the Palindrome"—the third movement is a musical palindrome. This clever piece goes forward twice and backward twice and arrives back at the same place. Similarly, Mozart's Scherzo-Duetto di Mozart is played by one violinist as written and by a second violinist with the same music inverted. In more recent times, we have Weird Al Yankovic's song "Bob" (from his 2003 album *Poodle Hat*), which consists of rhyming palindromes and parodies the Bob Dylan song "Subterranean Homesick Blues." The song "You Can Call Me Al" by Paul Simon features a palindromic bass run performed by Bakithi Kumalo.

DID YOU KNOW?

The longest palindromic word in the *Oxford English Dictionary* is the onomatopoeic "tattarrattat," coined by James Joyce in *Ulysses* (1922) to refer to a knock on the door. *Guinness World Records* gives the title to "detartrated," the past tense and past participle of "detartrate," a chemical term meaning "to remove tartrates." "Rotavator," a trademarked name for an agricultural machine, is often listed in dictionaries. The term "redivider" is used by some writers but appears to be an invented or derived term—only "redivide" and "redivision" appear in the *Shorter Oxford Dictionary*. The word "Malayalam," the name of an Indian language, is of equal length.

While researching this book, I came across some interesting facts about palindromes with regard to our own biology. As it turns out, palindromic motifs are found in DNA sequences and frequently in genetic instructions that code for proteins, which are biological structures we need to survive. But the meaning of "palindrome" in the context of genetics is slightly different from the definition used for words and sentences. Our genetic code—DNA (short for deoxyribonucleic acid)—is formed by two paired strands of molecules called nucleotides, which always pair in the same way—adenine (A) always pairs with thymine (T), and cytosine (C) always pairs with guanine (G). Together these two paired strands make up the well-known double-helix structure of DNA. Now, a single-stranded sequence of DNA is said to be a palindrome if it is equal to its complementary sequence read backward. For example, the sequence ACCTAGGT is palindromic because its complement is TGGATCCA, which is equal to the original sequence in reverse. Interestingly, I also learned that scientists have proved that many of the bases on the Y chromosome—the male sex chromosome—are arranged as palindromes. What's even more fascinating is that a palindromic structure allows the Y chromosome to repair itself by bending over at the middle if one side is damaged. Imagine that!

Finally, it's worth mentioning the semordnilap. Come again? Spell that word backward and you get "palindromes." "Semordnilap" is the name coined for a word or phrase that spells a different word or phrase backward. Semordnilaps are also known as volvograms, heteropalindromes, semi-palindromes, half palindromes, reversegrams, mynoretehs, reversible anagrams, word reversals, and anadromes. Sometimes they have also been called antigrams, but this term now usually refers to anagrams with opposing meanings. Semordnilaps are very useful in constructing palindromic texts; together, each pair forms a palindrome, and they can be added on either side of a shorter palindrome in order to extend it.

DID YOU KNOW?

The longest single-word English examples of semord-nilaps contain eight letters:

stressed/desserts
samaroid (resembling a samara)/dioramas
rewarder/redrawer

Other examples include:

was/saw
gateman/nametag
enoteca/acetone
deliver/reviled
straw/warts
star/rats
lived/devil
live/evil
diaper/repaid
smart/trams
spit/tips
stop/pots
bats/stab

Source: www.wikipedia.org/wiki/Palindrome

MORE SOLUTIONS ARE FOUND OUTSIDE THE BOX

When I wrote the first draft of this chapter, Steve Jobs was being memorialized in the media following his untimely death. He was a visionary who was always thinking outside the box. He was the Thomas Edison of our time—someone who understood early on the power of this important skill to extend the limits of what's possible. He forever changed how the world listens to music, downloads content, and uses phones, computers, and now tablets. As Jobs revolutionized the face of consumer technology, he owed his success to a mastery of ingenious thinking despite the mistakes he made along the way. He wasn't always a success, but he never gave up despite enormous failures, from miscues in his business pursuits to being fired from his own company. When he returned to that company later, he transformed it into one of the most valuable companies in the world, becoming one of the business world's greatest comeback kids.

Anytime you can think outside the box, you're upping your chances of finding new solutions to old problems. I mean that literally and figuratively. There are typically three or more ways to solve a problem, from equations in mathematics to life in general. When you realize this important truth, you gain the confidence to know that you can accomplish anything. You also increase your chances of standing out while at the same time defending your independence. This is an important point, because all of us like to think that we're "independent," but in fact this attribute is reserved for those who can truly stand on their own and who have faith that they can get themselves out of any predicament or disappointment. I witness a lack of independence in both children and adults, many of whom struggle both to solve their own problems and to make good decisions to carry them forward. There's no better way to overcome this handicap and boost your autonomy and self-reliance than to foster outside-the-box thinking. Being able to solve your own problems is critical to success in life—tackling not just the problems we encounter in a math class or in a project at work but all sorts of problems we face in everyday life.

Embrace every opportunity you have to think differently and be taken out of your usual routine or surroundings where you follow the same old rules. Always make up ways to do things and arrive at right answers your way despite the critics and naysayers. Give yourself permission to make up your own rules rather than always following someone else's. This is the essence of thinking outside the box, and it will reward you in innumerable ways—from augmenting your creativity and changing your perspective for the better to refining your logic, common sense, ability to make excellent decisions, and perceptual intuition—the productive thinker's holy grail.

Chapter Guide

I've given you a lot of ideas in this chapter on how to think outside the box. I encourage you each day to seek as many opportunities as you can find to do so. Make it a goal to hop outside your box from the moment you roll out of bed. Flex your imagination at breakfast as you catch up with the morning news and with family members. Then, as you step outside to start your day, set an intention to find at least three or four things on your way to work or school that will help you think differently. Remember, when you aim to live outside your normal box, you will be stoking your inner genius and making life more interesting.

The exercises in this chapter are meant to be done only

once as you read through, but you'll find lots of fresh exercises online that you've never seen before. Go to my Web site, www.MikeByster.com, for video demonstrations and additional resources to challenge your mental math shortcuts.

SOLUTIONS TO THE PROBLEMS IN THIS CHAPTER

Rebuses

1. man overboard
2. growing economy
3. win with ease
4. piece (*P*'s) of pumpkin pie
5. in between jobs
6. falling in love
7. on cloud nine
8. paradox
9. three blind mice (no *i*'s)
10. banana split
11. missing link
12. toucan
13. safety in numbers
14. ill in bed
15. makeup

Trippy Triangles

Triangle 1: 35
Triangle 2: 27

What's the Connection?

horn on a unicorn
one giant leap for mankind
52 cards in a deck
88 piano keys

Mental Math Shortcuts

$54 \times 54 = 2,916$; $59 \times 59 = 3,481$
$85 \times 85 = 7,225$; $35 \times 35 = 1,225$
$55 \times 65 = 3,575$; $25 \times 35 = 875$
$25 \times 45 = 1,125$; $55 \times 75 = 4,125$
$95 \times 94 = 8,930$; $96 \times 92 = 8,832$
$46 \times 46 = 2,116$; $42 \times 42 = 1,764$
$103 \times 105 = 10,815$; $104 \times 109 = 11,336$
$206 \times 205 = 42,230$; $208 \times 202 = 42,016$
$41 \times 61 = 2,501$; $91 \times 31 = 2,821$

Anagrams

stamp store
lives
they see
Old West action
I'm a dot in place
elegant man
organic

CHAPTER 6

Skill 5: Organization

Harry Held Little Baby Bobbie, Causing Nancy One Fantastic Nightmare

I've known countless people who were reservoirs of learning,
yet never had a thought.

—WILSON MIZNER

Harry, Bobbie, and Nancy were just one set of friends who kept me cruising through science class as a fifth grader. Yes, these are fictional characters, but they could tell me how to begin reciting the periodic table of elements anytime. Within that one sentence—"Harry held little baby Bobbie, causing Nancy one fantastic nightmare"—live the first ten elements, from hydrogen to neon. Many more sentences and characters followed, of course, taking me to the end of the table in organized fashion. My classmates thought I was a genius, but I knew otherwise. It was just a matter of using my imagination and stringing a few fun sentences together in groups of five to ten words. Simple as that.

Today I don't need to know the periodic table of elements

to get through my day. I encounter other types of challenges that are vastly more monumental (from my adult perspective now) to my ability to succeed, navigate challenges at work, and make a difference in the world. But I've used mental organizational devices since I first learned their value as a third grader decades ago, and I attribute many of my accomplishments over the years to this skill's uncanny ability to free up mental space, accelerate my problem-solving abilities, and help me to manage an untold amount of incoming data that constantly bombards my brain.

Lauren had a breakthrough moment within weeks of learning the fine art of mental organization. An audience member of mine during a presentation a few years ago, Lauren epitomizes what mastering certain organizational strategies can do for anyone who juggles the weight of "too much information" in daily life or, in Lauren's case, in her attempts to start a catering business that demanded she multitask to a degree that could drive anyone crazy.

Although plenty of experts have discussed the benefits of organizing one's physical space, that goal should come second to the task of organizing one's mental space. In fact, optimizing any physical space happens naturally once you've gotten your cognitive space organized. Just ask Lauren: While she was in the early stages of getting her business off the ground, which required that she manage competing demands from vendors and customers, all the while learning the ropes of being in business for herself (and hearing a lot of unsolicited advice) and overseeing a small staff, Lauren found it essential to find mental shortcuts to keep to-dos, promises, and responsibilities in check. She also came to rely on her mental organizing skills to manage the stress that accompanied being self-employed, for a lot of people depended on her as a leader.

I think it's fair to say that anyone who takes on such big roles in the working world has to find ways of keeping the mind well ordered and primed to handle the unexpected. But even people who aren't at the helm of a company and who don't have any interest in starting a business can benefit mightily from learning this skill. It has enormous benefits, from helping us remember a wide variety of things to seemingly unrelated endeavors like public speaking, prioritizing, accomplishing more at work, writing compelling and attention-grabbing articles or essays, managing a team of people, getting household chores done, collaborating with others, and solving problems in academic, professional, or personal situations. Put simply, the ability to organize the mind is what separates the high achievers from the nonachievers.

In this chapter you'll develop your power of mental organization. You'll learn how to sort through incoming thoughts systematically and create order out of the chaos of inbound information so that it can be stored and easily retrieved at a later date. We've done a lot of work with achieving higher levels of attention and mental capacity, creating associations and personal connections, and looking at things differently, but now it's time to bring all of these skills together and maximize your ability to manage massive amounts of data in an orderly fashion. The brain craves order and systemization. It likes predictability, too—knowing what it's dealing with so it can allocate resources and figure out the best way to handle the arriving information. Otherwise, reams of information can quickly become tangled, indecipherable, and effectively turned to mush in the mind's eye.

By now you should have already gotten your feet wet with strategies that entail organizing, but here I'll focus intently on establishing proven ways to mentally catalog information, especially when it involves the receipt of a lot of data at once. In doing so, I'll offer insights into how the brain operates when it receives a flood of information and how anyone can master techniques to immediately commit that content to memory without needing to hear it again—or even take notes! And how does the power of forgetting fit into this skill?

Being able to effortlessly organize thoughts has everything to do with the forgetting. The vast majority of the entire practice of continual mental organization has to do with ignoring and dumping the unimportant, which can clutter and clog your brain's precious processing channels. It's just like what happens when we organize our physical spaces: When we attack those untidy garages, closets, and cabinets, most of our efforts are spent on throwing away useless junk and outdated items. The proverbial spring cleaning is more about purging than adding. And the same is true of organizing our minds. This skill is primarily based on giving yourself permission to abandon certain thoughts and dispose of them as you would an old piece of clothing or an expired box of stale crackers.

The brain can hold a lot more than most people think, but unless you know how to register the details as they come in, your poor brain won't be able to hold much. With proper organization, you can access the particulars you need when you need them—fast. So whether you want to remember someone's talk that you heard during a seminar, recite a poem, or recall all of your weekly appointments and obligations without looking them up in your "organizer," the skills you learn in this chapter will make you your own personal organizer. No computer or notebook required. And as I stated earlier, this skill is immensely valuable and rewarding in more ways than one.

TWO REGIONS, ONE SEQUENCE

As I've already mentioned, it helps to symbolically think of the brain as having two "regions"—one part that memorizes information and another part that sorts and processes new information. Training these different regions to work simultaneously yet independently of each other is what will allow you to have a really fast and sharp brain. But as we've also seen, the brain cannot effectively accomplish two tasks at once when those two tasks entail complex functions, such as comprehending and counting. We can talk on the phone and play a video game like Tetris at the same time, but we can't really listen to two people talking to us at the same time and focus on both conversations at once. Neither can we do more than one brainy thing at a time, such as write a witty e-mail or blog entry while our spouse stands in front of us hoping to have a lively discussion.

Some commonplace activities, such as driving and talking on a cell phone, frequently go hand in hand, but when they do, it's likely that the brain is switching its main focus quickly between the two activities—perhaps a reason why this particular pairing has been so dangerous. What's even more dangerous is when one of the tasks sparks too many unrelated thoughts and our frontal lobes lose track of the other task. More evidence for the hazards of distracted driving.

The human brain is pretty quick, but there are limits to how much information it can process while juggling multiple streams of data. These limitations and the process of momentarily switching back and forth from one task to another in order to "multitask" make the skill of organization all the more essential so the brain can more easily perform those mental shifts swiftly, seamlessly, and reliably. The brain is constantly striving to keep track of two tasks or two sets of information, and organization is key.

With that in mind, let's turn now to my seven personal secrets to organizing incoming data. Some of this material will sound familiar, because I'll be reiterating concepts you've already acquired. See if you can really cement these ideas in your head. Although these strategies might not initially seem at all related to organizing thoughts and information in real life, work through learning them regardless. You'll be surprised by just how applicable these ideas are to streamlining data you encounter in everyday work and your personal life. At the end of the chapter, I'll give you a couple of games to play that gather all of these strategies together and help to further connect the dots between these concepts and their applications in the real world.

1. TURN NUMBERS INTO PICTURES: EMPLOYING THE POWER OF PEG

"One is a bun, two is shoe, three is a tree, four is a door, five is a hive. . . ."

In the mid-1600s, a man by the name of Henry Herdson linked digits with objects that resembled them. So, for instance, the number one became a candle. This would become known as the *peg system*: items to be remembered are pegged to—or associated with—certain images in a pre-arranged order. The system gets its name from the fact that the peg words act as mental "pegs" on which you can hang the information that you need to remember. There are several variations of this type of system today, another of which is the one based on *rhyming pegs*. In rhyming pegs, you remember items that rhyme with the numbers zero through ten, as in the following:

0 = hero
1 = bun
2 = shoe
3 = tree
4 = door
5 = hive
6 = sticks
7 = heaven
8 = gate
9 = vine
10 = hen

This system was introduced in England sometime around 1879 by John Sambrook. It's easy to use, and many people already know many of the standard rhymes from the nursery rhyme "One, Two, Buckle My Shoe." To use this system, start by memorizing this list, visualizing each item as you make the rhyme. Picture the items vividly—is the bun a hot-dog bun or a hot-cross bun? Is the shoe an old battered sneaker or a black high-heeled pump? Next, draw the item. The act of drawing helps you remember the rhyme, creating a strong mental association between the numbers and the words. By visualizing the object that each word represents as vividly as possible, you'll fix it securely in your mind, creating a strong mental association between the number and the word that rhymes with it.

Once you've formed an association between the numbers and the words that rhyme with them, you've constructed your pegs. Practice by saying each of the peg words out loud. Then try picturing the peg words in place of the numbers as you randomly jump among the numbers: 5, 3, 1, 8. Because the words rhyme with the numbers, you don't have to say the numbers to remember the words. If you want to remember a list, all you have to do is link each item with a peg: the first item with a bun, the second item with a shoe, and so on. To remember the list, call up each peg and you'll automatically remember the mental image linked to that peg.

Let's see how this could work for a short grocery list of milk, bread, eggs, and cheese—milk being item number one, bread being item number two, and so on. You could start out by visualizing a gallon of milk balancing a bun on its lid. Then imagine an old shoe squashing a loaf of bread. Then think of a tree filled with eggs. And finally, picture a wedge of cheese knocking on a door to be let in. When you get to the store and you think of one—bun—you'll think of a milk jug, and two—shoe—will bring to mind a shoe smashing the bread. Whatever image you choose, it should be evocative, bordering on the absurd. If you can make yourself laugh with the images you create, you're more likely to remember them.

The peg method is ideal for memorizing long lists because it's not dependent on retrieving items in sequence. In other words, you can access any item on the list without having to work your way through the whole thing. This method, however, is a bit more complicated to learn at first. In the peg system, first you must learn a standard set of peg words, and only then can you link the items you need to remember to the pegs. The peg approach can be used to remember ideas and concepts and to organize activities, as well as to remember lists for shopping and errands. In a work environment, you could use this system to recall certain facts or ideas that you want to present or highlight during a meeting when you're in front of colleagues and superiors and you'd rather not rely on notes or turn to a computer. It can also come in handy if you're giving a talk and want to remember the sequence of topics you're covering without needing a prompter or turning away from your audience to look at the accompanying slides on a projected PowerPoint presentation.

The various forms of the peg system all use a concrete object to represent each number. What's different among them is how you choose the object that represents each number. In addition to peg systems that rely on using pegs that look like the numbers they represent or pegs that rhyme with the numbers, another peg system relies on meaning, and yet a fourth peg system uses alphabetic pegs. There are potentially many types of peg systems, and you can invent your own peg system that works for you. My sister, for example, likes to use a peg system based on a group of random words that tell a story. Those random words are then the pegs for the new material she needs to organize and remember.

Alphabet peg systems are pretty easy to remember and use, like rhyming ones, because the alphabet makes a good system—it's naturally ordered and everyone knows it. In order to create concrete images for the letters, each image either rhymes with the letter of the alphabet it represents or has the letter as the initial sound of the word. The alphabet peg system might be: A = hay, B = bee, C = sea. Peg words can be chosen that rhyme with or sound similar to the letters of the alphabet they represent:

A = bay

B = bee

C = sea

D = deep

E = eve

F = effect

G = geology

H = age

I = eye

J = jay

K = quay

L = elm

M = Emma

N = end

O = open

P = pea

Q = cue

R = art

S = essay

T = tea

U = you

V = veer

W = double you

X = exit

Y = why

Z = zebra

If you don't like the rhyming aspect of the alphabetic peg-word system, you can come up with a list that doesn't rhyme but that simply uses the same letter of the alphabet to begin each word.

A = artichoke
B = bat
C = cake
D = dog
E = elephant
F = fireman
G = goat
H = horse
I = iron
J = jelly
K = kangaroo
L = llama
M = mouse
N = napkin
O = orange
P = pail
Q = queen
R = rat
S = shoe
T = tank
U = umbrella
V = vase
W = wagon
X = xylophone
Y = yarn
Z = zebra

The only problem with using the alphabet system is that most people don't automatically know the numeric equivalents of the letters of the alphabet, so they can't be directly retrieved as easily. For example, most people don't know, without counting, that *S* is the nineteenth letter, so if they wanted to recall the nineteenth item out of sequence, they would have to count off the letters and then retrieve the associated image.

You can also select peg words on the basis of meaning: one = me (there is only one "me"); three = pitchfork (three prongs); five = hand (five fingers on a hand). Numbers make good peg words because they have a natural order and everyone knows them. Unfortunately, this system is limited, because it's hard to find good peg words to represent numbers beyond ten.

2. CHUNK IT DOWN: THINK IN FIVES AND TENS

Why are Social Security numbers given in chunks of three, two, and four (999-99-9999) instead of as one unbroken number (999999999)? Why do phone numbers have hyphens in them? Because it's much easier to remember information when it's grouped into smaller chunks. I find that my brain prefers to remember things in groups of five, but maybe groups of four or eight will be your magic number.

Groupings allow you to organize information and sometimes apply other memory strategies, such as key words, a peg system, or a code you totally make up using your imagination. When my son memorized that long number, he grouped the numbers against the backdrop of a drum-filled song, which is an excellent example of grouping by sound.

But there are no rules to this technique. It's just a matter of breaking up information as you see fit and then finding a way to work with those chunks that is relevant to you. This method can be used for a wide variety of tasks, from recalling lists of items to remembering basic concepts, important points, or topics that you want to cover in a presentation at work or perhaps in approaching your boss for a raise. In a studying environment, if you're trying to figure out how to commit to memory a long batch of notes, see if you can break down your detailed notes into chunks of five main concepts. This will help you mentally organize all the material and recall the important facts.

3. DON'T BE DETAIL ORIENTED

When taking in a lot of new information, don't be detail oriented. If you try to absorb and mentally work with a truckload of material bombarding your brain, you won't be able to easily hold up a stop sign in time to begin sorting and organizing it well. It'll quickly become muddled and unyielding. What happens is similar to shoving too many things into the X-ray machine as you're going through airport security. In order to really see individual items, each object—some of which are filled with other objects—needs to be individually placed on the conveyor belt with a few inches of space in between. If you try to shove several items at once into the machine, suddenly you can't really see anything and the whole machine gets jammed and breaks down—or the conveyor belt screeches to a halt and the TSA agent has to separate out all your items.

Now, the mind won't ever literally break down if it receives too much information at once, but all of us have experienced being inundated with too much information to the point where we can't wrap our brains around any single piece of it. To maximize our ability to mentally organize incoming thoughts and ideas, we need to have a sorting system in place in advance and ready to work. We can't wait until the mind is already sinking under the weight of too much data. By then it's too late. This is when separating the *facts* from the *details* is paramount.

Facts are not the same as *details*. When trying to figure out the important parts of in-depth material to retain in your memory, it's critical that you separate the genuine facts from the distracting details.

Most important facts get repeated more than once, but they tend to be buried by distracting details. Indeed, facts are important, but they can be hard to find amid the details, some of which are truly interesting. Let's take a quick excerpt from Wikipedia about Mozart. See if you can pluck out the facts and disregard the details. Here's a hint: None of the facts are repeated, and this passage is quite tight to begin with.

Wolfgang Amadeus Mozart, baptismal name Johannes Chrysostomus Wolfgangus Theophilus Mozart (27 January 1756–5 December 1791), was a prolific and influential composer of the Classical era. He composed over 600 works, many acknowledged as pinnacles of symphonic, concertante, chamber, piano, operatic, and choral music. He is among the most enduringly popular of classical composers.

Mozart showed prodigious ability from his earliest childhood in Salzburg. Already competent on keyboard and violin, he composed from the age of five and performed before European royalty. At 17, he was engaged as a court musician in Salzburg, but grew restless and travelled in search of a better position, always composing abundantly. While visiting Vienna in 1781, he was dismissed from his Salzburg position. He chose to stay in the capital, where he achieved fame but little financial security. During his final years in Vienna, he composed many of his best-known symphonies, concertos, and operas, and portions of the Requiem, which was largely unfinished at the time of Mozart's death. The circumstances of his early death have been much mythologized. He was survived by his wife Constanze and two sons.

Mozart learned voraciously from others, and developed a brilliance and maturity of style that encompassed the light and graceful along with the dark and passionate. His influence on subsequent Western art music is profound. Beethoven wrote his own early compositions in the shadow of Mozart, and Joseph Haydn wrote that "posterity will not see such a talent again in 100 years."

Source: www.wikipedia.org/wiki/Mozart

Now, let's say that you have to take a test tomorrow on Mozart or give a short summary of his life to a team at work for a project. You have no idea what you're going to be quizzed on, and you also don't know exactly how your team at work will use Mozart's biography. You just sense that the important facts and anything unusual about his life should be featured. Of all the words and sentences in the above text, what do you think should be highlighted? Here's my list:

1756 composer
Classical era
600
Salzburg
age of five
royalty
Vienna
Requiem
light and dark
Western art
Beethoven
35

From these I can retell the story of Mozart. I don't need to know that his baptismal name is Johannes Chrysostomus Wolfgangus Theophilus Mozart or that he was "always composing abundantly" or that he "travelled in search of a better position." Those are details that my mind will absorb when I read the material but that don't need to be encoded by my key words. You'll note that the number thirty-five wasn't in the original text, and I didn't make "early death" a key word. I calculated that number myself because it's easier for me to remember that he was thirty-five years old when he died than to remember the year 1791 or the phrase "early death." If I remember the year he was born, 1756, and the fact that he lived to the age of thirty-five, then I can always do the math if I need to on a test that asks about his death. And the fact that his death was "early" and has been "mythologized" are details I can recall from this fact alone.

4. ONCE UPON A TIME: DON'T FORGET THE POWER OF STORY

As you read the details of Mozart's life in the Wikipedia excerpt, my guess is that you could picture him in your mind— even if you have no idea what he looked like. Stories make things memorable—and *organizable*—because they allow us to paint pictures and produce movies in our minds. They help us create order out of chaos by attributing a clear and tidy image to a piece of information. This in itself is a way of organizing thoughts and data. Stories inherently force order because they are themselves organized entities—they have a beginning, a middle, and an end. They convey facts in a streamlined flow. And they can hold a vast array of details, but because those details are held within the rich context of a story, they remain orderly and structured by the sequence of events. They are "well regulated" by the story itself.

The Wikipedia excerpt on Mozart doesn't even read like a story, but it gives the brain enough to conjure something that's like a story. I've made the point several times that storytelling is essential to memory and that being able to create stories in your mind, however absurd or ludicrous, is a fundamental memory strategy. But I want to be clear on an important point: This doesn't imply that you have to have a "photographic" memory. You don't have to have been born with a photographic memory (or any other special type of memory, for that matter) to maximize your ability to see things and immediately commit them to memory. People who train their brains to create instant associations and organize what they see do just as well as those with photographic memories—and even the people blessed with a photographic memory have to work on this skill to keep it in tip-top shape. Most people with amazing memories do *not* have a photographic memory—they simply know how to organize their thoughts.

Even if you don't feel like you're talented in visualizing or in transforming concepts and information into mental images, you can at least aim to organize data differently. Go with what works for you and, most important, what's *fun* for you.

My son Josh knows the importance of this all too well. Although he managed to memorize a two-hundred-digit number, he still meets tough challenges in his studies when the strategies he used to stick that number in his brain don't work. This is especially true with subjects he's not very enthusiastic about, and history happens to be one of them. When he came to me for help in preparing for a test on the Roman Empire, I guided him through a process of mentally "seeing" the key takeaways from each paragraph in his textbook and relating them to a sentence, vignette, or image. The secret is to learn the content thought by thought rather than verbatim. So for Josh to remember a whole section about the Romans' lifestyle, he had only to remember the sentence "The plumber got a job at the hotel." This signified to him that "plumbers"— the engineers who constructed numerous aqueducts to carry water and serve thousands of people—played an important role in Roman life at the height of the Roman Empire.

If creating stories out of key words isn't your thing, then try making up a mnemonic sentence instead. Find associations between the information you need to know and an area in your life you're passionate about. For example, I associate lots of information I need to retain with baseball. Maybe for you connections can be made with marathon running, cooking, tae kwon do, dancing, or painting. Watch out, though: You may keep on thinking you're not a "visual learner" or a good storyteller, but once you find ways to organize your thoughts around what you like to do, you may soon find yourself unconsciously telling stories. Stories make up the fabric of our lives, and they can be hard to avoid. However good you've been at avoiding this nightmare, what will you do one day when you're asked to give a speech? Learn this secret and you'll be ready.

5. FIND A SINGLE WORD FOR EACH THOUGHT

Another way to help classify and categorize large amounts of incoming data so you can mentally organize your thoughts and capture what needs to be permanently stored is to do what many expert orators do: label chunks of similar information with a single word or term. Not only can this technique help you hold the remote control when your brain is besieged with information, but it can be incredibly useful when you are asked to speak in front of a large group while mentally juggling a library of details to share in your remarks. The pressure to perform alone can smother your memory and steal the thoughts you're trying so hard to keep on the tip of your tongue. To this end, let's see how linking single words to sizable, intricate thoughts can be applied to the spectrum of circumstances that involve organizing massive amounts of data.

Most everyone is terrified of public speaking at first. Not only are we afraid of making a mistake or flubbing a word in front of a large group of people, but we fear that we'll draw a serious blank, completely forgetting what we're supposed to say, and find ourselves looking for an escape button. After all, they don't call it "stage fright" for nothing! Of course, presenting a formal speech or lecture in front of a live audience is not the only form that performance takes. You may find yourself teaching a course, playing a part in a theatrical production, participating on a panel, leading a group, presenting your ideas to your boss or a boardroom, getting up in front of a classroom to share your stories, giving a eulogy at a funeral or a toast at a wedding, or just saying a few words of thanks or telling an ice-breaking joke at your Saturday-night dinner party as you take the head seat at the table. In any of these situations, being able to say two or three sentences perfectly in a row can be hard and heart-stopping.

I'm surprised that most of us are not formally taught the art of public speaking in traditional school unless we're on the debate team or join the mock trial club. (And even then, sometimes the education system assumes we'll pick up the secrets to this important life skill on our own, largely through trial and error.) The problem with trying to learn the ropes of public speaking is that if you don't take to it easily at first (or if you have had the bad experience of totally floundering during a speech), you're much more likely to give up and avoid the spotlight for the rest of your life. It only takes one embarrassing gaffe for some of us to turn the other way and never look back, which is a shame. Contrary to what you might think, public speaking is not just for public servants and talented orators. It's also not just for people who plan to become captains of industry, CEOs, and leaders of groups. Anyone who wants to be heard and to convey their ideas, thoughts, and opinions needs to know how to speak in front of audiences big and small. Like so many other skills taught in this book, the ability to speak clearly and candidly to anyone will give you an advantage—a huge advantage. Speaking well and easily will no doubt make you stand out and make memorable to scores of others the most important thing in the world: you. Yes, *you*.

I'm going to use the word "speeches" to refer to all the various ways in which we can present information in front of others. A quick toast at a dinner party can be considered a speech just as the Gettysburg Address is considered a speech. All speeches—long and short—can be viewed as collections of ideas or thoughts. With a beginning, a middle, and an end, a speech typically flows from one thought to the next. The key to "memorizing" a speech is to create a code relevant to you that helps you recall all the chief thoughts in the speech. Your code will automatically help you organize your thoughts because it creates a methodical sequence and flow from one point to the next. You're not going to memorize everything word for word or even sentence by sentence. You're just going to memorize the thought process from beginning to end. In this manner you'll remember the speech thought by thought and let your mind fill in the blanks, fleshing out those thoughts as you speak them.

DID YOU KNOW?

"Speed-reading" is a total myth. Anyone who tries to speed-read isn't really reading every single word and line. If you know someone who claims to read two thousand words per minute, it's time to call that person's bluff. It's a well-documented scientific fact that it's physiologically impossible to read more than about eight hundred words a minute. Not only that, but it's also been proved that the structure and function of the eyes allow them to focus on only one small area of the page at a time, thus making speed-reading impossible. Just as I think there will never be a time when the human body can naturally run a mile in under a minute, there won't ever be a "genius" who can read a book in ten minutes. It happens in sci-fi movies but not in real life, so you can breathe a sigh of relief. That said, people who claim to speed-read are in fact employing a strategy to get through the material quickly: They are visually grabbing the thoughts and ideas ("skimming"), just as you'd organize a speech thought by thought, idea by idea. I should add that the fastest readers—and conversely the slowest readers—aren't always the ones who absorb and retain information the best. It's the people who, reading at a comfortable rate *for themselves*, need to read something only once to remember it.

How exactly do you go about preparing a speech? First I will say that it does help to write out what you want to say in longhand or on a computer. Include all the important facts or phrases you want to include in your speech. Read it over a few times, then break it down into thoughts and try to find a single word that's emblematic of each thought. What will happen is that you'll end up with a ten-page speech broken down into a dozen words that reflect all of the main points made in those pages. The key is to choose words that remind you of the entire thought. For example, if I were to begin a speech by telling my audience how I came to write this book, I might use the word "history" to inform my opening act. Then let's say I wanted to transition into an engrossing story about a student named Bobby who used my techniques. This anecdote could still be remembered under "history," but to make sure I didn't forget it I'd add the word "Bobby" to my list of key words.

Next would come the key word to get me into the second act of my speech. If I wanted to get audience members immersed immediately in a memory game, I could use the name of the game to direct me, such as "missing card trick" or some such phrase. The point is that I would pick certain words along my path that reflected the gist of what I wanted to say, and then I'd have to remember only those specific words.

I could even write down those words in order, just to be sure I got everything in sequence correctly. Ideally, I'd memorize the list of words using a simple sentence or story line and wouldn't even need a set of notes with me when I delivered the final speech.

The following is an excerpt from Franklin Delano Roosevelt's first inaugural address ("The only thing we have to fear is fear itself"), in which the newly elected president set forth his proposal for what would become the New Deal. The words or phrases I'd pick to create my memory code are marked in bold. After each paragraph, you'll see how zany this can get as I share how I'd try to mentally "picture" a story behind this speech in order to recall the order and gist of it. Bear with me:

> *This nation asks for action, and* **action now.** *Our greatest primary task is to* **put people to work.** *This is no unsolvable problem if we face it wisely and courageously. It can be accompanied in part by* **direct recruiting** *by the government itself, treating the task as we would treat the emergency of a war, but at the same time, through this employment, accomplishing greatly needed projects to stimulate and reorganize the use of our* **national resources.**

For this paragraph, I see a group of people with pickaxes and shovels (putting them to work) lined up outside an army recruiting office, building a path out of stone and dirt and water (natural resources, which is close enough to "national" resources for recall purposes) to the office. At the door is Uncle Sam (direct recruiting), with a huge sign reading ACTION NOW!

> *Hand in hand with this, we must frankly recognize the over-balance of population in our* **industrial** *centers and, by engaging on a national scale in a* **redistribution,** *endeavor to provide a better use of the land for those best*

fitted for the land. The task can be helped by definite efforts to raise the values of **agricultural** *products and with this the power to purchase the output of our cities. It can be helped by preventing realistically the tragedy of the growing loss, through* **foreclosure**, *of our small homes and our farms. It can be helped by insistence that the Federal, State, and local* **governments** *act forthwith on the demand that their* **cost be drastically reduced.** *It can be helped by the* **unifying of relief activities** *which today are often scattered, uneconomical and unequal. It can be helped by national planning for and supervision of all forms of* **transportation and of communications and other utilities** *which have a definitely public character. There are many ways in which it can be helped, but it can never be helped merely by talking about it. We must act, and act quickly.*

I see a man on a farm surrounded by a city skyline with belching smokestacks (industrial centers), with big stacks of corn, moving cobs from one pile to another (redistributing). In the scene is a home with FORECLOSURE on a plank nailed across the front door. He looks up as three Uncle Sams (small, medium, and large, representing the local, state, and federal governments) appear, with dollar signs above their heads (costs) that are rapidly shrinking away (drastically reduced). The Uncle Sams hold hands (unifying) as they approach a small lake where people are drowning. The Uncle Sams stop talking, and the biggest Uncle Sam, with a notebook and bullhorn around his neck, throws a bunch of raw materials into the lake. The drowning people use them to build roads and bridges and power structures (transportation, communications, and other utilities) to climb safely out of the lake.

> *Finally, in our progress toward a resumption of work we require* **two safeguards** *against a return of the* **evils** *of the old order: there must be a strict* **supervision** *of all* **banking** *and credits and investments; there must be an* **end to speculation** *with other people's money, and there must be provision for an adequate but* **sound currency**.

Here I imagine an old devil with two angels (safeguards) sitting on his shoulders. One is guarding a bank (banking), carefully watching who's going in and out (supervising); the other angel is in a casino, taking away a gambler's dirty, broken chips (end to speculation) and waving a wand to turn the chips into a pile of brand-new dollar bills with muscles (healthy, or "sound" currency).

This example is not meant to be something you actually memorize. I merely wanted to show you how I personally would go about trying to associate scenes and sentences with the words of the speech. By no means is this the only way to tackle the task of committing this particular speech to memory. Notice that each segment of my imagined story doesn't seem to relate to the next, and that's okay. So long as I can recall their sequence, I can create as many vignettes for the speech as I need to best remember it.

As we'll see in the next section, sometimes it helps to create an acrostic to provide another guide to the exact sequence of events or material, thus generating organization. Acrostics have been used for centuries as a way to manage ideas and incoming information. This ancient strategy has also been used to encrypt secret messages. Although I enjoy learning about the role of acrostics in history, I find them to be essential tools today for supporting my organizational skills and putting chunks of information into bite-size pieces that my brain can handle.

6. GET "ACROBATIC" ABOUT IT

An acrostic, whose name originates from Greek words that mean "top verse," is a form of writing in which the first letter, syllable, or word of each line, paragraph, or other recurring feature in the text spells out a word or a message. Traditionally, acrostics have been used as mnemonic devices to aid memory retrieval. A very famous Greek acrostic was made for the acclamation "Jesus Christ, God's Son, Savior." In Greek, the first letters spell ICHTHYS (ΙΧΘΥΣ), the word for fish. This explains the origins of the fish as a symbol for Jesus Christ from the early days of Christianity to the present time.

The classic mnemonic device for remembering the planets is another well-known example of an acrostic. You make the following sentence from the first letters of the names of the planets in order: My (Mercury) very (Venus) excellent (Earth) mother (Mars) just (Jupiter) served (Saturn) us (Uranus) nine (Neptune) pizzas (Pluto).

If you prefer to drop Pluto, then you can end the sentence with "served us nachos."

Acrostics are common in medieval literature, where they serve to highlight the name of the poet or his patron or to make a prayer to a saint. They are often found in verse works but can also appear in prose. A classic example of an acrostic poem in English was written by Edgar Allan Poe and aptly named "An Acrostic":

> Elizabeth it is in vain you say
> "Love not"—thou sayest it in so sweet a way:
> In vain those words from thee or L.E.L.
> Zantippe's talents had enforced so well:
> Ah! if that language from thy heart arise,
> Breathe it less gently forth—and veil thine eyes.
> Endymion, recollect, when Luna tried
> To cure his love—was cured of all beside
> His follie—pride—and passion—for he died.

Acrostics can be more complex than just making words from initials, and they can be a form of encryption. Using letters to hide a message, as in acrostic ciphers, was popular during the Renaissance. Various methods of enciphering were used, such as selecting letters other than initials based on a repeating pattern (equidistant letter sequences) or concealing the message by starting at the end of the text and working backward. Acrostics have also made their way into modern culture as an easy, sneaky way to deliver insults and political jabs at adversaries. In October 2009 the office of Arnold Schwarzenegger, governor of California at the time, sent a letter to the state assembly that contained an acrostic. The initial letters of each line spelled an obscene exclamation starting with the letter *F*. A spokesman for the governor called the incident coincidental. In January 2010 the CEO of Sun Microsystems sent an e-mail to his employees after the company had been successfully acquired by Oracle Corporation. The initial letters of the first seven paragraphs spelled

"Beat IBM." Coincidence? Probably not. Cleverness, more likely!

Acrostics can function as more than just a useful memory strategy. They can come in handy for organizing your thoughts to begin with—before they even become part of your memory. Anytime you have to create a lengthy story or sequence of substitute words or memorize a long list of items and you find that the peg system won't work for you, acrostics can be your strategy. Acrostics are also great for framing and organizing reminders in general, whether it's your to-do list, a checklist of items you need to pack, or a record of your weekly appointments and obligations. For example:

HAPS = homework, assignment notebook, pencil or pen, and spiral (how one kid remembers what to bring to class)

GO FISH = garlic, onion, fillets, iceberg lettuce, shallots, horseradish (a grocery store list)

DESK = dentist, eyeglasses, shower gift, kitchen light (a to-do list, with each word triggering something that needs to be addressed)

COPR (pronounced "copper") = catsup, onions, pickle, relish (how my sister reminds my brother-in-law what to order on her hot dog)

As with all of the mnemonic devices described in this book, there are virtually no limits to the types of acrostics you can create. The only rule you need to follow is making sure your creation has meaning to you. Note that your acrostic automatically establishes order, which is helpful when you need to rely on it to remember a certain sequence. Take, for instance, a list of tasks that must be done at work in a certain order if they're going to be accomplished on time: (1) e-mail boss, (2) prepare marketing campaign update for lunch meeting, (3) make doctor's appointment, (4) pay credit card bill, and (5) schedule dinner with Susan. You can create your own acrostic here by taking the first letter of the key idea in each task. BLABS (as in a person who blabs) could be your word here. *B* stands for boss, *L* stands for lunch, *A* stands for appointment, *B* stands for bill, and the final *S* stands for Susan. You won't mix up the two *B*'s because you know that your boss gets priority!

The key is to use acrostics when they come naturally to you and make sense to you. It does you no good to force them when they are difficult to create (and thus remember). But they do offer a brilliant way to organize your thoughts when they are easy to make. You can also employ them when you're trying to organize the chief sections of a long speech. Just as we created mental pictures out of lengthier chunks of material from the sample speech on pages 217–219, you can imagine an acrostic to generate the chief thought that needs to be conveyed in each sequential section. Try this right now. Go back to FDR's speech and see if you can create an acrostic using the main ideas expressed in each section. I encourage you to go online as well and share your acrostic at www.MikeByster.com. Let's see who comes up with the wittiest one!

7. BUILD A MEMORY PALACE: A PLACE TO GET ORGANIZED (AND COMFORTABLE)

At the World Memory Championships, top competitors memorize the order of twenty shuffled decks of cards in an hour and more than five hundred random digits in fifteen minutes, among other feats. Such amazing mental stunts take more than a quick mind and solid memory. They take exceptional organizational skills. Think you have what it takes, too? Believe it or not, almost everybody has the capacity to perform such incredible feats. But you will need more than just the collection of organizational strategies you have already learned in this book up to this point. You will need to weave together many strategies and techniques to create your own memory palace, an idea that's been around for centuries. Being able to go on wild expeditions in your mind that you control yourself, picture by picture, staircase by staircase, is key. This skill is useful for far more than just memory competitions and trivia. It can provide the mental bandwidth you need to pack more information inside your head while expanding your processing speed, mental sharpness, and overall brainpower. Let me explain.

A memory palace is an imaginary place where you can go to recall information. What you basically do is envision a large building (a "palace") in your mind and mentally decorate that building, filling it up from the inside out in ways that help you store information you need to remember. So, for instance, if I'm trying to memorize the signers of the Declaration of Independence, I might go to a parlor in my memory palace where all of the signers are sitting around the table. Or I could have a kitchen where my refrigerator is adorned with important telephone numbers. But memory palaces needn't be based on palaces per se. They can be based on a trusty route you take to work or a single room where you are most comfortable, such as your bedroom, or a favorite garden. The only rules you have to follow in building this fictional setting are to make it relevant to yourself and your life and to make it totally *bizarre*. You have to give yourself the freedom to fill your personal space with eccentric objects, situations, people, and even characters. Case in point: In one of my mind's bedrooms, I can "see" Harry holding little baby Bobbie, causing Nancy one fantastic nightmare (the first ten elements of the periodic table, as you'll recall).

With time and practice, anyone can build a memory palace, and again, your palace can reap a wide spectrum of benefits for you that go beyond a memory champ's achievements. You can use your palace at work to mentally stage your presentation at the next board meeting. You can use it at school to recall a year's worth of knowledge for a final exam or in an athletic setting to store critical information about plays or strategies. And you can use it in more personal ways as well, such as remembering important information like birthdays, anniversaries, your social calendar, and appointments. For instance, you could organize a year's worth of birthday dates by picturing a twelve-story building, with each floor designated as a month. January is the first floor, and your twelfth floor represents December. Within each floor you have mental pictures that signify the people and corresponding dates of their individual birthdays.

By now it should come as no surprise to you that the reason memory palaces are so effective is that they hinge on their creator's personal input. That is, they are "built" out of what's already familiar and comfortable. None of the presidents of the United States may be familiar to you, but place those presidents in your own living room a certain way and suddenly you can get to know Mr. Monroe and Mr. Garfield from a whole new perspective. Just as being in a comfortable and familiar place can boost your confidence and take the stress out of having to perform, taking abstract, lengthy, or complicated concepts, facts, and ideas with you to those familiar places can help you organize them and make them memorable, transforming hard-to-remember vital facts into easy-to-retrieve information and details. And as I've been suggesting over and over again, anytime you can add a bit of absurdity to your imagined scene you create a stronger, more organized memory. So see if you can use your wild imagination and have, say, Mr. Monroe sitting on your toilet reading *Men's Health* magazine; get Mr. Garfield to ride your orange cat, aptly named Garfield. I once had a student who mentally placed each president in a specific spot in his bedroom so that whenever he had to recall the presidents he could "look around" his room in his mind's eye.

Lots of Web sites will teach you how to build a memory palace. Most of them follow similar instructions, such as:

- Decide on a blueprint for your palace. Will it reflect your house? Your drive to work? A favorite vacation spot?
- Define a route with its specific locations and storage spots.
- Memorize your memory palace.
- Place things to be remembered in your palace, using symbols and images that are relevant to you and that reflect your creativity. This means you might not stock a closet with all of the planets. Instead, you'll "see" a mobile of the planets hanging over your bed with a string dangling from it that contains your mnemonic device, "My very educated mother . . ."
- Keep exploring your palace to lock it into memory, and make changes as necessary.
- Use your palace.

You may even want to draw your memory palace on paper the first time you do this exercise. See if that works for you. Memory palaces aren't for everyone, and they can take time and practice to get used to. But for some of us they can be astonishingly effective. You just might surprise yourself.

FINAL EXAM: THINK YOU'RE A GOOD ORGANIZER? TRY THESE!

From pegs to memory palaces, there are myriad ways to organize your thoughts. The seven I've given you in this chapter are just a small sampling; you can probably find other ways to sort and analyze incoming thoughts by employing your imagination and thinking outside the box. See if you can come up with your own unique methods in addition to the ones I've described, or simply use your own ideas and personal strategies to modify what you've learned in this chapter. You'll find that certain techniques work better for certain types of material. The goal is to train your brain to utilize the ideal system at a moment's notice so you don't have to exert too much effort in first choosing a tool and then applying it.

If you want to test out all seven of my organizing tactics in one fell swoop, pick a topic you know nothing or very little about but wish to learn more about, and gather information on it from various sources. For example, maybe you'd like to know more about the Enlightenment period or about enology (the science of winemaking), or perhaps it's the history of Pop Art and Andy Warhol that's got you curious. You don't have to go further than the Internet to collect your material—aim for a solid ten pages or so of content. Then try to organize all that content using every single strategy presented in this chapter, starting with the peg system. Notice which types of data in your collection can easily be matched with a peg system but not, say, an acrostic.

You needn't try to do this all in your head. Until you get really good at matching content with the best organizing technique, it helps to write out notes as you work through the process. Get a highlighter and pen and watch what emerges on paper as you play with the content and drum up stories, cross out irrelevant details, highlight facts, and identify patterns or letters that can become acrostics or other mnemonics. For an added challenge, pretend that you have to give a speech on your subject matter. What would you emphasize? How would you organize your presentation from beginning to end? How could you make it engaging and memorable to your audience?

We organize our thoughts all day long simply in order to think clearly, but rarely do we organize our thoughts on a level that would allow us to give lengthy live talks or to learn by heart an entire topic so we can recite facts and recall even the smallest details at our next dinner party. Yet when we become expert mental organizers, we can perform these impressive feats and break free from the pack. We can also nourish our brainpower and create more space for more information. Remember, an organized brain is a roomy brain. The more swiftly you can organize your thoughts, the more information you can take in quickly—and the more information you can learn.

Ready to flex your organizing skills some more? Below is a series of three exercises that will challenge your brain on every level. See if you can employ some of the strategies outlined in this chapter as you work through each exercise.

Not only will these exercises help you cement those techniques in your mind, but by proactively using them you'll be learning which ones come more naturally and easily to you, so you'll then be able to figure out which ones work best for you.

At first, these exercises may not seem to relate to the types of challenges you'll likely face in the real world, but doing these exercises is the equivalent of flexing certain "muscles" in your brain that you call upon every day in situations that demand you solve problems or quickly process incoming information. Lifting barbells in the gym to strengthen your arms isn't something you find yourself doing in the real world, but the results of flexing those muscles with the help of a weight will go a long way to prepare you for lifting all kinds of things and to support your body's healthy biochemistry in general. The same is true of exercises like those below; they have hidden benefits that you won't necessarily recognize until you're faced with a challenge at work or in a social environment and your brain can automatically think quickly and support your performance.

TEN ITEMS

Organizing items is a very simple game, but it's mentally empowering because it helps you improve your focus, mental capacity, mind organization, and memory. When the game is played at the expert level, it becomes very intense and takes a tremendous amount of concentration. The game can be played with two or more people and is usually best played around a nice-sized table, such as the kitchen or dining room table. Some household items are the only equipment you'll need: a stopwatch, a pencil and paper, and maybe a sheet or beach towel. Here's how to play.

One person chooses ten household items (it could be fewer or more depending on the number the players agree to) and covers them with a sheet. When the sheet is removed, the person who chose the ten items picks up each item one at a time and says what it is. For example, let's say the ten items are maple syrup, a calculator, a soda pop, a fork, a cell phone, soap, a book, a candy bar, a pen, and a belt. When the person finishes naming the ten items, he or she picks up the stopwatch and says, "Go," and the other person must rearrange the items in alphabetical order from left to right: belt, book, calculator, candy bar, cell phone, fork, maple syrup, pen, soap, soda pop. When the person finishes, he or she says, "Done," and if everything is in the correct order the stopwatch is stopped. If it's not all in correct order, the stopwatch keeps running until it's done correctly. If the person trying to alphabetize the items forgets what an item is named, he can ask, but fifteen seconds is added to his time for every item whose name is repeated. It's a good idea for the person naming the items to write down what he is naming them and read the list when naming the items to the other person so there are no arguments later on.

You might be saying to yourself: *What makes this game hard?* The challenge here is listening to the person articulate the name of each item and remembering exactly how the item is identified, because each item could have multiple names. For example, if the maple syrup is a bottle of Log Cabin maple syrup, the person laying out the items could call it any of the following: syrup, maple syrup, bottled syrup, pancake syrup, or Log Cabin syrup. Similarly, a cell phone could be a phone, a telephone, a mobile phone, an iPhone, a Samsung phone (or any other brand name), and so on. If the soda pop is a can of Diet Pepsi, he could call it soda, Pepsi, canned soda, a beverage, a drink, a carbonated beverage, pop, a soft drink, and so on. What he cannot do, though, is call it "lemonade" or personalize the word by saying something like "my favorite soda." He also cannot add an adjective, such as calling the syrup "delicious maple syrup." He can only call out what the item is, but that is what makes the game hard—you have to remember exactly what he says.

So, in this example, if the same ten items we used last time were named differently, they could be alphabetized this way:

1. Ballpoint pen
2. Bar of soap
3. Chocolate bar
4. Cola
5. Leather belt
6. Paperback book
7. Pocket calculator
8. Silverware
9. Syrup
10. Telephone

When the person is finished, the clock is stopped and the roles are reversed. The person with the lowest time wins the game!

STRATEGY

When I am the person who has to organize the items, I look at them and number them one through ten in my head from left to right before the other person reads me the name of each item. Then I remember the numbers of the ones from the first half of the alphabet (*A* through *M*) and mentally grab those first and alphabetize them. That way, if I do forget the name of an item later, I'll know if that name is from the first or second half of the alphabet, thus making it much easier to recall.

EXPERT LEVEL

You're empowering your mind tremendously as you get better and better at this game, but the expert level of this game can get pretty intense and difficult. What you need to do is take out four scraps of paper and write down the four different ways to alphabetize the items:

1. Alphabetizing
2. Alphabetizing based on the last letter of the word
3. Alphabetizing starting with the second letter of the first word
4. Alphabetizing starting with third letter of the first word

Before the person reads you the names of the items, pick one of the folded pieces of paper. If, for example, you pick the second way (alphabetized based on the last letter of the word), the ten items we used in the previous example (named as they were in the second example, not the first) would be alphabetized this way:

1. colA
2. telephonE
3. silverwarE
4. paperback booK
5. ballpoint peN
6. bar of soaP
7. syruP
8. chocolate baR
9. pocket calculatoR
10. leather belT

The reason why "telephone" comes before "silverware" is that, even though they both end in *e*, the last two letters of "telephone" read in reverse are *en*, while the last two letters of "silverware" read in reverse are *er*.

If you chose the fourth way of alphabetizing (starting with the third letter of the first word), the items would be in this order:

1. leAther belt
2. poCket calculator
3. coLa
4. teLephone
5. baLlpoint pen
6. siLverware
7. chOcolate bar
8. paPerback book
9. baR of soap
10. syRup

This game requires a tremendous amount of focus, con-centration, eye-hand coordination, and memory, and it is intense, fun, and sometimes immensely competitive. Every time you finish this game you will have had an amazing workout and improved several different areas of your mind.

> *Fact:* It's almost impossible to memorize and orga-nize a list of ten things without a strategy. Try one of the seven approaches mentioned in this chapter!

THE "13 − 1 = 10 + 2" TRICK

This card trick is meant to be memorized so you can perform it in front of someone else or a larger audience. I recommend that you go through all of the steps below a few times until you think you have this trick down pat. You have to keep the steps organized in your brain. For a live visual, refer to www.MikeByster.com. Oh, and if you're wondering where the name to this trick came from ("13 − 1 = 10 + 2"), I'm saving that explanation for after I've taken you through the steps. See if you can figure it out on your own!

HOW TO PLAY

- Start with a full deck of shuffled cards. (Ditch the joker cards; you should have fifty-two cards total.) Hold the deck of cards facedown in your hand.
- Flip over the top card, place it on a table, and note its number value. Let's say you turn over a six of spades. (Note: For the purposes of this trick, aces have a value of

one. If you flip over a face card—a jack, queen, or king—put it back in the deck on the bottom and choose another card until you get one with a value attached to it.)

- Continue to flip cards over onto the six of spades until you've flipped over the number of cards that, added to six, equals thirteen. In other words, don't bother taking note of these cards' values; just count out another seven cards, because six (the value of that first card, the six of spades) plus seven (another seven cards) equals thirteen. Once you've done that, you have pile 1. (Note: It's okay to lay down face cards as you count to thirteen; you don't have to put them on the bottom of the deck as you did when you were trying to find a "value" card.)

- After you've created pile 1, repeat the process and start a new pile. First, flip over a card from your original deck and place it on the table next to pile 1. Note the number (avoiding face cards), and then count out more cards until you reach thirteen. Let's say the second pile's first card is a three of hearts. You'll then flip over ten more cards and add them to pile 2. Repeat this process until you have four separate piles on the table.

- Flip all of the piles over so that they are facedown on the table.

- Get rid of *one of the piles* and put it back in your deck of cards (on either the top or the bottom, it doesn't matter).

- Starting out with the number ten in your head, turn over the top card from two different piles on the table. Add the top card numbers to the number 10. So if you flip over a three and a six (3 + 6 = 9), then your number is nineteen, because 10 + 9 = 19.

- Now count out nineteen cards from your deck.

- The number of cards *remaining* in that deck will be equal to the un-turned-over top card of the un-turned-over pile on the table.

Confusing? This trick is pretty straightforward, but you do have to be careful about the organization of the steps. It's perfectly fine to need to do this trick several times in order to commit the steps to memory. If you haven't figured it out by now, the name of the trick helps me to recall the steps. We create four piles by counting a particular way up to thirteen; then we remove a pile and place it back in the original deck. In the latter half of the trick, we start with the number 10 and add two numbers to it (from the top cards of the two piles).

If you take the last four letters of the word "twelve" ("elve") and last two letters of the word "one" ("ne"), you can spell "eleven" when you flip around the letters. And $13 - 1 = 10 + 2$ also reflects an anagram: In "twelve + one = eleven + two" all of the letters are the same! That's how I came up with the anagram of $13 - 1 = 10 + 2$ so I could recall that trick.

THE NAME GAME

In chapter 4, you learned secrets to remembering faces and names. I've always had a knack for recalling every name I've ever heard. I also have a propensity for remembering characters' names and the actors who play them on television. Take, for example, *The Brady Bunch.* I can tell you in seconds all of the characters' names and their real-life counterparts— Mike Brady (Robert Reed), Carol Brady (Florence Henderson), Greg Brady (Barry Williams), Marcia Brady (Maureen McCormick), and so on. This may just be an innate gift of mine, but I know that fast recall of names is a skill that can be developed, though it requires constant practice. I practice every single time I'm confronted with a new face, name, or character. So if you're not generally good at recalling names or other facts you want to keep stored in your brain for quick recovery, you simply need to practice more!

And here's the interesting part: This skill also entails a great deal of mental organization. While you may not have considered organizing your thoughts in chapter 4 as you learned how to memorize names and faces, you had to do some mental sorting just to keep incoming names in check. Now, however, we're going to take this to the next level by adding a deeper layer of mental organization. The Name Game is an excellent way not only to practice getting good with names but also to organize your mind. What you're doing is retrieving information and organizing it as quickly as you can. Let me describe the game first, and then I'll share a bit more about what this exercise is actually doing for you.

HOW TO PLAY

You can play this game with two or more people. First, take a piece of paper and write all twenty-six letters of the alphabet down the middle in one long column, like this:

A
B
C
D
E
F
G
H
I
J
K
L
M
N
O
P
Q
R
S
T
U
V
W
X
Y
Z

Now take a random set of twenty-six letters and match them up to this list. For the purpose of this example, I'm going to use the sentence "Actions speak louder than word" (not "words"), since it comprises twenty-six letters. However, you could just refer to an article or book and take the first twenty-six letters of any sentence. It's not important to use a string of real words or a full sentence. You just need to grab twenty-six letters from somewhere, and they can inlcude repeat letters. Alternatively, you can make up letters as you go down the column and write down one letter to go with each of the original set of letters.

In our list here, if we line up the letters from "Actions speak louder than word" next to our original alphabet, we've got the following:

AA
BC
CT
DI
EO
FN
GS
HS
IP
JE
KA
LK
ML
NO
OU
PD
QE
RR
ST
TH

UA
VN
WW
XO
YR
ZD

Each pair of letters now acts as initials. The goal is to come up with as many names as you can using this list of initials in a given time frame, say five minutes. The initials can relate to a fictional person, a famous person, or someone you know, so long as your fellow players are also familiar with that individual. (Otherwise, you could just make up names as you go along!) Here's how the scoring works:

- Each person gets one point for naming someone whom all the players know.
- Each person gets two points for naming someone in sports or entertainment.
- Each person gets three points for naming someone in history.

Why do historical people reap more points? Because they are often harder to recall. People you see and hear about on a daily basis are much easier to bring to mind; the names of individuals buried deeper in our memories require more mental energy, so they of course should be rewarded with more points. There are a few more rules to consider:

- The initials can be switched around, so, for instance, the second pair—BC—can also be viewed as CB. Try to come up with as many names as you can using the pairs of initials as they are read both forward and backward. In this example, we have Bill Cosby and Charlie Brown.

- You cannot use a modified version of someone's name. If a person is known as Bill and not William, then you have to stick with Bill. For example, William Clinton or William Cosby wouldn't be allowed. Norma Baker would not be allowed either, but Marilyn Monroe would.

- You can, however, use names that are iconic to a particular person but aren't that person's full name. Examples include Princess Di, Queen Elizabeth, and J. R. Ewing.

What makes this game so valuable for working on your name recall and organizing is that you're having to mentally handle multiple streams of information and manage them all as you go through a certain letter and find a pattern. Thinking about first names that begin with the letter *A*, for example, and then matching those to famous last names requires that you juggle the competing ideas and faces that come crashing into your brain. You'll find that you have to sort letters and names into categories quickly by common first names, common last names, famous faces, historical people, and so on. Then, as you hunt for the names that will give you the maximum number of points, you'll be adding yet another dimension of mental multitasking that demands organization. You'll be firing up your mental assembly line while at the same time flexing your mind's muscles to heave old data files from the back of your mind to the forefront.

You'd be amazed at what's already stored in your head. So much of our ability to recall information can be measured by our ability to recall names and faces. Thus, if you can strengthen and optimize your capacity to recall anyone's name in a split second, you're simultaneously fortifying and expanding your capacity to recollect *anything*. You're speeding up those parts of the mind that allow you to pluck out any piece of stored information in a flash, from snippets of small data like a name to the larger chunks of data that are encoded by details.

MY LIST

Admittedly, I had a tough time coming up with names for the initials OU, UO, XO, OX, YR, and RY. Nevertheless, I spent only about twenty minutes knocking all these names out, I avoided easy names from my personal life, and I didn't use the Internet or look anything up. What can you drum up? Go online and share your lists at www.MikeByster.com.

- AA: Alan Alda, Abigail Adams
- BC: Bill Cosby, Bill Clinton, Billy Crystal, Charlie Brown, Charles Bronson
- CT: Charlize Theron, Cheryl Tiegs, Tom Cruise, Top Cat
- DI: Don Imus
- EO: Ed O'Neill
- FN: Florence Nightingale, Nick Faldo
- GS: Ginger Spice, Steffi Graf
- HS: Saddam Hussein, Han Solo, Hilary Swank
- IP: Iggy Pop

- JE: John Edwards, Elton John, J. R. Ewing
- KA: Andy Kaufman, Anna Kournikova, King Arthur, Ashton Kutcher
- LK: Lisa Kudrow, k. d. lang
- ML: Mary Todd Lincoln, Martin Lawrence, Liza Minnelli
- NO: Ogden Nash, Oliver North
- OU:
- PD: Patrick Dempsey, Patty Duke, Princess Di, David Prowse
- QE: Queen Elizabeth
- RR: Robert Redford, Ray Romano, Ronald Reagan
- ST: Tupac Shakur, Tony Soprano, Shania Twain, Steven Tyler
- TH: Tommy Hilfiger, Hunter S. Thompson, Harriet Tubman, Teri Hatcher
- UA: Al Unser, Ursula Andress
- VN: Nia Vardalos*
- WW: Walt Whitman, Woodrow Wilson, Wendy Williams
- XO:
- YR:
- ZD: Zooey Deschanel*

*These are names that popped into my head even though I can't really tell you who they are or what they do. I must have seen these names somewhere in the media and my brain captured them subconsciously. Again, proof that we can retain way more information than we realize!

In the appendixes, I'll offer a few more games that will exercise your organizing skills. You'll have more opportunities to master cataloging and systematizing massive amounts of information. For now, it's time to learn one of the least appreciated skills in the business of developing a fast mind: forgetting. Knowing how and when to "forget" will ultimately help you truly master the orchestra that is constantly playing in your mind. It will further assist you in mobilizing and coordinating incoming information without losing sight of the important facts.

Chapter Guide

It helps to read this chapter once every few months, or at least twice a year, to remind yourself of all the strategies you can use to organize your thoughts and incoming data more effectively. Let's face it: When left to its own devices, the mind can quickly revert to disorganized chaos, handling information messily and sloppily. We all would do well to work on our mental organization on a routine basis. Aim to do the exercises and play the games described in this chapter as often as you can, especially the ones you find the most enjoyable.

And remember: Although the lessons outlined in this chapter may not seem directly related to tackling tough challenges in the real world and organizing "real information" in a business setting, in a social environment, or at school, they in fact work your brain the same way that you must think when trying to manage any kind of data. From the moment we wake up in the morning to the second our head hits the pillow at night, our brain is dealing with an enormous array of information—some of it trivial but a lot of it essential.

From checking e-mail and using social media to sitting in a classroom or meeting to listening to the radio or reading material during a commute to handling the rigors of a corporate environment that inundates us with constant data to remember, there's no end to the level of mental organization we force our brains to do daily.

Those who can make a habit of organizing information easily, simply, and quickly are in a much better position to achieve success sooner rather than later and to set themselves apart from others, which ultimately helps them to advance their careers. Even if you master just one strategy from this chapter and use it in your daily life, I trust you will notice a difference. And it won't just be in your ability to remember things and impress your peers; you'll find that everyday tasks get easier and the routine chores that used to annoy or frustrate you don't bother you anymore because you find ways to accomplish them in a more organized fashion. Indeed, as I noted at the beginning of this chapter, once mental organization becomes second nature, all other forms of organization come automatically, too.

CHAPTER 7

Skill 6: Forgetting

Memory's Linchpin

*Learning is not attained by chance. It must be sought for
with ardor and attended to with diligence.*

—ABIGAIL ADAMS

It seems counterintuitive: Why would you want to learn how
to forget in order to remember? But it's essential, as you no
doubt know by now. As I've been hinting at all along in this
book, forgetting is memory's linchpin—it's perhaps the ultimate secret weapon to powering up the mind and maximizing its capacity to hold information. And yet, like the other
skills you've already learned, this one is seldom taught in
formal education. In fact, when I teach this skill during my
live shows, students and adults alike express surprise that I
place so much importance on the word "forget" because it
sounds so paradoxical and they don't typically hear it used in
terms of learning . . . and learning *better*.

LEARNING TO FORGET

In chapter 6, I taught you how to organize your thoughts, but this skill cannot truly be mastered until you learn how to forget. Forgetting is a two-part process. First you have to know how to distinguish between what's "high quality" or important and what's "low quality" or insignificant, and then you have to be able to evict the petty, peripheral (and usually distracting) material from your mind—forever.

This is not a trivial point. Forgetting is hard to do intentionally! Of course, lots of things happen in life that we would prefer to forget, such as accidents or dreadful experiences, a bad grade or evaluation from our superiors, an argument with another person, a painful bout with an illness, or a period of enormous struggle and strife for whatever reason. But I'm not referring here to forgetting particular events or occurrences. I'm talking instead about the streams of information that constantly bombard our minds and that we try to take in as fast as they arrive. Whether we're sitting in a classroom or watching an informative TV show, we have a tendency to want to remember everything, including the pointless, which makes for very cluttered minds unable to think clearly or quickly.

When I picture how people must have learned to "forget" centuries ago, I imagine that it was a little easier to do then than it is today. It may have even come much more naturally, because people didn't have so many means with which to try to record all the minutiae coming into the brain. They simply held on to thoughts that were necessary for survival and unconsciously let the rest escape from their minds. There were no computers or handheld devices, and writing implements were inaccessible to most people.

And there certainly weren't any Post-it notes or reminder apps. Today, however, we live surrounded by these unlimited resources and with the constant urge to log everything and saddle ourselves with the impossible chore of sustaining it all in our minds.

Can you recall how many neurons I said a typical adult brain contains? If you say any number between fifteen billion and two hundred billion, you are right. That's a huge range. Assuming we use the lower figure, the brain is capable of remembering the amount of information in ten billion encyclopedia pages. And even that's a lot of data. The amazing capacity of the human mind revolves around its ability to be bombarded with millions of bits of diverse information every single day. It must also be able to store these and convert them into intelligent thoughts. It achieves this by evaluating, sorting, figuring, and redirecting information based on sequences and relationships. It discards the irrelevant bits of information and fills in the blanks with bits of information from its files.

What happens, though, when the brain has a hard time throwing out the rubbish? When the brain literally cannot forget anything? Like a clogged drain, it gets backed up. Information—both valuable and worthless—blends together in a cloudy mess. Brain fog sets in. And brainpower wanes. Which is why "evaluation" is so critical. By placing value on certain bits of information and forgetting the rest, we let the important information advance to the forefront and form a bigger part of our mental picture. We have the ability to do this temporarily (in short-term memory) or permanently (in long-term memory). Forgetting, in essence, is the art of neglecting or dismissing certain details from the incoming data in order to keep the brain clean, organized, and humming like a well-oiled machine. This, in turn, is what allows us to continue seeking out more information, assimilating it in our minds, and using it to our benefit.

On a grander scale, there's another hidden benefit to being able to forget that rarely gets attention. Forgetting what we know—at the appropriate time—can be an enormously powerful tool for gaining insight. Think about it: Without the ability to forget, our minds remain "stuck" with ready-made answers. We're not motivated to ask the questions that can lead our thinking to new ideas. To better grasp this concept, which I admit sounds abstract, consider the following: Legend has it that one day, on his regular walk past the local blacksmith's workshop on the island of Samos, the ancient Greek philosopher Pythagoras temporarily forgot that the banging sounds produced by the smith's hammering of iron bars were "noise"—his usual reaction. Instead he viewed them as "information" and soon discovered that musical pitch is a function of the length of the material being struck, which became his first principle of mathematical physics.

If we don't allow ourselves to forget once in a while, not only will we lose out on remembering the important information, but we'll also lose out on opportunities to gain new perspectives. We'll also cause so much congestion in our brains that we won't be able to accomplish tasks quickly and methodically. And it's no mystery that the potential for mental logjams looms large today given the colossal amount of data we are exposed to daily. "Data overload" is practically a cliché; though some people are more interested in the toll that data overload takes on our stress levels and psychology, I like to remind folks that above all it's undermining our mental acuity. It's robbing us of our potential and our paths to success.

Mentally and intentionally letting go of information requires practice, sometimes via exercises that at first seem entirely unrelated to the job of forgetting. The goal of this chapter is to help you become proficient in this critical skill and use it to accomplish a broad spectrum of challenges. Because this is one of the more advanced skills we'll be learning, you'll need to call upon your mastery of all the skills I've already covered in the previous chapters. The previous skills build to this master skill and make forgetting possible. So put your thinking, focusing, organizing, problem-solving, and concentrating caps on!

We're going to start with three of my favorite activities; then we'll have a recap of the importance of pattern recognition within the context of forgetting and end with a discussion about the lost art of note-taking in the realm of forgetting. You should master all of the lessons in this chapter—indeed, you should go over them as often as possible. They are the weight-lifting exercises for flexing your brain in (pardon the pun) mind-bending ways. Every time you perform these mental workouts, your mind will get stronger.

Remember: Everyone has the ability to forget. The art is *knowing when to use it* and using it wisely. As novelist Henry Miller once stated: "My 'forgettery' has been just as important to my success as my memory."

MULTIPLYING TWO-DIGIT NUMBERS IN YOUR HEAD

This may appear to be all about math, but in fact it's one of the most powerful ways to give your brain a calisthenics workout and employ the tricky art of forgetting. That's right: Learning how to rapidly multiply two-digit numbers in your head using my nifty shortcut will force you to forget certain information along the path to a solution. This exercise also reveals an aspect to forgetting that I haven't touched on yet: Sometimes we need to work with a piece of information momentarily and then expel it from our minds to make room for a new piece of information in that mental "space." Multiplying two-digit numbers easily without a calculator marvelously illustrates this skill, as you'll soon find out when you go through the steps. This skill can be applied to a wide variety of subjects, not just math, because every day we need to delete old, obsolete files in our brain so it can store new ones.

Coming up with this shortcut represented a pivotal time in my life. I was in the sixth grade at a junior high school where Arnie Benson, the eighth-grade math teacher, had a reputation for an unusually fast mind and an extraordinary ability to work with numbers. The first person I met who was really good with numbers (outside of my dad and his brothers), Arnie was someone I looked up to and would target as the person to surpass. When word got around that I might be able to beat him in a game of multiplying single-digit numbers with two-digit numbers, a competition was called. And I beat him. When the competition was over, Arnie said to me, "Mike, next time we're doing it all with *two-digit* numbers." He didn't realize that I had no mental shortcut for performing two-digit-by-two-digit multiplication. I could multiply single-digit numbers by two-digit numbers in my head all day long, but double digits by double digits? I had no idea how I'd pull that one off, so I sat down and vowed to figure out a simple shortcut that would work well enough for me to beat him again.

Luckily, we never met in competition again. But I did work out a formula for performing this kind of math in my head that set the stage for me to come up with other formulas and shortcuts. Once I realized that there was more than one way to solve problems, I knew that this principle could be applied to just about any problem in life. I no longer had to rely solely on the rules and steps that were given or taught to me. I could navigate through numbers, words, and other patterns however I wanted, paving a different path and arriving at an equally accurate answer.

Arnie is enjoying his life today in Dallas, Texas, and is as sharp as ever. We still keep in touch, for his influence on me and my time in his classroom were the defining moment in my life when the door opened wide for me to begin creating all sorts of shortcuts to stay ahead of everyone else. Arnie kept me on my toes; I never wanted to run into someone again who'd challenge me to a game that I couldn't win! To this day, the mere thought of being tested or outsmarted inspires me to keep thinking up new pathways to solutions and ever more shortcuts to successful outcomes.

Even if you hate numbers and math, I challenge you to attempt this exercise. I promise you that once you get the hang of it, you'll want to do it over and over again and show off this secret maneuver to your friends.

First let me take you through the steps of performing this calculation, and then I'll give you a few equations to try yourself. If you need to use a pen and paper the first time or two, go ahead. But at some point I want you to rely solely on your mental skills so your mind gets used to jumping through these hoops—picking up and dropping off information. This shortcut works like a charm every single time you want to multiply a two-digit number by a two-digit number; it's one of my own original inventions. At first it may seem long and tedious, especially when you try doing it all in your head, but once you have the steps down and have practiced them, it will become automatic.

> Reminder: In the following exercise I will use language like "tens digit number" and "ones digit number" as I explain the steps. This helps me to identify which numbers to use. You should already be very familiar with this language from previous chapters, but here's a cheat sheet again just in case:
>
> In the number 23, the 3 is called the ones digit number; the 2 is referred to as the tens digit number.

Here's the first equation:

$$\begin{array}{r} 32 \\ \times\ 51 \\ \hline \end{array}$$

Step 1: Multiply the tens digits together: $3 \times 5 = $ **15**. *Hold that number in your head.*

Step 2: The second and third steps are the hardest. First, cross-multiply the numbers: $5 \times 2 = 10$ and $3 \times 1 = 3$, then add $10 + 3$: **13**.

You'll need to keep this number, 13, in your head. You will use this number to make an adjustment to the first number, 15, which should still be in your head. If it helps, you can think of the number 13 here as just a 1 and a 3.

Step 3: Now add the tens digit number of the new number, 13, which is 1, to the first number in your head (15 + 1 = 16), then tack on the 3 to get 163. This is the new number you'll need to remember. Drop all previous numbers from your head and keep only **163**.

Step 4: Finally, multiply the ones digits in the original equation (1 × 2 = 2) and tack the product onto the end of 163. And now you have your answer: **1,632**.

Confused? Bewildered? Lost? Let's do this exercise again with a new set of numbers. Once more, if you need to use a pen and paper to drill down each step and create a mental image of the process, feel free to do so. Okay, let's try the following:

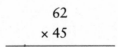

$$\begin{array}{r} 62 \\ \times\, 45 \\ \hline \end{array}$$

Step 1: Multiply the tens digits (6 × 4 = 24). Keep the number **24** in your head.

Step 2: Cross-multiply (6 × 5 = 30; 2 × 4 = 8) and add (30 + 8) to get **38**.

Step 3: Recall that you had the number 24 in your head from the first step. Now you're going to use this new number, 38, to modify the first number. Take the 3 and add it to 24, which gives you 27. Then tack on the number 8, and you arrive at **278**. *Keep this new number in your head and ditch the previous one.* Say it a few times: two-seven-eight, two-seven-eight. Then it's in your head and it will stay there.

Step 4: Go back to the original equation (62 × 45) and multiply the ones digits (2 × 5 = 10). Uh-oh, the last time we did this exercise we didn't get a two-digit answer. So what do we do here? We cannot just tack on a 10 to the end of 278. What we have to do is one more little step, similar to what we did before. We add the tens digit of our number, 10, which in this case is the number 1, to 278, and we get 279. *Then* we can tack on the ones digit number, 0. Now you have your answer: **2,790**.

Did you follow that? Are you still feeling queasy? Don't panic if you're not totally in sync with me yet. That's normal, as this trick can take time to get down, much less commit to heart. If you don't feel fully confident enough in the methodology to proceed, go back to the beginning of this section and review every step for both examples using all of your focus and concentration. Make sure you don't have any distractions keeping you from absorbing this systematic process. When you're ready, it's time to try this calculation on your own and *in your head*.

Below are two more sets of equations. See if you can do this without pen and paper (or a calculator!). Work at your own pace as you master this shortcut. Don't worry if you struggle the first few times you do this exercise. You'll find the solutions to these equations at the end of the chapter. For a video demonstration of multiplying two-digit numbers, go to www.MikeByster.com.

Tip: As you work through these problems, really focus on the forgetting part. Be mindful of the numbers you have to keep in your brain at every step, and when you reach a crucial intersection where you need to mentally drop a number and pick up a new one, see if you can be acutely aware and hyperconscious of that exchange. The "drop off and pick up" juncture is a place of vulnerability. If you're not paying attention, you can lose track, make an unintentional fatal mistake, and end up with the wrong answer. It's like you're working on an assembly line that processes different numbers. As one number comes your way, you speedily tend to it and then you have to let it go as it moves on past so you can handle the next number coming down the line. If you take too long tending to a certain number, the whole assembly line can get backed up—or break down and stop entirely. Keep it going by staying focused on the task at hand. Maintain a steady cycle of "find and forget" in your head until you have your answer.

Self-Test 1

$$\begin{array}{r} 31 \\ \times\ 53 \\ \hline \end{array}$$

Self-Test 2

$$74$$
$$\times\ 52$$
_____

Now let's turn to the next exercise, which will help you improve another aspect of the forgetting skill: evaluating information and immediately dumping the superfluous or no longer relevant. Again, this lesson employs numbers, but training your brain using an activity like this will help you "forget" automatically when it comes to other subjects, including everyday tasks like instantly picking out the highlights from a lengthy article or fishing out the bottom-line message in people's presentations or in crucial conversations you're having. This particular exercise puts your listening skills to the test, so pay attention!

THE SECRET NUMBER

This game requires at least two people and works best in groups of three or more. Here's how it works: One person picks a number between 100 and 1,000. The other players have to guess what that number is while the person with the secret number says "higher" or "lower," depending on their guesses. The person who states the correct number after the fewest guesses wins.

How does this game help sharpen your forgetting skills? Well, during every round of calling out numbers and narrowing down the range, a new range of numbers is considered while all other numbers outside that range are thrown out. So, for example, if your secret number is 437 and someone guesses 500, you'll say "lower"; if the next guess is 300, you'll say "higher." Now the range of numbers is between 300 and 500. Future guesses will constantly shift this range. This forces players to continuously keep only a certain defined series of numbers in their heads at any given time and to forget about the rest. If you try to keep all the numbers in your head, you'll quickly lose focus and won't be able to stay on track. Ditching and forgetting the disqualified numbers is key to staying in this fast-paced game and to winning. The game's added bonus is that it also enhances everyone's listening skills. Often the person who wins this game isn't the person with the fastest mind—it's the one who can totally focus on the "active" numbers, concentrate on the direction the person with the secret number gives ("higher" or "lower"), and stay on top of the moving flow of changing numbers. All of these skills require forgetting, but they also demand an intense level of listening.

You can also build in other rules to make this more difficult. You could, for instance, eliminate or penalize people who go the wrong way when they are told "higher" or "lower." If you're playing with just yourself and one other person, the goal is to become faster and faster at arriving at the secret number with the fewest guesses (and outpace the other person when it's their turn to try guessing the secret number).

Once you start playing this game repeatedly with new numbers, you'll start to feel your brain working harder and harder and picking up speed. It's an excellent game to use in the car or when you just want to kill time with someone. The swift movement of constantly changing information in your brain—some of which you need to remember, some of which you need to forget—is a hard-core training session for your brain. Similar to the burn you feel when you work a set of muscles intensely, you'll probably feel a "burn" here in the form of fast breathing, racing thoughts about numbers, and a higher level of energy!

AABEGHIILNPTZ DORSW

Did you get that? Let's switch gears here and consider another exercise that's good for developing the art of forgetting but that involves words and letters rather than numbers. The letters in the heading above are the letters of the phrase "alphabetizing words" put in alphabetical order. As you know from chapter 2, this is one of my favorite pastimes, and I do it all day long—as I drive, read mail, and even listen to people talk. (I confess, I also like to count how many letters are in the sentences people say, but that's another game I'll save for later.)

What I didn't touch upon in that earlier chapter, however, is the fact that this exercise is very effective for building your forgetting muscles. How so? Like the previous tasks that compel you to work with constantly changing information and focus squarely on the critical data at hand in order to arrive at a correct solution, this one calls for a clever allocation of mental space throughout the procedure. As your mind works through the process of alphabetizing a word (without pen and paper!), it has to "forget" which letters have already been taken care of and which ones are left to put in order. Take, for example, the word "alphabetize." This one starts off easy because we have the first letter of the alphabet already in place. But there are two *a*'s in this word, so we have to drag that second *a* to the beginning and put it next to the first *a*. Once that is done, your mind has to "forget" about the *a*'s and move on to seek letters further down the alphabet. In addition to the *a*'s in the word, we have a *b*, then *ee*, *i*, *h*, *l*, *p*, *t*, and finally *z*. Note that having the *z*, the last letter in the alphabet, close to the end of this word also makes it slightly easier to alphabetize. In fact, from a visual standpoint, when we look at the word "alphabetize" as a whole, our eyes coordinate with our brains so we can instantly see that there's an easy *a* at the start already and a *z* close to the end, which follows the pattern of the alphabet. But did you find it more difficult to think through the exact placement of the middle letters, especially the *h*, *i*, *l*, and *p*? Perhaps you didn't even notice that I made a mistake above when I listed *i* before *h* in alphabetizing the word "alphabetize."

It turns out that certain sections of the alphabet are much harder than others to break down in our heads and recall their letters' exact order in relation to one another. We are really put to the test knowing on the spot whether *i* comes before or after *h* or even if *g* precedes *h*. It's quite amusing to think we can struggle with knowing the precise order of our alphabet's twenty-six letters—an alphabet that allows us to create intricate words and sentences, including lyrical poems and compelling stories. Yet it's a harmless weakness of the complex human mind.

There are three characteristics that make some words easier to alphabetize than others:

1. For most people, it seems to be easier to alphabetize two shorter words than it is to alphabetize one longer word, even if they consist of the same number

of letters. The compound word "waterfall" is harder to alphabetize than the words "water" and "fall." Obviously, you're having to take in more letters at once and arrange them in your head alphabetically when you work with "waterfall."

2. Words that have two or three of the same letters are much easier to alphabetize than words in which each letter appears only once. So the word "anthill" is easier than "knight."

3. Words that do not have three or more consecutive letters in the alphabet in the word are also easier to solve. The only exception to this rule is when the three or more consecutive letters are at the beginning of the alphabet (*abc, bcd, abcd*). So the word "English" is troubling for most people because it contains the three consecutive letters *g*, *h*, and *i*. Its correct alphabetical spelling is "Eghilns." But a word like "bracket" contains an *a*, a *b*, and a *c*, and no one mixes those letters up. It takes less effort to alphabetize: "abcekrt."

Is there a trick or shortcut to alphabetizing words in your head automatically? Actually, there isn't. You have to figure out what works for you. I give you full permission to use your hands if you have to. One way that works for many people is to count on their fingers: The letter *A* is the left pinkie finger, and the rest of the alphabet follows, moving left to right, over and across the right hand. Each finger can stand for a letter, or you can designate one finger for a certain section of letters. Your left pinkie finger, for example, could be *A* through *E*, and so on.

Another strategy is to first assess how many letters are in

the word you're trying to alphabetize. Let's say the word is "Washington." That's a total of ten letters, which can be represented by your ten fingers. As you work your way through the alphabet and knock off the letters you've placed in order, you can follow along with your fingers so you know where you are and whether or not you might have missed a letter or two.

Yet another technique that seems to work really well these days among the texting-savvy younger generation is to consider the letters on a keypad or telephone that reflect certain numbers. The letters *ABC*, for instance, represent the number 2 on a phone keypad. The lower numbers are closer to the beginning of the alphabet, whereas the higher numbers are closer to the end. For the older folks who haven't gotten used to the art of manipulating keypad letters on a telephone, I don't suggest trying this method. It takes some "built-in" experience and is best left to those who are already extremely deft with those keypads.

I'll give you one more tactic to consider: Don't think about the actual word you're trying to alphabetize in your head. If the word is "automobile," you don't have to think that you're spelling "automobile" every time your mind goes back to the whole word to figure out what letters are still left. Just look at the word as a collection of letters in a certain order. You have to unscramble them so they are in order from *a* to *u*.

Ready to try this yourself? Following is a list of 10 eight-letter words that go from easiest to most difficult in terms of alphabetizing. See how fast you can put the letters in each of these words into correct order. Perform this exercise as often as you can when you're out in the real world. When you come across a road sign or a menu at a restaurant, try to whip those letters into alphabetical shape before they leave your field of vision. Next time you're waiting in line at the supermarket, take words on a magazine rack and alphabetize them before it's your turn to pay.

Self-Test 3

1. NOTEBOOK
2. BASEBALL
3. BUSINESS
4. HOMEWORK
5. BACKYARD
6. PRACTICE
7. STRANGER
8. STRAIGHT
9. CHILDREN
10. QUESTION

Here are some additional challenges that up the ante:

1. Alphabetize the numbers 1 through 8 spelled out:

O N E T W O T H R E E F O U R F I V E S I X S E V E N
E I G H T

2. Alphabetize the first six months of the year spelled out:

J A N U A R Y F E B R U A R Y M A R C H A P R I L
M A Y J U N E

3. Alphabetize the Great Lakes:

S U P E R I O R M I C H I G A N H U R O N E R I E
O N T A R I O

4. Take an entire headline or sentence and try to alphabetize it! Or you can go in reverse—alphabetize a word from Z to A.

If you haven't figured it out by now, these exercises require that you try hard to organize your mind efficiently. You're constantly going back and forth, working with the information that's left and still needs to be organized. That is why these mental gymnastics are such excellent workouts for becoming an expert note taker and studier. How can multiplying two-digit numbers and alphabetizing words have anything to do with the tasks of note-taking and studying? They have everything to do with each other.

PATTERNS, HABITS, AND FORGETTING

I cannot reiterate the importance of making a habit of noticing patterns in the world and of forgetting where doing so is essential to retain the critical information and make room for even more data. The brain is an incredible machine with an enormous capacity, but if it's not groomed for superior processing, it cannot function at its highest level. Pattern recognition has been a theme throughout the book, but let's take a moment here to examine more patterns and see how they tie into the art of not only creating associations but also forgetting. As it turns out, pattern recognition lies at the heart of all the skills in this book and provides the ultimate foundation for making a habit out of forgetting.

To start, let's try a few patterns to get your brain churning:

2, 4, 6, 8, 10, __, __, __. (Can you figure out the next three numbers?)

That was an easy one: The pattern is a series of even numbers. How about the following?

77, 49, 36, 18, __. (Can you figure out the next number?)

Here's how that one works: 7 times 7, the two digits in the first number, equals 49, which is the second number in the series. Now do it again: 4 times 9 equals 36, which is the third number in the series. Repeat: 3 times 6 equals 18, which is the fourth number in the series. Repeat: 1 times 8 equals 8, the missing number at the end of the series. Cool, huh?

Sometimes we can find patterns in other, subtler ways. Now I'm going to show you a series of solutions to math equations. See if you can figure out a pattern in the way they are solved. You might not "see" it right away, so take your time with this one. The exercise in itself is a mighty good one for waking up your brain.

105	102	109
× 107	× 104	× 106
= 11,235	= 10,608	= 11,554

Hint: This pattern works only for multiplying two numbers between 100 and 109. All answers must be five-digit numbers.

Answer: The first digit in the answer is always a 1. The next two digits in the answer, or the "middle" number, are found by adding the ones digits in each problem. Hence, in

105 times 107, you add 5 plus 7 to get 12; in 102 times 104, you add 2 plus 4 to get 6. But wait: The "middle" number must have two digits, so you have to place a 0 in front of the 6. In 109 times 106, you add 9 plus 6 to get 15. Finally, to arrive at the final two digits in each answer, you multiply the ones digit in each equation. So in 105 times 107, you multiply 5 times 7, which equals 35; in 102 times 104, you multiply 2 times 4 to get 8. Again, this number cannot be a single digit, so place a 0 in front of the 8. And in 109 times 106, you multiply 9 times 6 to get 54.

You can try a few more on your own below. This exercise is less about knowing how to perform the shortcut for multiplying numbers between 100 and 109 than it is about forcing your brain to work through patterns that have you mentally jumping through hoops. (Remember, solutions are found at the end of the chapter.)

102	105	109
× 103	× 101	× 108
=	=	=

Okay, let's take it up a notch. Below is a pattern in squaring a number in the fifties. Can you find it?

$56^2 = 3,136$
$53^2 = 2,809$
$58^2 = 3,364$
$54^2 = ????$

Hint: Take away the 5 and look for a pattern.
Answer: 2,916.

Solution: In every case, the ones digit squared (6^2, 3^2, 8^2) gives you the last two digits of the answer (36, 09, and 64, respectively). This is why I told you to take away the 5, so that you might see this. Now what you do is square the number 5 (5^2), which gives you 25. Then add the ones digit to 25. So, in 56^2, we have 25 plus 6 to get 31; in 53^2, we have 25 plus 3 to get 28; in 58^2, we have 25 plus 8 to get 33. Let's do 54^2 together:

- Square the ones digit, so 4 times 4 equals 16. This gives us the final two digits in our answer.
- Take 5 times 5, which is 25, and add the ones digit to it, so 25 plus 4 equals 29. This gives us the first two digits in the answer.
- Answer: 2,916.

Did you follow that? If not, go back and think through it. Get to a point where you can do this exercise in your mind quickly. Here are others to try:

$57^2 = $ _____
$55^2 = $ _____
$59^2 = $ _____
$51^2 = $ _____
$52^2 = $ _____

Patterns don't necessarily have to reflect a complex array of different numbers or things. They can be as "simple" as a complex array of the same numbers or things. Binary code is a prime example of this. The word "binary" refers to something with just two parts. We often hear that binary code is a way of representing text or computer-processor instructions by using the binary number system's two binary digits, 0 and 1. This is accomplished by assigning a so-called bit string to each symbol or instruction. For example, a binary string of 8 binary digits (bits) can represent any of 256 possible values and can therefore correspond to a variety of different symbols, letters, or instructions. Even if you don't understand what that really means, suffice it to say we owe much of our ability to build computers and their complex programming to simple digital patterns that use 0's and 1's to create codes.

THE WILD WORD COUNTDOWN

Another game I like to play that's based on alphabet codes is called the Wild Word Countdown. This one is fantastic for getting better with numbers and mathematics. It's pretty simple: Each letter in the alphabet corresponds to a number, starting with the letter A, which equals 1. The rest of the alphabet follows in sequence: $B = 2$, $C = 3$, $D = 4$, and so on, until you get to the last letter, Z, which equals 26.

To play the game, there should be one leader and any number of players or teams. Have the leader give a random number from 60 to 100, which becomes the target value. In three minutes, each player or team must think of three words that come closest to the target value. For example, let's say the target value is 83. One word you might try is "tennis." Let's see what that would add up to:

T E N N I S

20 5 14 14 9 19
20 + 5 + 14 + 14 + 9 + 19 = 81

Since 81 is only 2 away from 83, this word gets 2 points.

The goal is to amass the fewest points by finding words as close as possible to the target value. You can try playing the Wild Word Countdown with any target value. If you don't have an opponent, you can even practice by yourself to get a terrific mental workout anytime, anyplace!

The Wild Word Countdown makes you think outside the box, requires quick calculations, and helps you practice mental math. A secret to playing the game is to memorize the values of common endings of words or suffixes. For instance, here are some common endings of words and their values using the A = 1 . . . Z = 26 code:

S = 19
ING = 30
ER = 23
ERS = 42
ED = 9

Using a verb as your word makes it much easier to get close to the target value. Say your target value is 68. The word "walk" is worth 47 points, and by adding suffixes the word becomes "walks" (66), "walking" (77), "walker" (70), "walkers" (89), or "walked" (56). So "walks" and "walkers" turn out to be pretty good words.

For a more advanced level of play, pick a certain number of letters the word can have in addition to the target value.

Games like the Wild Word Countdown may not feel like they are adding anything to your pattern-recognition ability or "forgetfulness," but they are.

Once your mind has a grasp of the game's rules and you've become familiar with the patterns that emerge between the letters and their "values," your brain is fully tuned in to its own pattern-recognition software, if you will. It's also in a groove whereby you force yourself to forget along the way as you continue to search for new words while forgetting the previous ones. With your mind flexing its pattern-recognition and forgetting muscles, chances are that the next time you're faced with a hidden pattern you'll identify it much sooner and not be distracted by competing information. So while it may seem impractical to play games that are about numbers and arbitrary words rather than real-world problems, the fact is that they can help you speed up those areas of your mind that you enlist when you're trying to "read" your colleagues and bosses, or when you're trying to concentrate really hard, or when you're planning the future and hoping to make a re-alistic prediction of what's to come based on patterns you're seeing now. In other words, these kinds of exercises will help you solve real-world problems in the long run.

ATRPTNSE, AKA PATTERNS

Here's another game that will show you what happens when your brain is fired up by patterns and will help you sharpen the right areas of your brain to accelerate pattern recognition in general. I'm going to give you five letters, and I want you to come up with as many real words as possible using all five letters. The words I will give you will be scrambled, much as the letters *a-t-r-p-t-n-s-e* spell "patterns" when they are switched around. This is an excellent way of forcing your brain to look at things differently and seek patterns via different mental paths. Okay, here we go. Let's try the following (remember to use all of the letters):

EISML

How long did it take you to arrive at all four words? Don't worry if you didn't time yourself the first time around. We're going to do this again (and you can find answers at the end of the chapter). Notice that it might have taken you only a few seconds to get the first three words but then several minutes to get the last word. Let's try another one. Below is a new scramble of letters. Shift them around to find six real words. Yes, six different words.

AELST

Still stuck on a few of the words? If you find yourself stumped on the fourth or fifth word, then try really hard to switch the words around. Here's a hint: Write down the scrambled word differently and see how that changes the way your eyes look at it and how your brain interprets it. So, for instance, rather than staring at AELST, try playing with LATSE or SETLA instead. Watch how a visual shift in letters can instantly allow another word to pop up right in front of you. Bam! Why does this happen?

When you sit and stare at a set of letters, your brain starts to go in circles. It becomes all the more challenging to switch the letters around in your head to arrive at a new word, especially once you've found the relatively obvious ones. What you need to do in this case is visually mix up the letters again so your mind is forced to see another pattern somewhere. Put another way, you need to see letters in altered states in order to see more patterns. Like a broken record, the mind can get stuck seeing just one pattern.

Let's try one more. This time I'm going to give you a six-letter jumble. Find the five words that can be found in it. Remember, when you get stuck, try mixing up the letters again to see another pattern, which will probably bring you another word or two.

SIETLN

For more fun games like this, I encourage you to play Word Whomp by going to www.pogo.com, signing up for a free account, and clicking on the Word Whomp link. Or go to www.MikeByster.com and use the direct links there.

THE LOST ARTS OF NOTE-TAKING AND STUDYING

All too often I watch kids and adults alike struggle to take useful notes. Sadly, I don't think we are ever formally taught how to take notes or study. It's largely assumed that we will learn on our own as we progress through school, but too often that doesn't work out as well as we'd like. As you already know by now, I'm a firm believer that people who excel in school and life aren't necessarily smarter, but they do study smarter. They know what's important. And they know how to ignore—forget—the irrelevant.

When I was in college, I had a roommate who rarely slept. He was always studying, and whenever I looked over his shoulder to peer into his textbooks, I'd notice that he had a habit of highlighting pretty much everything. He couldn't decipher the important from the unimportant and focus solely on the critical information. To him, everything needed to be remembered; he treated all the information the same, so rather than separating what had to be permanently stored for quick recall from the stuff he could just disregard, he tried to pack it all in. This would be the equivalent of re-membering every single number in my shortcut to two-digit multiplication. Virtually impossible.

Because of my roommate's inability to distinguish be-tween what was constructive and, frankly, *destructive* to his memory, he retained very little of the information and the important content got overrun with gunk. His grades weren't all that great, either. It didn't help his ego that I managed to get really good grades with minimal studying. I always felt bad for him, but at the time I didn't know how to help him. Now, however, I would give him a few pointers, starting with making him aware that he doesn't need to encumber his brain by stuffing it with every piece of information.

When it comes to the broader tasks of dissecting and ingesting massive amounts of information, such as a whole chapter in a textbook or an hourlong lecture, learning how to pluck the good from the bad takes practice, as well as trial and error. Sometimes you'll find that it's quite easy to distinguish between what's important and what's not. Other times it won't be so easy, and you'll have to take the long road before you realize where those shortcuts are. My roommate stayed on that long road for far too long. If you ever find yourself stuck on the long road, endlessly trying too hard to retain important information, then it's probably time to stop and take a step back. Remind yourself that you don't need to know everything, that there are hidden clues to differentiating the pivotal from the pointless, and that it's okay to give yourself permission to let certain details go. Also remind yourself that it's impossible to shove all that you encounter into your brain, which craves order and extra space. In a lot of ways, the skill of forgetting is the master key to all of the previous skills I've taught you. I mentioned at the start of this chapter that forgetting allows you to become an expert at mental organization, but it also provides the foundation upon which you can truly master the arts of focus and concentration.

Even though the exercises in this chapter don't seem to relate directly to note-taking, studying, cramming an entire year's worth of history into your head for a final exam, or preparing for a hugely important presentation at work, they will subconsciously help you build your mind's "muscles" for discarding information that you either don't need or don't need anymore. The following are some additional tips to consider.

BE SELECTIVE

Remember, to a large degree the art of memory is the art of selecting what to remember in the first place and forgetting the rest. Don't treat everything the same. If you fall into this trap, your brain will fall into a trap as well, because it has only so much active space in which to work with information. Another way to look at this is to consider the fact you have only so much time to do a certain number of tasks. Your brain likewise shares these limitations. Just as you would prioritize your to-do list in everyday life to maximize your time and optimize your energy, you need to help your brain figure out how to prioritize its mental tasks and make the most of its power.

As you dig into your textbooks, playbooks, business materials, and notes, make choices about what is most important to learn. Imagine that you are going to create a test on the material and consider the questions you would ask.

When reading, look for chapter previews, summaries, and review questions. Pay attention to anything printed in bold type. Also notice visual elements—tables, charts, graphs, and illustrations. All of these are clues pointing to what's important. During lectures, notice what the instructor or presenter emphasizes. While at practice for a hobby or sport, focus on what your coach or teacher requires you to repeat. Anything that's presented visually—on the board, on overhead projections, or with slides—is also key.

When listening to a lecture or presentation, notice what nuggets of information are given more than once. (Hint: find patterns in the delivery of the material that's meant to be retained.) This may seem like obvious advice, but I watch people treat material that's repeated over and over again as equal to what's mentioned only briefly one time. Again, don't make the mistake of treating everything the same! I realize that we all as humans want to be treated equally, but when it comes to information we must discriminate!

DON'T CREATE UNNECESSARY ASSOCIATIONS

We covered this in chapter 2, but it bears repeating as it relates to forgetting. The data already encoded in your neural networks is arranged according to a scheme that makes sense to you. When you introduce new data that you want to recall, you can remember it more effectively if you associate it with similar or related data. Avoid creating associations with data that you don't need to remember.

GIVE YOUR BRAIN A CHANCE

Sometimes the way you combine studying or retaining information with other activities can affect how well you remember the material. The trick is to avoid what psychologists call *retroactive inhibition*, something that happens when a new or unrelated activity interferes with previous learning. Acclaimed educator and leadership coach David B. Ellis writes about this in his seminal work *Becoming a Master Student*, a popular college text now in its thirteenth edition.

As an example that demonstrates this phenomenon described by Ellis, let's say that you've just left an intoxicating presentation about astronomy that included a fascinating lecture on the origins of the universe. Within seconds of letting the details really soak into your brain as you reflect on them, you find yourself checking your cell phone for messages and realizing that you have tons of unanswered calls and e-mails to address. Suddenly, your mind is yanked out of the thoughts from the lecture and becomes totally immersed in the relatively menial tasks you have yet to complete for the day. You begin to analyze how you'll check items off your to-do list and soon find that you can think of little else. The key concepts of the astronomy lecture are pushed aside by your gripping concern about these other responsibilities.

Although we may think that our minds can multitask, they often falter when they are coerced into juggling competing thoughts, especially if one of these thoughts isn't all that set into the brain yet. That thought then becomes fleeting and cannot be restored again. I have no doubt that this partly explains why there's been an inverse relationship between our multitasking demands (going up) and our critical-thinking skills (going down). The good news is that we can reverse this trend if we change how we choose to operate.

Consider another version of the astronomy-lecture scenario. Let's assume instead that you go to the lecture with a friend. On the way home the two of you talk about what you heard and how you thought about it. The discussion ignites into a lively debate as you and your friend take opposite stands on belief systems with regard to who or what created the universe. Later, just before going to sleep, your brain can now process the key points of the lecture, which will come in handy the next time you want to spark a conversation on this very subject or perhaps be quizzed on it formally. Keeping your head in the subject matter of the lecture rather than letting yourself get distracted by other menial tasks made all the difference. Those synapses and neurons in your brain worked long enough to create a rock-solid memory. In the first scenario, you didn't give yourself time and the details quickly vanished from your short-term memory before they could safely be stored and stockpiled in your long-term memory bank.

These pointers aren't just for kids and students. Adults will find these techniques for filtering information helpful to maximize and optimize their own mental organization for everyday life. For example, if you're a corporate executive who religiously writes down every word during a meeting or tries to learn by rote memory a speech that will help you gain a promotion, you're doing a great disservice to your poor brain. Your ability to perform well at work or think on your feet is also severely compromised. Think back to the story I told at the beginning of this chapter about Pythagoras. Momentarily forgetting, taking in a new piece of information, and treating it entirely differently from before was what allowed him to make a new discovery. That's the kind of insight that the combination of organizing and forgetting can achieve. We rely on conventional wisdom all the time, but what would happen if you forgot the obvious answers that spring to mind and searched instead for new ones? I think you'll find that you'll be much more creative, inventive, and solution oriented.

Being able to cherry-pick repeated information and lock it into your memory while you throw out the remainder is perhaps one of the greatest skills that anyone—including bona fide savants and memory champs—can have. And anyone can achieve this skill with practice. Use the exercises in this chapter as often as you can to make forgetting an automatic function in your brain.

REAL-WORLD HABITS

Despite all the commitments we juggle daily in our lives, rarely do we forget to tend to the important stuff—like brushing our teeth, eating when hungry, picking up our kids from school, paying bills, buying groceries, and responding to friends in need. These activities are all habits we keep that come automatically and reflect the rhythm and beats—*patterns*—of our lives. And we have an innate ability to disregard the stuff that can wait until later or be placed lower on the list of priorities. We know the difference, for example, between responding to a crying baby, upset spouse, or screaming boss and returning e-mails that can wait. Some things in life are relatively easy to prioritize without any thought. The subtle things, however, can be harder to triage or know how to deal with on the spot and can disrupt our rhythm and slow us down. This is especially true when it comes to the influx of information that needs to be sorted out in the brain before any action is taken.

The whole point of the exercises in this book has been to help you more naturally process incoming information so you can think productively and have plenty of mental storage space to preserve the facts and details that ultimately allow you to reason, remember, and carry out your everyday tasks easily, quickly, and efficiently. Of course, another goal of these exercises has been to facilitate more creative thinking and become an excellent problem solver. These are the qualities that shape productive thinkers who can achieve more in less time. I mean that literally and figuratively. After all, we all have the same twenty-four hours in a given day, 365 days a year. So how is it that some people seem to defy finite time constraints and achieve a tremendous amount more than others? How do you explain why others are able to accomplish a great deal more with the same resources and talent as everyone else? The answer lies in whether or not the people behind those achievements have formed habits that leverage the six skills maximally in the real world.

You don't need to know how to compute difficult equations quickly in your head (unless your job relies on math), and you don't need to alphabetize words to become a successful entrepreneur or CEO of a *Fortune* 500 company or otherwise have an impact in the world. But you do need to possess a collection of practical tools that help you to navigate real-world challenges and problems you'll encounter on the road to success. And you'll be surprised by how connected the exercises in this book are to working the brain in those real-world scenarios. If you make a habit of flexing your brain in the ways I've been describing, all the habits you keep become painless—including the coveted habits of, say, a highly successful person and someone others look up to. And you won't forget the important stuff.

My guess is the title to this book initially threw you off. But by now I hope you've come to appreciate the power of forgetting in a whole new way. It's through the lens of forgetting that we can keep our brains clutter free, primed for creativity, and poised to change the world. Just make a habit of forgetting as you would remembering. Use the skills learned in this book to balance the competing demands your brain is constantly handling to stay sharp, mindful, fast, insightful, and at times forgetful. Soon enough you'll become the sharpest, smartest you.

Chapter Guide

As with the previous chapter, it helps to reread this chapter once every couple of months or twice a year to remind yourself of the "forgetting" strategies and recognize patterns more frequently. See if you can perform the exercises in this chapter as often as possible. I like to alphabetize words on a daily basis as I'm driving and noticing words around me. Multiplying two-digit numbers in your head might not be something you want to do every day, but the more you train your brain to take this particular shortcut—"forgetting" along the way—the sharper and quicker your brain will be.

SOLUTIONS TO THE PROBLEMS IN THIS CHAPTER

Self-Test 1: $31 \times 53 = 1,643$

Self-Test 2: $74 \times 52 = 3,848$

Self-Test 3:

1. BEKNOOOT
2. AABBELLS
3. BEINSSSU
4. EHKMOORW
5. AABCDKRY
6. ACCEIPRT
7. AEGNRRST
8. AGHIRSTT
9. CDEHILNR
10. EINOQSTU

Additional Challenges
1. E E E E E E F F G H H I I I N N O O O R R S S
   T T T U V V W X
2. A A A A A A B C E E F H I J J L M M N N P R R
   R R R U U U Y Y Y
3. A A C E E E G H H I I I I M N N N O O O O P
   R R R R R S T U U

Number Patterns
Pattern 1: 12, 14, 16
Pattern 2: 8

Multiplying Numbers in the Hundreds
$102 \times 103 = 10,506$
$105 \times 101 = 10,605$
$109 \times 108 = 11,772$

Squaring a Number in the Fifties
$57^2 = 3,249$
$55^2 = 3,025$
$59^2 = 3,481$
$51^2 = 2,601$
$52^2 = 2,704$

Word Patterns
EISML: smile, slime, limes, miles
AELST: least, steal, teals, tales, slate, stale
SIETLN: listen, tinsel, silent, enlist, inlets

Prosperous, Productive, and Prolific

Memory is the library of the mind.

—FRANCIS FAUVEL-GOURAUD

(NINETEENTH-CENTURY FRENCH AUTHOR AND TEACHER)

No matter what you do in life or how far you take your formal education, you never stop learning. The key to life, and perhaps to the universe itself, is to never stop learning. Just as I truly believe that parents are the most important component in a child's reaching his or her full academic potential, you are the most important component to reaching your own fullest potential in your adult life. We all learn basically the same things in traditional schooling. What we learn and experience outside of formal education is what sets each one of us apart. The people we meet and the mentors we keep can change from year to year, but we essentially remain the same. We may get our information at school or at work, but learning habits and strategies often come from elsewhere—in the things we do at home and in our personal time.

Perhaps nothing is more gratifying than being praised for a job well done or told that you're "brilliant" upon solving a complex problem, achieving a major accomplishment, or coming up with some great idea. Can anyone be brilliant? Is there a productive thinker in each of us that can pave the way to monumental success in life? Do we each have a "smart switch" somewhere deep inside that we can turn on by using memory strategies, exercises, and systems like the ones I use?

We may be no better at appreciating just what makes the human brain so remarkable and, in some ways, unpredictably extraordinary than our grandparents were, but we do have a much greater understanding of how it operates, what contributes to both its health and its decline, and the myriad ways in which we can optimize its functionality, including its ability to process information and safely store it for future use. Though people like to talk about our beating heart being the center of our lives (after all, it's the heartbeat we seek in those first few weeks of life), it's really the brain that takes center stage. Our heart wouldn't beat without our brain, and it is our brain that allows us to experience the world on every level—to feel pleasure and pain, to love and to learn, to decide what to do, and to participate in life in ways that make life worth living!

Until we meet a health challenge that affects our brain's capacity or functionality, we tend to take our mental faculties for granted while we worry about so many other pressing things, from our daily responsibilities to our long-term goals and aspirations. We assume that our mind will travel with us wherever we go and be there for us. But what if that won't always be true? And what if we can in fact accelerate our brainpower hundreds of times over just by actively nurturing it in the ways I've been describing?

The idea that we have a master "smart switch" hidden

somewhere in the recesses of our brain is as fascinating as it is mystical. Maybe one day we'll be able to come much closer to understanding what turns on one person's brain to full power while another person's brain lags behind, all other things—including genetics—being equal. Maybe we'll also find out that our control over our smart switch relies more on how we are trained to use our minds in everyday life than on anything else. I believe this is very realistic, because what I attempt to do every single day in my work—guiding people through this mental training—is producing results that I cannot attribute to just luck or giftedness or talent or even genes.

We live in a vastly different world now from just a generation ago; few people will dispute the profound impact that technology has had on all of us. Could you go a day without your cell phone? A week without checking e-mail or responding to texts? A month totally unplugged from the Internet? How about a year sans any comforts of modern life, such as access to all things computer-related or digital? While you'd like to think that you could do it, chances are you'd have a tough time. These technologies afford us the opportunity to be more efficient, productive, and knowledgeable. They also can help us be healthier and happier. But with all this comes a profusion of potential distractions as well as costs to our health if we end up feeling overwhelmed, stressed, and anxious and living on the brink of a meltdown as we grapple with an unending to-do list. I don't think it's a stretch of the imagination to connect our high-tech world and the inherent expectations that it places on us with an increase in health challenges from insomnia to depression.

As much as we've gotten used to the blessings of electronics to make life easier, we've become accustomed to chronic interruptions that can slow our productivity down and cloud our creative minds. The pace of technology has, unfortunately, moved faster than our brains can adapt. Which is why we increasingly find ourselves feeling rushed, scatterbrained, and depleted. This is not a frivolous point. Study after study shows that we're more stressed out than ever before. We're overworked, underslept, and overscheduled; we chronically feel like we're behind the eight ball with responsibilities both at work and at home. We are confronted with an increasing amount of stimuli and information, which is to say we're encountering more and more opportunities *and* distractions. The question is, how can we better mine all this incoming data that our brain accepts at face value and determine what to pay attention to and what to disregard? How can we keep up with our frenetic world, all the while working faster and smarter throughout the day?

The solution isn't to take on less or try to do more, as we have in the past (and have failed at miserably). The answer lies in mastering a few skills that will allow us to optimize our time and in fact accomplish more with less effort—and not feel frazzled, stretched to the limit, and utterly exasperated. Brain clutter and attention-deficit disorders needn't be realities we embrace as necessary by-products of our modern world. As I stated clearly in the introduction: *If we can learn to minimize the idle, ineffective clutter and maximize the stuff that future successes are made of, then we can go far. And mastering the art of forgetting is the ultimate key to that achievement.*

To say that you've accomplished a lot by 9:00 a.m. because you've dealt with numerous to-dos in a flurry of electronic activity (all the while getting ready for the day and taking care of household chores, too) may sound heroic, but that can set you up for an unproductive day if you've burned through all your mental energy and cluttered the brain with pablum. Indeed, there are limits to our ability—and mental capacity—to "do it all."

None of us can possibly fathom the persistent synthesizing that our minds do on an hourly, daily, weekly, and monthly basis throughout our lives. When I make decisions today, including those that guide me through complex problems, I am basing the course I take on the existing library of my mind. It's filled with knowledge past and present, however practical or impractical that knowledge may seem to be on the surface.

I believe that highly productive thinking on a regular basis is achievable by most anyone—regardless of IQ—because of two fundamental facts that I've been instilling in you since the beginning of this book. One, many of the attributes of an efficient thinker are very teachable—and learnable; and, two, the mind is an incredibly mysterious organ that we just don't fully understand yet. I've witnessed people who believed they were doomed to mediocrity radically transform their lives in a matter of weeks just by implementing some of my techniques and gaining a little more confidence to keep going, to keep trying. There's never been a better time to establish strategies that can soothe the ongoing storm that modern technology foments and maintain a cool, calm, collected mind that supports peaceful well-being—the cornerstone to productive thinking.

Productive thinkers don't all belong to the same tribe. There are as many different breeds of productive thinkers in the world as there are species on the planet. This explains why there can be so many disparate subject areas, industries, professions, and callings to pursue. So of course, part of occupying your own brilliance is a matter of finding your tribe and then thriving in it. Again, that entails making the most of your learning so you can spot the opportunities and capitalize on them. I am fortunate to be able to see these kinds of achievements in people across the world, both on the formal-education side and out in the real world where people are trying to get ahead in their personal and professional lives.

CHOOSE TO BE PROSPEROUS, PRODUCTIVE, AND PROLIFIC

America has always promoted the belief that each person can create his or her own success. We love being independent— the rights of the individual are very much enmeshed in our culture. Independence Day is one of our finest national holidays and a cornerstone of the American mind-set. But somehow that idea of personal independence gets lost when it comes to learning and education. When we don't do as well as we'd like to in school or in our jobs, we point a finger elsewhere rather than hold up a mirror. We forget that our founding fathers tried everything in their power to ensure that we would thrive on independence, which I would think entails a great deal of personal integrity, fortitude, and responsibility.

I've been hinting at the importance of taking learning into your own hands since the beginning of this book, and I want it to be firmly planted in your mind as you move forward now and take the necessary action to control your educational life and opportunities. Every January 1, if you want to make just one New Year's resolution that's actually do-able, incredibly powerful, and sustainable for the entire year, make it your goal to refresh your mind on the strategies in this book and schedule time to work your brain every single day in ways beyond your normal routine. If there is a master switch somewhere inside you, only you can ultimately decide to flip it on. My hope is that I've given you plenty of ideas to at least begin to make a tremendous change in your life. The six skills outlined in this book reflect the essence of produc-tive thinking. They will facilitate whatever it is you want to accomplish in life.

I know the value that being productive brings to people because I see it day in and day out. I also see what lack of confidence, defeatism, and chronic failure can do to people, no matter how privileged they are or how many people love them. Without a well-functioning brain, life is much more difficult. But when you do have a strong brain, pretty much anything is possible. Things tend to fall into place when your mind is ahead of everyone else's. Whatever you hope to gain from reading this book, I hope that you at least em-brace its call to personal action. Always question how you can do something faster and more effectively. Always seek new solutions to age-old problems; when you get stuck, sim-ply find another way. And always think back to the idea of forgetting—what you eliminate from your convoluted mind will position it to better manage problems and prompt mo-ments of discovery. This will ultimately make you a more ef-ficient human being and a more prosperous individual. After all, isn't that all any of us wants in life? To be more (effort-lessly) prolific in all that we do? The rewards go far beyond the financial ones. I think it's safe to say we'd all be pleased to leave a legacy that associated us with the words "prosperous," "productive," and "prolific."

Alvin Toffler, an American writer and futurist, might have said it best when he stated: "The illiterate of the 21st century will not be those who cannot read and write, but those who cannot learn, unlearn, and relearn." As parents, teachers, mentors, and general contributors to the world at large, it behooves us to be fierce advocates for our own future, including the future of our society. I don't know any better way to do this than to learn the lessons of memory, which are really the lessons of learning, and to share those with as many people as possible. It just may be your stroke of genius.

Q & A

Odds and Ends and a Few More Reminders in the Classic FAQ Style

Live as if you were to die tomorrow.
Learn as if you were to live forever.

—MAHATMA GANDHI

This appendix includes some frequently asked questions I get from both children and adults. In many of these answers, you'll find echoes of information from previous sections of the book. If you have a question that isn't answered here, just log on to my Web site at www.MikeByster.com and ask me there.

GENERAL QUESTIONS

Q: The idea of "forgetting" and being more efficient in all that we do seems absurdly counterintuitive. Remind me: How can you be "forgetful" and super efficient at the same time?

A: I didn't just put these two concepts together to

confuse readers. There's tremendous power in the ability to forget. Although the human brain can take in and retain an enormous amount of information, it's not all that great at processing and working with tons of data at once—which is what we're increasingly having to do in our work and personal lives. If we can make a habit of instantly forgetting nonessential details we come across, we can make mental room for the information we need to have on hand to solve problems and get more done. Too many of us try to remember everything, rather than be choosy about what to bank in our memories and forget the rest. But the people who discriminate against the trivial and savor the essential are the ones who succeed.

Q: Are you a prodigy or genius?

A: I don't like these labels because they are impossible to define, even from a scientific perspective. I am just a super productive thinker—someone who sees relationships and patterns in the world that most people don't see but could if they tried. And my real gift is being able to teach the skills that allow people to amaze their friends, improve their minds, and become excited about learning. It doesn't take a "genius" to learn my program: Adults and students across the spectrum—from the learning disabled to the most gifted—have had great success in learning my strategies. I believe we all have the potential to become astonishingly productive thinkers, whether or not you call that being a prodigy or genius.

Q: How do you create the shortcuts?

A: I naturally see relationships among numbers. Some of my shortcuts are the result of painstaking trial and error, while other shortcuts come to me at random moments (while watching TV, for example). Some of the shortcuts I've come up with are ones that I found out later were first documented by others, while other shortcuts I believe are unique to me. The shortcuts I present in the book are really just alternative ways to approach a problem. The shortcuts do not bypass reason and problem-solving skills but do help people identify patterns. The ability to recognize patterns is one of the documented tests for cognitive ability.

Q: Why aren't you in Las Vegas making a living gambling?

A: While the math and memory exercises that are a part of my program probably would make anyone better at understanding the odds involved in card games, the truth is that I am much happier helping individuals become more productive in their everyday lives than trying to beat the odds in Vegas. And the casinos have made it clear that they would rather I stayed away from them anyhow.

Q: Why is it important to do math problems in your head when you have a calculator?

A: My system is about much more than multiplying large numbers without using a calculator. It's about exercising your brain and training it to organize information. I like to say that your brain is like any other muscle—the more you exercise it the stronger it will become, and the stronger your brain is the more you can do with it. I've designed my system with this goal in mind.

Q: How hereditary is productive thinking?

A: How we each think is hereditary, but more important, learning strategies such as those that help us organize our thoughts and be creative are highly learnable. These are the very skills that make someone a productive thinker. I like to say that you're never too old to change your brain, but it helps to start early, as there's more time to shape the brain, build on the features that commonly characterize efficient thinkers, and bring out that inner brilliance.

Q: What's the difference between being "naturally gifted" and being a "hard worker"?

A: I see both types of people all the time, and sometimes you cannot tell the difference in their achievements. But I will say that I've also seen plenty of people who are naturally gifted who don't make much of an effort. These people rarely reach their fullest potential and rarely catch up to the average folks who simply work hard.

Q: What is the most powerful memory strategy of all?

A: The one that works for you. Experiment with all of the strategies and see what resonates with you and your abilities. There is no single "right" strategy—beyond the one that makes sense to you and that you find easy to implement.

Q: Will these strategies help me prevent dementia or general senility?

A: While I cannot make any specific health-related promises or guarantees, I will say that science has now proved that challenging the brain in the ways I describe in this book can improve the brain's functionality and help stave off the onset of progressive age-related brain disease. There are still lots of missing clues to the science of the brain and exactly how and why it declines over time.

I don't doubt for a second that we'll come to learn more about the true power of mental exercise in disease prevention—not just in the mind but also in the entire body. Until we have all those clues figured out and solid proof of what we can do to extend the longevity of our minds and bodies, I think we would do well to keep our minds and bodies engaged as much as possible. This means physical challenges to the body and cognitive challenges to the mind. Even if you're someone who is destined to get a brain disease owing to age or genetics, delaying its onset for even a few years by maintaining an active brain could dramatically improve your quality of life.

QUESTIONS FROM PARENTS, TEACHERS, AND EDUCATORS

Q: Can these ideas help American schools overcome their problems with math and science education?

A: My strategies are intended to be a fun and creative supplement to the amazing work that teachers do every day in the classroom rather than a way to supersede it. I aim to unleash the brainpower that is already inside people and help them see the potential they have in all subjects, not just math.

Additionally, I believe that people who have learned to love something when they are young more often than not will continue to love it and practice it for the rest of their lives. My hope is that this book will help parents and teachers change the attitude some kids have about learning, math, and memorization into a more positive one. I also hope that they come to appreciate the utility of forgetting in a whole new light that enhances their brainpower.

Q: Why does my son perform so well on homework but then struggle with test taking?

A: In a word: confidence. Once you make a mistake, it can haunt you for a long time. The first couple of times I did a show, if I made a mistake, I thought the show was done, over with, finished. I always felt that it was the end of the world. But I eventually learned to sustain—and more important, to nourish—my confidence. Fueling one's confidence amid mistakes and the occasional (serious) fall is easier said than done. But there are things you can do to help your son regain his confidence and nurture it for a lifetime of success—and challenges. It helps to start by sharing with him the ways in which he can prove he's smart while not under pressure. Teach him a few card tricks or mental math shortcuts that he can share with friends or in front of an audience. Help him produce a live show in front of family members and friends at your next informal dinner party.

Q: How can I motivate my daughter more?

A: First, realize that motivation begets motivation. When a kid gets her first A, that becomes her expectation, as well as her source of motivation every time she wants to achieve another A. While you want to help your child set realistic expectations, you also want to make those expectations as high as possible. Until she lands an A, she won't have that expectation.

Second, as you know by now, I'm a proponent of keeping learning fun, cool, and exciting. Get your daughter to love and enjoy what she has to learn. Use the strategies and games in this book to push her memory building. Help her organize her thoughts better. If you're helping her prepare for a test, go back to my exercises where I make it fun and cool and transport those concepts back to traditional schoolwork.

It's an attitude thing more than anything. I see kids who love a certain subject and who do so much better than other kids who are actually smarter but don't like the subject. If your daughter truly doesn't like a subject, you have to just make it more enjoyable for her. Create rewards for her—incentives for a job well done, or for at least trying. Unlike many adults, most kids are extremely open-minded and willing to try new things. Kids don't give up as easily as adults do, either. They will happily accept second and third chances. What's more, kids are used to having to do some things that they don't like. But still, if you can make even the most mundane tasks fun for your daughter, it will change everything.

Q: How can this system help someone who has autism, ADD, or learning disabilities?

A: I try to tell kids and adults that to learn a lesson, they must do it four, five, or six times until they've got it mastered (that is, they get it and get it well), then go out and show it off. For these individuals, this may be the first time in their life they feel smart. It's like running a marathon: Everyone will run it at a difference pace but still arrive at the finish line. Of all the people I work with, those with disabilities are the ones who most often come back for more. They are so motivated and excited about feeling smart for the first time.

Q: My child is falling behind in school. What can I do?

A: Many parents who come to visit me after I've performed a show lament that their child has serious anxiety about math or is doing terrible overall in school, and they may tell me they've resorted to expensive tutoring to figure out "what's wrong" with their child and help him or her get up to speed with peers. But what I typically find is not that a child is delayed developmentally or that he or she isn't smart. Much to the contrary—and much to the parents' relief—all that's missing usually is a little confidence and help with focusing. (Do I sound like a broken record by now? I know I've been harping on these issues for the greater part of this book, but they must and should be repeated.)

Unfortunately, tutors rarely teach kids how to learn. They review what the child is supposed to retain but offer no help in effortlessly retaining that information. And that's what I'm teaching here. The other problem with tutoring is that private teachers charge, on average, $75 an hour—so at six hours a week, which is customary, parents are paying roughly $450 per week, or close to $20,000 a year! (Tutors at some private schools can cost upward of $35,000 a year—in addition to the tuition.) That's a lot of money that few families have at their disposal.

Try this exercise: Create a random two-hundred-digit number and have your kid memorize it, just as my son did. At bedtime, do one or two numbers at a time. Every night or every morning, add another number. Help your kid find a strategy that works to keep the growing number in his or her head. Try this exercise with letters, too. Or numbers and letters. Mastering all two hundred digits will make your kid feel like he or she can do anything!

Q: I'm a teacher who loves this memory system. But how can I teach these ideas without my students losing interest in the traditional route, especially when it comes to math?

A: Even though my book outlines shortcuts and untraditional ways of arriving at solutions to problems, especially in the math department, I'm not suggesting that the traditional methods do not have value. Much to the contrary, students need to learn how to add, subtract, multiply, and divide in the usual manner before they can fully appreciate and master the shortcuts. They also must have their multiplication tables down flat. All of my strategies act as supplementary and complementary material to whatever it is you want to teach, whether it's traditional arithmetic, history, complex calculus, or even carpentry. They are geared to help students optimize how they learn and to take the "overwhelming" factor out of the learning curve.

One way you can teach memory strategies and foster a classroom of students who learn to think on their own and to manipulate concepts from various sources is to send them home with a list of twenty items. This list can encompass any subject matter, from pop culture (such as a list of the top movies of the century or favorite restaurants) to an academic list of biology definitions or important historical events. Instruct them to go home and find a clever way of memorizing the list in a certain order. The following day, have each student share how he or she created a memory technique . . . and suddenly you'll have a whole new collection of unique memory strategies homegrown from your homeroom!

Q: I've heard that certain television shows and videos are "bad" for young kids' developing brains. What do you think of that? Can some TV shows and videos turn preschoolers' minds to mush?

A: Kids should be introduced to numbers and patterns as soon as possible, long before they can learn their multiplication tables, and this can be achieved without any use of a television or computer. I also believe that children need to be introduced to certain programming when their brains are equipped to handle the information appropriately. These days, kids typically start watching television at four months of age; the average preschool kid watches more than ninety minutes of television a day.

As I was piecing this book together, a new study emerged that said it's not only how much but also what they're watching that can have an impact on children's attention spans. The study, published in the *Journal of Pediatrics*, explored how fast-paced programming can affect what psychologists call executive functioning, which is your ability to stay on task and not be distracted. More technically, executive functioning is a collection of skills that govern how we behave and that involve working memory, delayed gratification, and problem solving—all the skills we need to function well. Executive functioning is what allows us not only to remember things and solve problems but also to plan. This particular study looked at 60 four-year-olds and broke them into three groups. One group watched a nine-minute clip of *Sponge-Bob SquarePants*; a second watched a nine-minute clip of *Caillou*, a realistic PBS cartoon about a preschool boy; and the third group drew pictures for nine minutes instead of watching television. Immediately afterward, when the researchers tested each group's executive functioning, they found that the PBS-viewing and picture-drawing groups performed equally well on the tests. The *SpongeBob* group, however, scored significantly worse—the implication being that watching a full half hour of a fast-paced cartoon show could be detrimental to a preschooler's executive functioning. The researchers speculated that *SpongeBob*'s more rapid pace and fantastical characters—such as a talking, pants-wearing kitchen sponge who lives under the sea—might be too much for preschoolers' brains to take in. Granted, *SpongeBob* is not intended for this audience, but many parents still expose their young ones to these programs from a very early age. As parents, the question we really should be asking ourselves is: How can we prepare our youngsters to build this executive function?

According to the experts, one answer is by promoting good old-fashioned play, which entails many skills I've outlined in this book—getting kids to use their imaginations, be creative, focus and concentrate, and listen to and follow directions so they can reach a goal. Educational, age-appropriate programming might have a positive effect, but the key term here is "age-appropriate." (The American Academy of Pediatrics recommends that kids under age two not watch any television.)

The other thing to bear in mind is that we need to set good examples. As adults, we're constantly trying to do too many tasks at once, such as texting, being on the computer, and talking on the phone all at the same time. Kids mimic their parents, and unless we teach them how to focus and concentrate on one task at a time, especially during those formative years when the brain is developing, we're not preparing them optimally to establish lifelong good habits and behaviors.

QUESTIONS FROM BUSINESS MANAGERS, EXECUTIVES, AND CEOS

Q: I am a business executive who has always struggled to make myself stand out, especially when it comes to my ideas, so I can change my organization and gain the promotion I deserve. In addition to applying the strategies in this book, what else can I do?

A: Your question addresses an important branch of the memory topic: the art of making yourself memorable. In fact, this book wouldn't be complete without a final nod to the concept of memorable ideas. I don't know anyone who doesn't want to make their ideas better known by more people, whether to sound smart, to write a provocative essay or speech, to strategize a brilliant campaign of some sort, to win an election, to be a better leader, to get their message to resonate as loudly as possible, or just to be heard, taken seriously, and able to make a memorable impression that stands the test of time. Mark Twain once observed, "A lie can get halfway around the world before the truth can even get its boots on." His observation rings true: Urban legends, conspiracy theories, and bogus scare tactics and claims circulate effortlessly. (Just consider the number of Internet hoaxes the spread virally or check out your spam folder that quarantines junk.) Meanwhile, people with important ideas—businesspeople, educators, politicians, journalists, and others—struggle to make their ideas "stick." And therein lies the heart and soul of the wonderful 2007 book *Made to Stick* by Chip and Dan Heath. The authors answered these important questions: Why do some ideas thrive while others die? And how do we improve the chances of worthy ideas?

The Heath brothers bring up a good point: As our knowledge and expertise increase, our creativity and ability to innovate tend to taper off. Why? Because the walls of the proverbial box in which we think thicken along with our experience. The more we know, and the more we specialize in a certain field, the harder it becomes to yank ourselves out of our little boxes and tap areas of creativity that were easier to access when we had more to learn. It's an interesting paradox, but what I find even more intriguing is the Heaths' claim that we can continually foster innovation by focusing on the art of communication: We can better convey our ideas, they assert, by using elements that maximize memory, such as simplicity, unexpectedness, concreteness, emotions, and storytelling. (These key words, in fact, became their acronym for their six principles; note that the initial letters spell out "success"—well, almost.) Here's a great case in point that they use to demonstrate a most memorable event.

When Art Silverman of the Center for Science in the Public Interest (CSPI), a nonprofit group that educates the public about nutrition, was charged with conveying to the public that movie-theater popcorn is unhealthy, he could have told moviegoers that their bag of popcorn contained thirty-seven grams of saturated fat. But rather than just state the fact, he instead decided to craft a message that put the fact into a context that people could quickly understand.

At a press conference on September 27, 1992, he said: "A medium-sized 'butter' popcorn at a typical neighborhood movie theater contains more artery-clogging fat than a bacon-and-eggs breakfast, a Big Mac and fries for lunch,

and a steak dinner with all the trimmings—combined!"
The people at CSPI added insult to injury by laying out the
full buffet of greasy food for the television cameras. And
the message was heard loud and clear, causing an immediate sensation in the media. The story was featured on CBS,
NBC, ABC, and CNN; it made the front pages of *USA
Today*, the *Los Angeles Times*, and the *Washington Post*'s
Style section; Leno and Letterman cracked jokes about fat-
soaked popcorn; and reporters had some fun with the news,
too, writing headlines such as: "Popcorn Gets an 'R' Rat-
ing," "Lights, Action, Cholesterol!" and "Theater Popcorn
Is Double Feature of Fat."

Well, the idea wasn't going anywhere. It stuck. Moviegoers, repulsed by these findings, avoided popcorn in
droves. Sales plunged. Service staff at movie houses grew
accustomed to fielding questions about whether the popcorn
was popped in coconut oil, the "bad" oil. Soon after, most
of the nation's biggest theater chains—including United Artists, AMC, and Loews—announced that they would stop
using coconut oil.

I won't go into the details of the Heaths' main lessons
other than to say that you should read their book and all of
the richly detailed stories from their research. While the book
isn't designed to help you maximize your personal memory,
it can undoubtedly assist you in mobilizing more of your creative energy and expressive talents, which can in turn nourish your mind's overall processing abilities—in short, your
ingeniousness.

Q: I am a manager. How can I use these techniques to
keep my team sharp and motivated and morale high?

A: Once you master the six skills, you should automatically find that your job, including the component of managing others, gets easier. Now that you understand the value of these skills in your own personal and professional life, you can show others by way of example how to value the same skills and develop them over time with conscious effort. You may find it helpful to set aside an hour or join your team over lunch and share your experience with the information contained in this book. Just as you've worked at strengthening your own logical, creative, and imaginative side and honed your ability to organize data efficiently and retain more information in your brain, you can encourage your colleagues and teammates to do the same. Create a culture that celebrates unconventional thinking and new ideas that make old ways of doing things obsolete. Push your staff to think outside the box at meetings and employ the power of forgetting to make the most of their day and mental bandwidth.

Help your team members, especially the underexperienced employees, to organize their thoughts—and their time—better when it comes to tricky projects or campaigns and inspire them to find their own solutions to problems, even if that means doing things differently. And be sure to reward the good work that results from their focus and concentration. Just as kids need to be complimented and to feel a strong sense of independence and uniqueness, so do adults—especially in corporate or business settings. Remember, it is in these settings that we can feel invisible because we're surrounded by peers who share similar qualities and levels of competence. Breaking away from the pack and standing out becomes all the more challenging. Yet when you help members of your team do just that, it will go a long way toward motivating them while stimulating their loyalty and generating their best efforts.

Q: In addition to your Web site and the sites you mentioned in the book, what other Web sites are good for math resources, games, and other mental challenges?
A: In the following sections are a few you might find useful.

PUZZLES, GAMES, AND MENTAL EXERCISES FOR EVERYONE

• Lumosity: www.lumosity.com
Lumosity is one of the most developed Web sites for mental fitness and brain training. A lot of money has clearly been put into the site, which means your experience is great. The games are fun and interesting. There is a free seven-day trial, if you want to give it a try.

• Play with Your Mind: http://playwithyourmind.com
This Web site has over one hundred original mind games, puzzles, and other brain exercises. Spend some time surfing here to find games that appeal to you and to see the full range of ways to exercise your brain.

• Happy Neuron: www.happyneuron.com
Happy Neuron is a Web site with games and activities divided into five critical brain areas: memory, attention, language, executive functions, and visual/spatial. The Web site

costs $9.95 a month and has a free trial offer so that you can see if you like the approach.

• My Brain Trainer: www.mybraintrainer.com

The online Brain Gym costs $9.95 for three months. It is full of games, puzzles, and other challenges to improve your mental fitness. The Web site recommends ten minutes of brain training twice a day for the best effects. The Web site also has a twenty-one-day basic training program that claims to improve your mental speed.

• Queendom: http://queendom.com

Queendom is a completely addictive and free Web site that has thousands of personality tests and surveys. Queendom also has an extensive collection of "brain tools" for you to use in exercising and testing your brain.

• BrainBuilder: www.brainbuilder.com

Founded in 2004, BrainBuilder offers cognitive exercises, an online "trainer," tracking of your brain progress, and baseline testing to provide comprehensive brain training. The fee is $7.95 per month, with a free seven-day trial offer available.

• Braingle: www.braingle.com/math.html

Visit Braingle for tons of user-submitted tricks and tools for a bunch of cool concepts. You can also learn more about cryptography, probability, and optical illusions.

• Sporcle: www.sporcle.com

I go to this site every day. It's a great place for a variety of word games and other mental challenges. I love the Daily

Dose, a word-based quiz that changes every day. You can also keep track of your scores and invite your friends to challenge you.

- BrainBashers: www.brainbashers.com

I know that some of us just can't get enough of brainteasers, puzzles, games, riddles, and optical illusions, and the people at BrainBashers seem to also know this. Check it out.

- Boatload Puzzles: www.boatloadpuzzles.com

You get what you'd expect on this site: a boatload of puzzles to try.

- JigZone: www.jigzone.com

For a jigsaw puzzler's paradise, go here. Anyone who needs more help in pattern awareness would do well to check out this site.

- Puzzle Baron: www.puzzlebaron.com

Puzzle Baron comprises a family of sites filled with challenging exercises and games, including cryptograms, acrostics, and logic puzzles. The printable-puzzle site at www .printable-puzzles.com is where you can download print-quality, high-resolution PDF puzzles to solve the old-fashioned way, with pencil and paper.

- The riddle page of the National Institute of Environmental Health Sciences: http://kids.niehs.nih.gov/games/ riddles/index.htm

Even though kids are this site's target audience, any adult can find its brainteasers, puzzles, and riddles fun and engaging.

- The Brain Boosters page of Discovery Education: http://school.discoveryeducation.com/brainboosters/

This site features an archive of "brain boosters" that you can solve.

MATH RESOURCES FOR EVERYONE

- Wolfram MathWorld: http://mathworld.wolfram.com

If you're looking for a place with a huge amount of math resources, this is a good place to start. MathWorld covers everything from the simplest to the most complicated subjects.

- The Math Forum: http://mathforum.org

A great resource for learning and connecting with people for anything math related. Puzzles, mentoring, research—it's all easy to find here.

- Math Is Fun: www.mathisfun.com

You've been learning all along in this book that math can be fun, but if you need a reminder, the Math Is Fun Web site will help with that! It even includes a mathematics dictionary with more than five hundred definitions.

- Coolmath 4 Kids: www.coolmath4kids.com

If you're an adult, don't be dissuaded by the "kids" factor. Coolmath 4 Kids is a really fun site that can help with all sorts of math concepts, whatever your age. If you need some math flash cards or want to learn some new games or methods of division, I encourage you to check this out.

- Math Maze: http://library.thinkquest.org/05aug/01951

Go to this site to read a great history of mathematics, as well as some info on famous mathematicians. For even more fun, there are some entertaining games to play, too.

- Cut the Knot: www.cut-the-knot.org

At Cut the Knot, you will find hundreds of Web-based programs to explain many different mathematical concepts—from algebra to calculus and beyond, you won't run out of things to learn here!

- SuperKids Math Worksheet Calculator: www.superkids
  .com/aweb/tools/math

Again, don't be put off by the "SuperKids" in the name if you're looking to improve your math skills, as this site appeals to everyone. You really couldn't ask for a more useful Web site than this worksheet creator. As you have learned, the best way to learn new math concepts is through repeated practice. Here you can make customized worksheets and answer sheets for averages, fractions, and much more.

Additional Games to Engage Everyone from Nine to Ninety-nine

Plus Tricks to Amaze Your Family and Friends

Learning is not compulsory . . . neither is survival.

—W. EDWARDS DEMING

This appendix is meant to supplement all the chapters in the book and provide additional exercises that will reinforce the six essential skills. These exercises aim to work your brain in ways that maximize its fullest potential while making the process entertaining and engaging.

Whether you're playing with a nine-year-old or a ninety-nine-year-old, the goal is to extinguish any anxieties you may still have about math—and learning in general—and to increase your chances of success in all that you do. I'll start with fun games for everyone, and then I'll mention a few games that specifically help kids empower their minds so they have the greatest chance to succeed academically. Note, however, that kids aren't the only ones who can play these super-kid-friendly games. You might find these tricks enjoyable to try out yourself on friends and family at your next social gathering. They'll leave you feeling like the smartest person in the room.

FUN GAMES FOR EVERYONE

GHOST

This game is best for just two players. The object is to outwit your opponent by thinking two or three steps ahead. Here's your chance to put all your spelling, vocabulary, and organizational skills to good use. It gets easier the more you play, so give it a try.

How to Play

Player 1 thinks of a word that he keeps to himself. He then tells player 2 the first letter of that word. Player 2 now thinks of a word starting with that letter and then tells player 1 what the second letter in that word is. It's then player 1's job to think of a word starting with those two letters. He then tells player 2 the third letter of this new word. Once a word is four letters long and a player says a letter that forms this into a full word, that player loses and has to record a G. The first person to do this five times and record G-H-O-S-T is the loser.

Here's how to challenge and outwit your opponent. If you say a letter and your opponent thinks that he can't use this letter to think of a word, he's allowed to challenge. If you then can't think of a word, you get a G. If you can, your challenger loses and gets the G. Let's take an example:

- Player 1 comes up with the word SUPER and says the letter S.
- Player 2 thinks of STOMACH and says the letters ST.
- Player 1 thinks of STAND and says the letters STA.
- Player 2 thinks of STAMP and says the letters STAM.
- Player 1 thinks of STAMMER and says the letters STAMM.

If player 2 is stumped at this point, she would challenge player 1, who would state STAMMER. Player 2 now has to record a G. But if player 2 does think of STAMMER, she would say S-T-A-M-M-E. Now it's player 1's job to think of another word, because if he spells out STAMMER he will lose. Player 2 took control of the word. It's strategy in action. So the name of the game is trying to outwit your opponent and get him to finish spelling the word.

THREE MISSING CARDS

Throwing a party this weekend? Then master the art of this one beforehand, and when people look like they need a new form of entertainment late into the evening, bring out a deck of cards.

To perform the following, have a full (without the jokers), newly shuffled deck of cards in your hand facedown.

Pick three people and have them sit across from you at a table. Each person will pull a card out of your deck and look at it (without showing you), and then you'll place each card facedown in front of each respective person. You can even designate each person with their card: person 1's card, person 2's card, and person 3's card. I'll use this labeling system in describing the rest of the trick. Here's what we have so far:

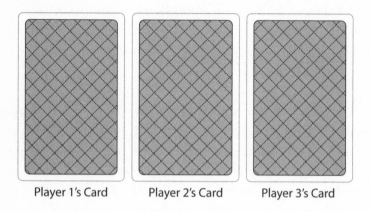

| Player 1's Card | Player 2's Card | Player 3's Card |

Now you're ready for the trick:

Step 1: In front of player 1's card, put ten cards facedown. This is pile 1.

Step 2: In front of player 2's card, put fifteen cards facedown. This is pile 2.

Step 3: In front of player 3's card, put fifteen cards facedown. This is pile 3. Take the leftover cards (there should be nine in total) and put them aside for now. This is your "unused" deck.

Step 4: Pick up player 1's card and put it on top of pile 1.

Step 5: Pick up pile 2 and ask someone in the audience to give you a number between 1 and 14. Let's say someone shouts out, "Seven." What you'll do is count out seven cards from pile 2 and place them on pile 1. Put the remaining cards in pile 2 back down. Pick up player 2's card and place it on pile 2.

Step 6: Pick up pile 3 and again ask someone in the audience for a number between 1 and 14. Let's say this time someone shouts out, "Five." You'll count out five cards from pile 3 and place them on pile 2. Put down pile 3. Pick up player 3's card and place it on pile 3.

Step 7: Take the unused nine cards and place them on pile 3. Now take that new pile 3 and place it on top of pile 2. Pick up this new pile 2 and place it on pile 1. You should have a full deck again.

Step 8: Make two piles by going through the deck like this—one card face*up*, one card face*down,* one card face*up*, one card face*down.* . . . Go through the entire deck until you have one faceup pile and one facedown pile.

Step 9: Get rid of the faceup pile. You don't need these cards anymore.

Step 10: Repeat steps 8 and 9 with the remaining deck. Don't forget to get rid of the faceup pile.

Step 11: Repeat steps 8 and 9—but this time switch the order of your pile-making so it goes like this: one card face*down*, one card face*up*, one card face*down*. . . . Rather than start your pile-making going up-down-up-down, you're going down-up-down-up. Once you've created your piles this time, get rid of the faceup pile, as you did previously.

Step 12: In this last step, you'll once more set out two piles starting with a faceup card, but you'll place all of the facedown cards in front of your players. These cards will be the original missing cards!

This trick is a lot easier than it plays out on paper here. To see a video of this trick in action, go to www.MikeByster .com and watch how it's done. Then you'll be able to remember the steps and do this trick yourself.

BIZZ-BUZZ

This game is great for a group of people. Position your friends in a circle. Designate someone as the starter (that can be you), who begins the game by saying the number "1." Going around the circle, each person will call out the next number in sequence. So the second person in the circle will say "2," the next person will say "3," and so on. But here's the catch: certain numbers cannot be said. The banned numbers are:

- Any number with a 7 in it, such as 47, 67, or 73
- Any multiple of 7 (7, 14, 21 . . .)
- Any digits that add up to 7, such as 25 (2 + 5 = 7)

If one of the banned numbers comes up when it's your turn to say a number, you say "Buzz" instead. If you say the banned number, you're disqualified and must step out of the game. The goal of the game is to reach a high number, and the last person in the circle wins!

This game can be played at different levels of intensity and difficulty. For instance, you can up the ante and add another set of banned numbers; that's where the "Bizz" part comes into play. You'll say "Bizz" for certain numbers and "Buzz" for others. It all gets even trickier when you have to account for numbers that could go either way. For example, if you designate all numbers with a 7 in them as Buzz numbers and all multiples of 7 and digits that add up to 7 as Bizz numbers, then there will be times when your number meets the criteria for both kinds of banned numbers, in which case you say "Bizz-Buzz." Once this game speeds up to a rapid-fire pace, you'll be surprised at how many times the players happen upon a random number combo that they don't catch as a Bizz-Buzz moment.

676 COMBINATIONS

Did you know that there are 676 combinations of three-letter words with one letter in a certain spot? I know, it sounds impossible, but it's true. According to the mathematical rule of combinations, the fact that there are 26 letters in the alphabet means that there are 26 times 26 different combinations—and potential words—that can be created if one letter remains constant in all of those combinations. Don't panic if this sounds confusing. Once you go through the motions of this game—which gets your mind thinking *fast*—you'll understand what I mean as your mind spins through the combinations.

You need just one partner, a piece of paper, and a writing implement.

Below are two piles of "clues":

A   E   D   L   N   R   S   T

1   2   3

What you'll do is pick one letter from the top row and one number from the bottom row. Let's say you choose the letter L and the number 1. Now you have to try to come up with as many three-letter words as you can that start with the letter L (in other words, that have L in the first position), as in:

LAB
LAD
LAG
LAP
LAM
LAW
LAY
LEG
LET
LID
LIE
LIP
LIT
LOB
LOG

LOP

LOT

LOW

LUG

LYE

Or let's say you choose the letter *R* and the number 2. The list begins:

ARC

ARE

ART

BRA

CRY

DRY

ERA

ERG

FRY

IRK

ORE

ORT

PRO

PRY

TRY

URN

WRY

Ideally, this game is played with a partner and you time each other. The person who can create a comprehensive list of words from the same set of clues in the shortest amount of time wins!

HOW DID YOU DO THAT?! IS SEEING BELIEVING?

The next trick I am going to teach you wouldn't be complete without a brief tangential discussion of optical illusions (not that I want to give away my trick before explaining it!).

The following images illustrate that we cannot always trust our visual perception—what we see isn't always what we get! The components of an object can distort the *perception* of the complete object. In other words, our brains can interpret what we see differently from what's really there, for several reasons. For one, there can be design elements or background patterns that affect how our eyes see a certain image. Or we can be thrown off as a result of thinking about what we *should be* seeing versus what's right in front of us. How we perceive things has a direct correlation to how we react. Games like bingo and poker provide only partial information, and the players have to make decisions based on their intuition. A hand can be perceived as either weak or strong depending on the strategies used to intimidate opponents, such as betting and bluffing.

Optical illusions have been studied for millennia. The ancient Greeks used a technique known as *entasis*, which incorporates a slight convexity in the columns of the Parthenon to compensate for the illusion of concavity created by parallel lines. Psychologists and artists alike have popularized many of the following illusions, which you'll find at various Web sites that talk about optical illusions and how incredibly challenging they can be for the brain. For more of these, I encourage you to check out www.scientificpsychic .com/graphics and http://en.wikipedia.org/wiki/Optical_ illusion. And for an incredibly trippy optical illusion in action, Google "the spinning dancer." If you perceive the dancer's foot touching the ground to be the left foot, she appears to be spinning clockwise; if you see the foot touching the ground as her right foot, then she appears to be spinning counterclockwise!

WARPED SQUARES?

There are no curved lines in these figures. You can use a ruler to check it out. The diagonal patterns created by the tiny squares distort our perception of the figures.

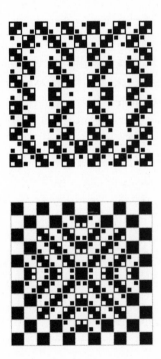

WORD COLOR TEST

For this exercise, get out a piece of paper and a set of markers. Using a green marker, write the word YELLOW at the top. Using a red marker, write the word BLUE beneath the top word. Continue down the page: using a blue marker, write the word ORANGE; using a yellow marker, write the word BLACK; using a purple marker, write the word RED; and using an orange marker, write the word GREEN.

Now, do not read the words, but say aloud the *color* of each word as you look down your list of words. How hard do you find it to say the correct color and not be distracted by the word itself? This is a type of psycholinguistic test that poses some difficulty because the portion of the brain that handles language has the conflicting tasks of verbalizing the color of the written words while ignoring the meaning of the words representing colors.

VERTICAL LINES

Let's try one more.

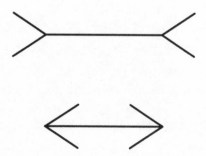

Do you think the vertical lines are the same exact length or different? Turns out that they are the same length. Our eyes cannot always be trusted (nor can we always trust the part of our brain that tries to accurately interpret what our eyes are seeing), and there are lots of tricks to be played based on this weakness.

GOTCHA!

One of my favorite crowd-pleasers is Gotcha. Here's how to dupe your best, smartest friends.

Ninety percent of people will fall for this card trick. Your victims—ahem, audience—might think you're playing with a fixed deck, but they won't think that you've fixed the deck in the way I'm going to tell you to fix it. So yes, for this trick you'll need to rig a deck of cards such that the first four cards off the top of your facedown deck are:

- the 9 of spades
- the 8 of clubs
- the 9 of clubs
- the 8 of spades

Perhaps you already see the pattern, but hang on a second. What you'll do is ask someone to take the top two cards from your facedown deck, look at them in private, and then return them to anywhere in the deck, which you'll fan out for them in your hand. Say something like "Abracadabra" over the deck, or maybe smash the deck behind your head and flip through it without shuffling them. Then turn over the top two cards, show them, and ask: "Weren't these your cards?" These two cards won't be the exact cards they first chose, but they will be similar enough that your audience won't know the difference. They'll think that you've actually rigged the deck to have two 9 of spades cards and two 8 of clubs cards and that they are looking at the same exact cards they first pulled. In other words, their mind won't instantly say, "Oh, I must not have looked at the suit carefully."

How does this happen? The numbers and colors are too close for the mind to quickly distinguish. Obviously, you could do this trick using any set of four cards that are close in color and looks, such as a 9 of hearts, 8 of diamonds, 8 of hearts, and 9 of diamonds. Once again, your victim won't be able to register the cards exactly in terms of suit and number—unless he or she is paying exceptionally close attention or has a hunch that you're bending the mind in this unique way.

THE SHOE GAME: "REMEMBER WHEN . . . ?"

This game—an updated version of the classic *Newlywed Game*—works best when it's played among couples who know each other pretty well. Each couple pair is a team, and one other person needs to be the leader and cannot be part of a team.

Now, position each couple back to back; they can be sitting down on the floor or in chairs. Each person holds a shoe from his or her partner in addition to his or her own shoe. So if I'm playing this game with my wife, she'll hold one of my shoes and one of her own shoes in her hands, while I hold one of hers and one of mine in my hands. We can't see each other because our backs are lined up. The leader starts by asking a series of questions related to who is better or worse at particular tasks. The players respond to each question by holding up the shoe of the person they think is better or worse. Let's say the question is, "Who is the better cook?" If my wife and I hold up the same shoe, then we're in agreement and we win a point. If we don't agree, our shoes won't match and we don't get any points. After a round of twenty questions, the couple with the most points wins.

Below is a list of questions that can be used. The leader is encouraged to make up other questions as well, especially as they pertain to the group at hand.

1. Who is the better cook?
2. Who is the better driver?
3. Who is on time more often?
4. Who loses their temper more easily?
5. Who is sloppier?
6. Who is in the mood for fast food more often?
7. Who was more nervous on your first date?
8. Who is funnier?
9. Who worries more?
10. Who is in better shape?
11. Who sleeps better?
12. Who is more thoughtful?
13. Who is handier?
14. Who is the better athlete?
15. Who has the bigger brain?
16. Who takes longer to get ready?
17. Who does more work around the house?

18. Who has better taste in clothes?
19. Who has the better pulse on pop culture?
20. Who sings with a better voice?

How does this game improve your mind? These questions are designed to stimulate your memory and plunge your mind back in time. You'll find that these types of questions force you to recall situations and events in your life to validate your response. If you and your partner disagree on an answer, explain to your partner why you answered the way you did. Think back and cull the details and facts you need to make your case. This isn't about fighting over a response— it's about being able to quantify and qualify your memories.

Many of us don't reminisce unless we're forced to. But when we do, we're actually working our brains in ways that can help us optimize their functionality. The mere act of pulling data from the farthest reaches of our brains taps all the six essential skills (focus, concentration, information retention, thinking outside the box, organizing, and even forgetting). It also verifies the full extent and power of your brain. As I've been reiterating throughout this book, the mind can retain and work with much more information than we typically think it can. We just need to push it to unleash its fullest potential. Games like the ones in this chapter help you do just that.

MEMORY MONSTER GAME

One of my favorite mind-sharpening exercises is to take an ordinary sentence, assign three letters to most of the words in the sentence, and try to memorize all the letters in a few seconds. It's a great mental exercise because it teaches you how to process information quickly. Plus it helps train your mind to work with patterns and use mnemonic devices.

On the next page are four sentences and a list of three-letter sequences that correspond to them. The smaller words that aren't as critical for recalling the sentence—such as the pronouns (*my*), prepositions (*on*), and articles (*the*)—are not included; hence they are not shown in all-caps here. Pick one of these four sentences and try to memorize it and its nine three-letter sequences—then turn the page and see if you can recall all nine sequences!

1. ATE DINNER WITH my PARENTS at a RES-
   TAURANT. WAITER POURED COFFEE on my
   FATHER.
2. PLAYING VIDEO GAMES, TRYING for WORLD
   RECORD. My BROTHER UNPLUGGED the
   MACHINE.
3. SKATEBOARDING down the SIDEWALK,
   FLIPPED OVER, but LANDED TOTALLY on my
   FEET.
4. I was WATCHING TV'S ALONE; my mom
   YELLED PICK UPA your CLOTHES. I SAID
   LATER.

Sentence 1	Sentence 2	Sentence 3	Sentence 4
AIT (ate)	PLI (playing)	SKE (skate)	WCG (watching)
DIN (dinner)	VIO (video)	BOR (boarding)	TVZ (tvs)
WTH (with)	GMS (games)	IDE (side)	ALN (alone)
PRS (parents)	TRG (trying)	WAK (walk)	YED (yelled)
RET (restaurant)	WRL (world)	FPD (flipped)	PIQ (pick)
WAI (waiter)	REC (record)	OER (over)	UPA (upa)
POR (poured)	BRT (brother)	LDE (landed)	CLS (clothes)
CFE (coffee)	UNP (unplugged)	TOL (totally	SED (said)
FHR (father)	MCH (machine)	FET (feet)	LET (later)

Okay, so working with one sentence at a time, try to remember all of the letter sequences in each one. You can recite it out loud or write it down.

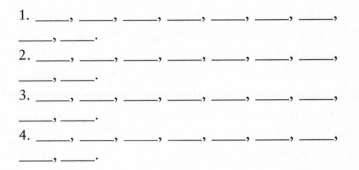

1. ____, ____, ____, ____, ____, ____, ____, ____, ____.

2. ____, ____, ____, ____, ____, ____, ____, ____, ____.

3. ____, ____, ____, ____, ____, ____, ____, ____, ____.

4. ____, ____, ____, ____, ____, ____, ____, ____, ____.

How well could you do this? Did you look back to find letters that you missed? Obviously, the pattern that you're supposed to identify is the use of letters that convey a whole word without using the entire word, and using only those words that communicate the main thrust of the sentence. So as your mind is having to go back to that original sentence, it's simultaneously picking out the chosen letters in an organized fashion. It's doing this task over and over again, as if jumping through hoops. This back-and-forth mental motion is the equivalent of a pencil sharpener. The chronic yet intentional maneuvering of your thoughts hones your mind and fuels its processing speed.

SUPER-KID-FRIENDLY IDEAS

BUILD CONFIDENCE WITH NUMBERS

Attention, parents of kids younger than ten: confidence building cannot start early enough in life, especially in the math department. Number awareness in young children can set the stage for a lifetime of success. Simply encouraging kids to count the stairs as they climb or descend, or to count the sugar packets on a restaurant table, are wonderful exercises that don't require serious math. And here's a trick you can teach anyone who can count to 10. I'll explain how it works as if you're performing the trick, and then once you learn it you can teach your youngsters in your own words.

First, take out a sheet of paper and create three columns that look like this, making sure you use the numbers provided—do not change anything or the trick won't work!

Column A	Column B	Column C
124	244	316
322	343	118
223	145	217

Now find ten pennies and put them into a pile. Pick a three-digit number from each of the columns above. Let's say you choose the numbers 124, 343, and 217. The goal is to add these numbers up quickly, which will be an impressive feat for someone who can only count to 10!

Obviously, you're not going to actually "add" the numbers up traditionally. And you're not going to use a calculator. You're going to apply a shortcut that works with these particular numbers.

To start, what you'll do is look at the hundreds digit from each of the three numbers, and then pull pennies from your pile to create a new pile based on those numbers. For example, in the number 124, the number 1 occupies the hundreds digit, so you'll take one penny from your pile and start a new pile. Then you'll do the same for the next number, 343, whose number 3 occupies the hundreds digit. So you'll remove three pennies from the original pile and add them to the new pile. Repeating again with the third number, 217, you'll remove two pennies from the old pile and place them in the new pile. Now you're ready to find your answer using the final three steps:

Step 1: Ask yourself: how many pennies are in the new pile? Answer: 6. We got six pennies because we moved 1 + 3 + 2 over to the new pile. This is the first number in the answer.

Step 2: Remembering that the middle number is always 8—always!—now ask yourself: how many pennies are left in the old pile? Answer: 4. This is the third and final number in the answer.

Step 3: Now you just have to figure out what the first and last numbers are based on steps 1 and 2. Hence, 124 + 343 + 217 = **684**.

When you teach a young one how to perform this shortcut, obviously you'll want to avoid using the terms "hundreds digit" and "ones digit"; you can simply tell them to look for the "first number" or the "third number" in each three-digit number. Your youngster will also want to ask the audience to choose which three numbers to add. Doing this trick in front of several people can be a huge crowd-pleaser. When adults watch a child add three big numbers like that, they are impressed and the child gains a lot of positive reinforcement to his or her self-esteem.

SPIN THE CONVERSATION

My son and I rarely share a quiet ride in the car. We're constantly engaging each other's mind on some crazy level. It's rewarding for me to be able to interact with him in such an innovative manner that not only strengthens our bond but also manages to spin my own brain around in fun and stimulating ways. Here are two of our favorite games—no pencil, pen, or computer required. Try them the next time you're traveling with children!

Have a Conversation Without a Certain Letter in It

In 1939 a novel by Ernest Vincent Wright was published that was called *Gadsby* and whose subtitle says it all: *A Story of Over 50,000 Words Without Using the Letter "E."* That's right: this man wrote an entire book without ever using the letter *e*! Hard to believe. Though self-published and little noticed in its time, the book is a favorite of fans of what's called *constrained writing* and is a sought-after rarity among some book collectors.

I had never heard of constrained writing until I was doing some research on this unusual tome. Or at least, I never knew that there's an official term for the literary technique whereby the writer is bound by some condition that forbids certain things or imposes a pattern. Such constraints are very common in poetry, but they also are what give us many of the devices I've talked about in this book—namely, palindromes, acrostics, and anagrams. All of these are prime examples of constrained writing in action.

So I guess you could say that my son and I enjoy the art of constrained conversation. That is, we like to conduct full conversations that abide by certain rules, one of which is just what Mr. Wright did when he penned his book: avoiding the letter *e*. Here's how one of these exchanges might unfold:

"Josh, how was school today?"

"Not bad, Dad. But my instructor was boring."

"Josh, I don't want to say this, but you cannot drop out of school if your instructor is boring."

"Why not? What kind of law is that?"

"Josh, I know it's not fair. But that's how it is."

Try it sometime! You can make this game as easy or as hard as you like based on the rules you enforce. The one who breaks the rule first loses.

Have a Conversation in Which Each Sentence Has Only Five Words (And It Must Make Sense!)

This game is a variation on the same theme as the previous game, as it entails conducting a conversation based on a preset rule or set of rules. For example, you could conduct a conversation like the one below in which each sentence can only be five words long:

"Let's go to the park."

"I don't want to go. The park is so lame." (Two distinct sentences, each with five words.)

"Josh, I love the park. What are you talking about?"

"Dad, it's the twenty-first century."

"Let's go to the beach."

The sky's the limit when it comes to what kinds of rules you want to impose. Just be sure to keep it challenging and, above all, fun.

PRODUCE A SHOW

I'm also a big believer that everyone needs to be famous—for something! All people, kids especially, need a way to show off once in a while. It builds confidence and self-esteem and encourages them to perform in ways that will help them interact successfully with the world for the rest of their lives.

Here are two tricks that you can teach your kids before helping them put on a "magic" show at home in front of family and friends. Trust me, these tricks will impress the most educated folks in the room. Teachers, too, can facilitate such shows in the classroom, just by choosing a student to be the star of the show (or two students, in the case of the Magic Box) and taking them through the how-tos of performing these tricks, either after school or when everyone else is at recess.

You can embellish this activity by devising a makeshift stage in the living room or den and dressing your kid up in wizardly clothes, which you can find in any costume shop. The goal is to make your child, who has some amazing skills to display, the center of attention. Not only will having to memorize the steps in each trick work your child's brain, but the challenge to perform in front of a live audience and shoulder the stress of being "onstage" will be a learning experience in itself.

I'll explain both tricks to you as if you were learning

them yourself. Once you've got the steps to these tricks down, work with your child to explain them in your own words, coming back to these explanations as necessary. I'll start with the easier trick of the two.

The Magic Box Mind-Reading Trick

Lots of simple tricks seem mysterious and inexplicable to those who are not in on the secret. This one is great crowd-pleaser for two people to try on a group of people. Start by putting the numbers 1 through 9 in a three-by-three box, like this:

1	2	3
4	5	6
7	8	9

Ask someone to be your secret partner. This person will already know the trick, because you will teach it to him or her beforehand. When you begin the trick, have your partner leave the room (or turn around) so that when someone else in your audience silently picks a number, your partner won't know what it is. Using the trick, your partner will be able to guess the number that was chosen. Here's how it's done.

- With your partner looking away or out of the room, ask someone in your audience to hold up a number from 1 to 9, using his or her fingers. This is the secret number. Now ask your partner to turn back around or return to the room.

- Begin by pointing to the number 1 box and asking your partner, "Is this the number?" But when you touch this first box, make sure you touch the *subsection* of that box as though it were a miniature version of the three-by-three grid. In other words, if you were to break down the number 1 box, it would look like this:

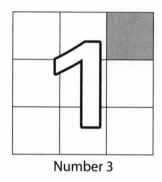

Number 3

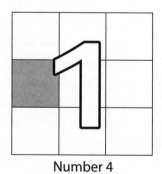

Number 4

Number 9

- The shaded areas indicate where you'd point in the first box to immediately clue your partner in to what the secret number is on the larger grid.
- Continue pointing from box to box until, when you reach the correct one, your partner says, "Yes, that's the one!"

The Black Horse Trick

Similar to the Magic Box Mind-Reading Trick is the Black Horse Trick. Again, pair up with a secret partner, as you did before. In fact, you can even say, "Now we're going to perform the same trick—but without touching the number at all!" Just a few words spoken by you will let your secret partner know the correct number. Here's how it works:

Set up two words in advance that correspond to a set of numbers. Here we use BLACKHORSE, where each letter symbolizes a number from 1 to 10. Note that these words have no repeated letters.

B	L	A	C	K	H	O	R	S	E
1	2	3	4	5	6	7	8	9	10

When your partner comes back into the room, say something like, "All right, try to guess this one." The key is that the first letter of the first word you say will correspond to the correct number—in this case the number 3. A question such as "So, you really think you know it this time?" would signify the number 9! Anyone you play this trick on will certainly be begging you to tell him how you managed to pull it off. Not only does it work every time, but it employs lots of brainy activity. You're forced to come up with a crafty sentence to convey to your partner what the number is, and you also have to remember the BLACKHORSE code. Just don't start counting on your fingers or your audience might catch you out. As your mind thumbs through the letters of the word and translates them into the numbers, you have to inwardly juggle information that ultimately exercises those mental muscles.

The Missing Number Trick

This is an extremely cool trick, but one that does require focus and concentration. You'll probably have to take yourself through this a few times before you teach it to others.

I like the Missing Number Trick because it is easy to do and you can do it over the phone. People will believe you are psychic after you do this trick for them. There are several ways to perform it, but I will teach you just one. All you need to be able to do to perform this trick is to follow a few simple steps, add up some one-digit numbers, and know the multiples of 9 up to 36. Here are the steps:

Step 1: Have someone type a three-digit number into a calculator.

Step 2: Ask that person to add up the sum of the digits and subtract it from the original number.

Step 3: Have him or her multiply the new number by a whole different three-digit number.

Step 4: Have the person circle one of the digits in the final answer—any digit except a 0—and then read you the rest of the digits, but not the circled number. After he or she reads them to you, you can announce what the circled number is.

If the person follows all the directions correctly, the sum of all the digits, including the circled number, will have to add up to a multiple of 9 (9, 18, 27, or 36). Here's an example of the trick using actual numbers:

Step 1: The person types a three-digit number into the calculator (836).

Step 2: The person adds up the digits of this number ($8 + 3 + 6 = 17$) and then subtracts the total from it ($836 - 17 = 819$).

Step 3: You multiply the new number by another three-digit number ($819 \times 523 = 428{,}337$).

Step 4: Have the person circle one of the digits in the final answer—except for any 0's—and then have him read you all the digits except the circled number. So, if the person circled the 2, he would read you "4, 8, 3, 3, 7," and as he read, you would add up the numbers ($4 + 8 + 3 + 3 + 7 = 25$). The next-highest multiple of 9 after 25 is 27, and you know that the sum of *all* the digits, including the missing number, has to equal a multiple of 9; since $25 + 2 = 27$, the missing number is 2.

Say the digits the person reads you already add up to a multiple of 9, like $3 + 2 + 4 + 1 + 8 = 18$. The missing number in that case can be either a 0 or a 9, since $18 + 9 = 27$. You told the person not to circle any 0's, so you know the missing number must be a 9.

The key is to memorize directions so you can explain what you're doing to your audience and do a little mental math. Those are the only requirements for successfully performing this trick.

FEELING SUPER SMART YET?

Productive thinkers rarely rest on their laurels. Once you've mastered all of the strategies and exercises in this book, seek out more ways to bend your mind and keep it in tip-top shape. Don't forget to go to www.MikeByster.com for online resources and videos.

Maintaining a sharp, fast mind requires constant attention and work. Just as bodybuilders never stop lifting weights and watching their diets, none of us can let our brains just sit there. The encouraging news is that you don't have to go far to engage your mind in ways that support and expand its power. I hope I've given you plenty of ideas that you can use throughout your daily life. No computer or playing partner is required. All you need is your own thinking brain and its well-groomed skills to turn any everyday experience into an effortless path to a smarter, wittier, brainier, and brighter you.

ACKNOWLEDGMENTS

When you have been practicing your craft and trying to better yourself and your abilities for more than four decades, a great many people come into your life who help you in various sorts of ways. This book reflects the culmination of not just my lifetime work in teaching the skills of learning and working with numbers, but also my collaboration with a small army of bright, talented people who surround me every day. An entire book could be filled with the names of those who have shaped who I am today, for I owe everyone I've ever worked with through the years a heartfelt thank-you. The unwavering support of family members, friends, and colleagues has also paved the path to this book. Your guidance, insights, and feedback have been indispensable; *The Power of Forgetting* is as much yours as it is mine.

First, I give a resounding thanks to my family. You cannot pick your family, but I am really lucky to have been blessed with an amazing group. I would like to thank my parents, Gloria and Dave; my wife, Robin; and son, Josh; my sister, Beth; her husband, John; my sister-in-law, Liz; and my in-laws, Harriet and Gil. I am greatly indebted to cousins Norm and Jackie and my uncle Shelly, who was the first to showcase my abilities, albeit to his potential girlfriends at the time. And a special shout-out to our golden retrievers Winnie and Wrigley (Cub fans, now you can sympathize with some of my trials and tribulations), who kept my blood pressure low no matter what the situation.

I am eternally grateful to my friends whom I have known for decades and who have always believed in me even when I did not believe in myself so much. Thank you for always saying the right thing at the right time: Lee Grossman, Dave Charman, Pat DeLacey, Howard Gartzman, Steve Kost, Rick Drucker, Neal Golden, Brett Keeshin, Kim Scott, Michelle Barger, Beth Weis, Don Lanphere, and the Dirty Dozen from the University of Illinois.

There have been many teachers, principals, and administrators who always kept the doors to their classrooms or their schools open so I could try out new theories or games that I had come up with. A special thanks to Jennifer Atterman, Linda Kahn, Barbara Wolke, Sue Chaplik, Jamie Hindin, Joanne Fuller, Jennifer Greene, Ellen Gaffney, Kerry DiFusco, Sharon Phares, Judy Wheatley, Mark Klaisner, Edna Bazik, Ann Butcher, Arne Benson, and Frances McTague.

I would like to thank some members of the television and radio industry who made my times working with them all the more interesting as they engaged me in lively conversation while also trying to stump me with difficult problems in front of live audiences. Thanks to JuJu Chang, Alison Lynn, Bob Sirott, Harry Porterfield, Gayle King, and Jay Levine.

I am very fortunate to have a great group of people at Brainetics. When you are your own boss for more than twenty years and then you become part of a team overnight, sometimes that is a tough transition. But these people made it happen seamlessly, and they are an absolute joy to work with every day. Thanks especially to Joel Appel, Angela Mooney,

Rhonda Fabian, Jerry Baber, Tim O'Brien, Luke Sword, Kristin MacLaughlin, John Grover, Adam May, Derrill Rodgers, Frank Kvietok, Allison Sauve, and Willard Cowan.

When Bonnie Solow first called me to ask about doing a book, I wasn't so sure about that. I didn't know if I'd have enough to say, and I was, frankly, intimidated by the process of putting a book together. But she kept encouraging me to share my knowledge in a way that my DVD program couldn't. I eventually surrendered, realizing it was finally time to reach more than just kids, teachers, and parents. I also realized that I had a lot to say. Thank you, Bonnie, for paving the way for this book to reach everyone; your leadership, guidance, and enthusiastic support of this project have been invaluable. Your creative stewardship, intrepid attention to details, and commitment to overseeing every step are appreciated more than you know. I can't thank you enough.

Thank you, Kristin Loberg, my collaborator, who spent countless hours listening to my disorganized ramblings and coming to (organized) live shows—transforming it all into a smooth-flowing, simple piece of writing like only you could.

And a special thanks to the wonderful people at Random House, especially Tina Constable, Mauro DiPreta, Julia Pastore, Annie Chagnot, Jennifer Reyes, Tammy Blake, Ellen Folan, Catherine Cullen, Meredith McGinnis, and everyone at Crown Archetype who made this book possible. I suggest everyone write a book so you can experience the warmth and tremendous professionalism that I have experienced working with the Random House team. Thank you.

INDEX